102/BV

NATURAL HISTORY
WITH A
CAMERA

NATURAL HISTORY
WITH A CAMERA

L. W. BROWNELL

Author of "Photography for the Sportsman Naturalist"

1942
AMERICAN PHOTOGRAPHIC PUBLISHING CO.
BOSTON

Printed in the United States of America
The Plimpton Press, Norwood, Mass.

To my two daughters
Betty and Joan
who have followed in my footsteps
in their love of the outdoors,
this book is lovingly dedicated

PREFACE

It has always been my belief that, in order to be a really good nature photographer, one must have at least a fairly accurate working knowledge of the lives of the things that he is desirous of photographing. His knowledge of the natural sciences need not be profound, but he should know where and when to look for his subjects and, when he finds them, should be sufficiently well acquainted with them to be able to call them by name. If he does not possess this elementary knowledge of the wild things he will be all too apt to discover, before he has been long at this work, that he is not doing any too well in obtaining the photographs that he would like to have. Also, many of the subjects which he may find, and photograph, he will be unable to properly identify, which will make the photographs practically worthless for any really useful purpose.

Therefore, rather than write entirely from a photographic viewpoint, treating extensively the various methods and materials used in different types of nature photography, I have made this rather subservient to the main purpose of the book. I have tried to tell about the habits of the wild things, where and when to look for them, how to find and handle them, and how to know them when they have been found. At the same time, however, I have endeavored to include sufficient information on apparatus and methods, so that the beginner in this work may learn how. This knowledge, however, can best be obtained through experience.

The photographic illustrations in this book were all made by myself from the living wild things, in many instances in their natural habitat. Some were made from specimens in captivity, which in many cases is necessary in order to obtain the best results or, in fact, often to obtain any results at all. The moths and butterflies, in most cases, were photographed from specimens reared from the eggs or larvae in breeding cages, which is the best way in which to obtain perfect specimens of these insects. I have never, however, made a photograph from a dead or mounted specimen, except once of a group of passenger pigeons, which bird has been extinct for forty or more years and, therefore, a photograph of it could be obtained by no other means.

I would like to advise those who are entering this field of photographic endeavor to stick always to absolute truthfulness. While the temptation is often great to resort to faking in order to obtain certain photographs they must not, under any conditions, allow themselves to be led into doing so. Once a photograph has been found to be a fake, and this is bound sooner or later to happen, all the work of the person who made that photograph is discredited, no matter how excellent some of his other efforts may be.

I have written this book in the hope that it may lead many to enter a field that is prolific of results and in which I have spent many of the most enjoyable days of my life.

L. W. B.

Paterson, N. J.
May 27, 1942.

CONTENTS

ILLUSTRATIONS

EQUIPMENT

NATURE photography, while it has gone a long way beyond its infancy, is still a fairly new branch of photography and one that has taken great strides in the past few years. The earliest nature photographs were poor when compared with those made nowadays, but they were a beginning. It was not so many years ago that publishers of works on biology began to see the advisability of using these photographs to supersede the old-time, often very crude, drawings or paintings as illustrations. It is undeniable that this was in most instances a very great improvement, and that first-class photography of nature subjects is infinitely better than the best efforts of artists. This is true, however, only so long as the photographs are honest portrayals of the living wild things. As soon as nature photographers allow themselves to descend to faking, the value of the photograph, from any point of view, is completely lost.

Some forms of nature photography require so much time, patience, and hard work to do them honestly that it is easy to understand why some unscrupulous workers, impatient to get results, resort to trickery of one kind or another. One of the commonest forms of such dishonesty is photographing stuffed birds and animals, and dead insects, and passing the results off as having been made from living specimens. These subterfuges are always sooner or later detected, and photographs by the man who made them are always thereafter suspect. Because this aspect of nature work is so important, perhaps it would be well to start off this chapter on apparatus by showing under what conditions it is necessary, and to what extent permissible, to alter natural surroundings; and to describe some of the appliances used to obviate that necessity as much as possible.

I can readily understand why it is that some nature photographers, too anxious to obtain results, will allow themselves to be led into these falsehoods, especially if their conscience is not in very active operation. The photographing of the wild things is always more or less difficult, and anything that tends to lessen the obstacles that must be overcome and make them easier to surmount, is bound to be welcome. To take advantage, conscientiously, of any means that will help to lessen, or eliminate, any of the difficulties is perfectly legitimate so long as the means do not in any way detract from the realism of the finished product. Unfortunately there are some people who apparently do not consider it at all necessary that the photograph be realistic, so long as the image of the subject is large and well defined.

I have in mind a book published some years ago which advocated the photographing of birds by the removal of the nests containing young, with the branch upon which they were built, to a spot where a tent was erected inside of which the operator concealed himself with his camera, and outside of which the nest was again set up. This he termed " control of the nesting site," and he stated that it was of no special importance to either the old or young birds. I consider that this method, under some extremely peculiar conditions, may be permissible, but just twice in my long experience as a nature photographer have I employed it. Of these two instances I intend to speak later and more fully in another chapter. Ordinarily I consider it a most pernicious practice. Aside from the fact that a photograph of the nest in its original site is not being obtained, the danger to the young birds is so great, especially if they are quite young, that the results obtained do not fully justify the means. Furthermore there are few birds that will not be deterred for an indefinite length of time from returning to a nest that has been removed from the spot where it was built.

Birds are, probably, about the most difficult of all nature subjects to photograph. They are naturally shy and their fear of mankind is inherent. This is, however, overcome to a considerable extent in the breeding season when they have their young to feed and protect. In the attempt to make the birds more at ease during the photographing of them, various types of blinds have been advocated by different photographers in which to hide both their cameras and themselves from the suspicious and prying eyes of their subject. A well-known English ornithologist used an artificial tree trunk apparently with considerable success, but he confessed that he frequently endured torture from the heat and the stinging insects that managed to obtain entrance to his retreat. Many photographers use a small tent which has a slit in one side through which the lens of the camera may protrude. An umbrella with a long stick may be stuck into the ground and have draped from its edges a tube of cloth long enough to completely cover the camera and operator down to the ground. The material for both of these appliances should be green, and it may be of some light semi-transparent stuff, such as cheesecloth, through which one may easily see from the inside but be fairly well hidden from the outside. If any heavier material is used, a peep-hole must be made in the side of the tent through which the camera may be pointed, and through which the operator may watch the movements of his subject. Such devices allow the photographer to occupy the enclosure with his camera, and they provide room for a campstool for his comfort during what often proves to be quite a lengthy wait for the birds to return to their nest. These blinds may be further camouflaged by attaching foliage, or other natural objects, either real or artificial, to the outside. They are often very useful, but they add considerably to the paraphernalia of a field trip and, if one is to do much walking, this is something to be taken into consideration.

But anything suddenly appearing near the nest, no matter how well camouflaged, is an object of suspicion to birds and must be well looked over and appraised by them before they will approach. I have been fully as successful in obtaining results with the camera uncovered as with any kind of blind. In ninety per cent of my bird pictures, after finding a nest containing about half-fledged young (it is dangerous to younger birds to keep their parents away from them for any length of time, and older birds are apt to struggle from the nest when they become impatient for their food), I set up my camera at a sufficient distance from it to insure an ample space on each side for the parent bird to appear fully in the picture, no matter where it may alight. I then eliminate as carefully as possible, without leaving any evidence that this has been done, all foliage or other extraneous matter that intervenes between the camera and the nest, so as to obtain a free view of the latter. Then having focused, set my shutter, inserted the holder and drawn the slide, I attach the end of a hundred-foot rubber tubing to the shutter release and lay it along the ground to a hiding place which I have previously selected, taking care that there is no kink in its entire length, and that nothing is pressing upon it to interfere with the free passage of air. The bulb I use for making the exposure is a six-inch spray bulb which may be purchased at almost any hardware or rubber goods store. For more modern shutters, which do not have pneumatic releases, it is a simple matter to build an electrical device operated by a battery and long wires, by which the shutter can be worked from any distance. The camera must be well covered with a focusing cloth to prevent possible fogging of the film when the vagaries of the birds impose a lengthy wait. This should be fastened down securely so that no loose end will show any movement in what breeze may be stirring. Almost any bird will quickly become reconciled to a new object near its nest if it is stationary, but any movement of any part of that object may deter the bird from approaching for an indefinite period. When all arrangements are made, the operator simply has to wait in patience until the bird decides to take a chance and return to the nest. I have on occasion camouflaged my camera somewhat by the addition of branches or leaves in an attempt to lessen the time of waiting, but have never been quite sure that any advantage was gained by so doing.

For certain forms of controlled work, every nature photographer should possess at least one glass tank and one cage, and it is better still to have several of each, of different sizes.

With the majority of amphibians, the frogs, toads, salamanders, etc., the best photographs can be made in a tank. For photographing fish and many of the mollusks or crustaceans, a tank is indispensable and there are a very large number of water insects that can be photographed by no other means. The small inexpensive aquariums that may be purchased in several sizes at any pet store, are admirable for the purpose. Two slots should be cut in the rim on each side, one about two inches from the front and the other about halfway between that and the back, in which may be slipped a pane of glass which will confine the subjects closer to the front, thus making it much easier to keep them in focus. The bottom of this tank should be covered to a depth of about two inches with perfectly clean sand. The front glass, at least, must be kept spotlessly clean and the water with which the tank is filled must be absolutely clear. If the glass is at all dirty or spotted, or if the water is the least murky or has floating pieces of dirt or debris in it, the photograph will not be so good. Sea water must be used for all sea creatures and this must be dipped some distance from the shore where it is clear. Many of the inhabitants of the sea cannot exist if placed in fresh water.

A cage can be built with the front and both sides of glass, and the back of some opaque white material. Wood covered with tin and painted white will answer the purpose. This makes an excellent cage for those who prefer a dead-white background for their pictures, and it is easily made. Personally I much prefer to use the tank as a cage, as it is much more convenient and answers the purpose perfectly. I think that the out-of-focus background seen through the rear glass of the tank is much preferable to the dead white background, as it gives things the appearance of being photographed in the open. Small mammals like lizards and snakes may be confined in this cage for photographing, although I have never found it necessary to do so with the latter. Any kind of setting that is suitable to the subject can be built in the cage by the use of a few stones, small plants, pieces of sod, and other natural objects, and much better photographs made of these quick-moving subjects in this way than in any other manner. Nor can this by any stretch of imagination be classed under the head of faking. With larger mammals, such as woodchucks, skunks, opossums, etc., I have sometimes used a larger enclosure built on the ground, of wire mesh, which contained any accessories necessary to the picture. In this the subjects were allowed to roam about at their will, and an exposure was made whenever the opportunity presented itself. I have made excellent pictures in this way with a tripod camera, but it is much easier to obtain results with a Graflex or a miniature camera.

The necessary outfit for a nature photographer, at all events for one who is just starting in this field of activity, is neither extensive nor expensive. Many of the gadgets that are advertised and exploited as aids to the making of fine photographs in the field of nature photography, are really of very little use and are often entirely superfluous. One can do excellent work with a simple outfit, and it is frequently an advantage to have it as small and compact as possible. I do not mean to imply that the best work can be done with cheap implements or without the proper accessories. If one would be successful in this work, he needs proper apparatus. For serious work in this field one should invest in the very best camera and lens, of whatever type he may decide upon, regardless of size or cost.

It sounds very well to say that a good workman can do good work with any tools. In some trades this may be so, but I wish most emphatically to state that it is very far from being so in nature photography. For instance, it is an absolute impossibility for anyone to photograph a rapidly moving object with slow lenses, shutters, or emulsions. For photographing living wild creatures, fast lens and shutter speed is frequently needed. An exposure of 1/1000 second may sound extreme, but it is necessary to stop action in the wings of a flying bird, and is entirely inadequate for photographing a butterfly whose wings are rapidly fluttering. However, this speed is not very often necessary, and I would advise the beginner not to attempt such shots until he has familiarized himself with much easier subjects. For ordinary work one does not need a faster speed than 1/150 second, and in the majority of cases a shutter speed of 1/50 second will be found entirely adequate.

I would advise, for anyone who expects to do really serious work in nature photography, a 5 by 7 view camera having both front and rear extension of bellows, fitted with a lens working as fast as f:4.5, and with a shutter capable of giving exposures ranging from time to at least 1/150 second. Contact prints of this size are suitable for reproduction without enlarging. With a camera of this type I have made fully nine-tenths of the more than ten thousand negatives which I have in my collection. I would advise also, as a more or less necessary adjunct to this outfit, a reflecting camera such as the Graflex. A camera of this type is almost an absolute necessity to the nature photographer, for there are many times when a photograph can be obtained with no other camera. I use a $3\frac{1}{4}$ by $4\frac{1}{4}$ size with an f:4.5 lens. In choosing a lens, it is immaterial which of the various standard makes is selected, but it must be one of the better ones and fairly fast, for no matter how good a man may be, he cannot secure satisfactory results in this particular line of work with a poor lens.

A telephoto attachment is often a very considerable aid to the nature photographer when either from the inaccessibility of the subject or because it objects to his presence, he is unable to approach close enough to obtain a sufficiently large image with the ordinary lens. With the telephoto attachment at a distance of twenty-five or more feet, one may obtain a sufficiently large-sized image. Of course the telephoto attachments slow down the exposure somewhat, but snapshots are possible with them on a reflex type of camera. Speed in a lens can often very profitably be sacrificed to depth of focus, especially with such more or less stationary objects as plants, bird's nests, fungi, etc., where it is essential to have every part of the subject sharply defined.

I advocate a 5 by 7 view camera as the very best for all kinds of nature work if one is confined to a single camera and hopes to use his photographs for commercial reproduction. It should have an extension of bellows both at the rear and in front. The worker is handicapped by a camera with only a front extension of bellows, even though the length of the bellows may be considerable. There have been innumerable times when it would have been impossible for me to obtain the photograph for which I was trying if I had been unable to focus from the rear. For example, rear focusing comes in handy when photographing a rattlesnake all set to make a strike, with the front end of the camera within striking distance of the snake, as I have done on various occasions. When making images near life size or larger, focusing is much more easily accomplished by using the rear rather than the front extension. When the lens is within a foot or so of the subject, the point of sharp focus changes so materially with each forward movement of the lens that it is frequently extremely difficult to obtain a really sharp focus by the use of the front extension alone, especially if the subject is likely to move. Moreover, if you wish to make a greater enlargement, such as can be made with the auxiliary lens about which I will have something to say later, a sharp focus cannot possibly be made except with the rear focus, for when the lens is always within an inch or two of the subject, the movement of a small fraction of an inch throws the image completely out of focus.

While the type of camera that I have recommended is the one that meets most of the requirements of nature work, some excellent results may be obtained with smaller cameras of less bulk and weight. I have seen some very acceptable work done with a small pocket Kodak fitted with a fast lens. A friend of mine has built up a most admirable collection of nature photographs, covering practically the whole field, with only a 3¼ by 4¼ Graflex which can be used equally well as a hand camera for instantaneous exposures, and on a tripod for time work. The 35 mm cameras have great possibilities for nature work when properly handled. They are small, light, easily carried, and can be handled in situations where it would be impossible or dangerous to use a tripod outfit, and they hold a roll of eighteen or thirty-six films at one loading. The small negatives save considerable space in storage, and if care is taken in exposure and development, they can be enlarged to at least a five by seven size without any material loss of definition. Most people do not realize how much more difficult it is to hold a light camera steady, than it is to hold a heavier one. For exposures slower than 1/100 second any 35 mm camera should be used upon a tripod and the shutter should be released by the wire cable, if critically sharp enlargements from the negative are expected. Therefore if you have any small camera, no matter what type it may be, go out and try your hand at this work. You will get many worth-while results, and at least gain considerable experience which, if you later wish to continue to work with nature and to purchase a more expensive and extensive outfit, will be of real value to you in your further efforts.

Buy a tripod for strength and rigidity, rather than for lightness or price. The tripod of a nature photographer is bound to be more or less roughly used. Of course a heavy tripod adds to the burden which one must carry on a trip, but absolute rigidity is essential in this work and the lighter makes of tripods lack this quality, nor will they stand the racket. A tilting and panoraming top saves much time and vexation on rough ground. It is, of course, entirely possible to photograph low objects without the use of an adjustable tripod top, but it is much easier to do so with one, and with much less strain on the tripod. For photographing the nests of ground-breeding birds and other objects on the ground, I have for years used with great success a tripod with single-piece legs about eighteen inches long. With such a tripod the camera can be placed fairly close to the ground so that a much truer view angle of the subject may be obtained than with the ordinary tripod even though the legs are telescoped to the smallest length. Anybody with ordinary mechanical ability can make the legs from a fairly hard wood that will not easily split (willow is excellent), and fit them to any tripod top.

A ball-and-socket clamp is frequently extremely useful for attaching the camera to a branch or limb of a tree where it is impossible to use the tripod, as it can be tilted in any direction or at any angle. It can be bought in several sizes, but it is best to use the largest, as it is difficult to fasten any but the lightest cameras rigidly enough with the small-size clamp to prevent them from slipping, and a slip is unfortunate, especially if it comes just as an exposure is about to be made. I have sometimes lashed the legs of the tripod to the branches of a tree and used the tilting top. Many of my pictures of the nests of tree-building birds were made in this manner. A ball of fairly heavy twine is extremely useful not only for this, but also for other purposes connected with nature photography.

For a beginner an exposure meter is useful. When photographing birds or small objects that cannot be approached closely, a reading may be hastily snatched by pointing the meter at one's own hand or coat sleeve or anything else that approximates the tone of the object, taking care that the light hits it at the same general angle. Such a reading can be made in five seconds, and while not an exact method of working, it gives quite a good general idea of the exposure needed, and may make all the difference between a good picture and a worthless one. If the angle of view of the meter covers more than the object, one cannot meter the light reflected from a small object without having the reading affected by the surroundings. In such cases, the reading is again taken from the hand or something else of similar tone to the object. A crumpled white handkerchief gives a good reading for white or light-colored flowers. When taking readings in this manner, the exposure will be correct for the principal object, and if anything has to suffer it will be the surroundings, which are less important.

A meter is not infallible. It must be used with intelligence, and in the light of experience, but for the novice who might have little idea what the correct exposure should be, it is a valuable guide. Experienced photographers, working with the image plainly visible in its full intensity upon the groundglass of a view camera or in the hood of a reflecting camera, soon learn to judge exposures fairly correctly without mechanical aids. But a correct exposure is so essential to successful photography that the beginner should use a meter until experience can be substituted for it, and even then it is often wise to use one as a check upon one's judgment if the light is at all tricky or unusual. It is better to be sure than sorry in the matter of exposure, for a grossly inaccurate exposure will let your quarry escape where you can never catch it again — not in that pose, anyhow.

While most of my work has been done with glass plates, that is largely so because my work extends back into the years when the best emulsions were available only upon glass. Plates still have advantages for laboratory work where they are largely used, but for field work the advantage is now all with film, which has only a minute fraction of the weight of glass plates, and no danger of breakage. Film, especially cut film which can be used in plate-back cameras and Graflexes, is now coated with all the best emulsions. As the general practice is to process all modern films by tank in total darkness, by time and temperature methods, this presents no hardship under makeshift conditions while on a trip. By the use of a changing bag which weighs no more than a shirt, even darkness is not necessary for processing the fastest films available.

The early panchromatic emulsions left a great deal to be desired in the rendition of color in terms of black and white, which is of the utmost importance in nature work. But later emulsions (typified by Eastman's type B panchromatic) like Eastman's Panatomic X and Agfa Finopan, render color in tones practically the same as the eye sees them, without any filter. These films are not of extreme speed, but are fast enough for most any work, and they have a grain so fine that there is practically no loss in any ordinary degree of enlargement. As they are available in 35 mm, in all the regular rollfilm sizes, and in cut film, they are a good choice for nature work with almost any kind of camera. Sometimes color contrasts upon these films can be falsified to good advantage for special effects by overcorrecting them by the use of K1 or K2 filters, which increase the exposure respectively one and a half, and two times. This is sometimes necessary, as for example when red flowers or red berries are shown with green foliage and the two colors are of such saturation that they come out practically alike in tones of gray. The color contrast between them is so great to the eye that they do not appear natural when reduced to the same tone of gray, and the reproduction is really more truthful if they are overcorrected so that one of them (usually the red) comes out lighter than the other. Many of the extreme speed panchromatic films (Eastman type C panchromatic, for example) are oversensitive to yellow, orange, and red. Greens can be made to show their relative color upon such films only by the use of green filters which increase the exposure about five times, thus throwing away the only special advantage of the films by making them slower in operation than films of normal speed which are used without filters, or with the rapid K filters. These films can, however, be used to good advantage without filters to make reds come out lighter than greens, as under the necessity mentioned above. Orthochromatic films can be used without filters for the opposite effect, making the greens come out lighter than the reds.

But for most ordinary shots, panchromatic film of Eastman type B, used without a filter, gives all the correction necessary for rendering color exactly as the eye sees it.

Much of the perfection of the finished photograph depends upon the use of the proper paper in the printing. Contact papers are made in several degrees of contrast, some of them in as many as six. As an example, in the Eastman's Azo papers which I use exclusively in my work, the grade F which is a paper with a very high gloss to be used on ferrotype plates, and a good paper for reproduction purposes, is made in six degrees of contrast, denoted by numbers from 0 to 5. No. 0 is an extremely soft emulsion for use with negatives that are very contrasty. It softens down the extreme contrast and produces an excellent print from a negative that would give a poor result if printed on an ordinary paper. No. 5 has an extremely hard emulsion for use on very flat negatives where there is little or no contrast between the highlights and the shadows. The numbers between these two are for use with negatives of varying degrees of contrast. I have found that Nos. 1, 2, and 3 give sufficient range for nearly every negative, although it is well to have some of No. 0 and No. 5 on hand for extreme cases.

Much can often be done to improve the picture by a little judicious shading during the printing. One quickly learns to tell at a glance what part of a negative should receive less exposure than the rest. Prints that need much dodging are better printed in a printing frame rather than in a regular printing box, unless one has one of the expensive printers that have a built-in device to allow shading during the exposure. Hold the printing frame no closer than a foot from the electric light. The bulb should be the frosted kind which gives better diffusion of light. Hold your hand, or a piece of cardboard, for a short time over that part of the negative that needs the least exposure, moving it slightly all the while so that there may be no sharp line of demarkation. One soon learns by experience just how long and in what manner this shading should be done in different cases, to give the best results. Also, in trimming the print, much can often be done to improve its looks by cutting off all extraneous objects which appear in the picture and detract from the general effect.

When printing by enlargement, papers are available in many surfaces and many different degrees of contrast, among which choice can sometimes be made to good effect. But the experienced worker will usually have most of his negatives so timed and developed that they will all print upon the same paper. This is good practice because the worker thus gains a facility in the use of that paper that he can never acquire when constantly switching from one paper to another. Bromide papers come in a wide enough variety of surfaces and contrasts to meet any needs, but the slower chlorobromide papers are the choice of many workers. While these are usually furnished in only one degree of contrast, this is sufficient for most negatives if they have been carefully made for printing upon that paper. Chlorobromide papers have a longer scale than most bromides, and they give a richer print. The scale can easily be compressed or extended by shading or by spot printing during projection, for those negatives which demand something a little different from the normal exposure scale of the paper. The surfaces of Eastman's Illustrator's Special and Defender Illustro are ideal for reproduction, and they do not need to be squeegeed as glossy prints do.

Chlorobromide papers tend to develop to a warm tone unless the exposure and development are correlated to give a pure black, as can easily be done. Many workers develop the print in amidol which gives a blue-black tone naturally. The warm tone is pleasing for many effects, but if the print is to be reproduced, the tone should be as black as possible.

MARCH

INSTEAD of commencing our nature studies with the calendar year, it has seemed more appropriate to follow nature more closely and begin with her own fiscal year which starts in March. It is then that Mother Earth wakes up from her winter slumber and starts into operation that progression of growth, bloom, and fruit, and of giving birth to young, hatching eggs, and raising the offspring to maturity, that makes the endless cycle of her charms.

Although spring begins in March, it is really a sort of in-between month in the seasons for the nature photographer. In the early part of the month, the brooks and ponds are still more or less ice-bound and snow is apt to linger in drifts in the woods and protected hollows where the sun does not strike too strongly. Even then there is far from being a dearth of animal or plant life, and as the month advances nature comes to life and the chances increase for the photographer to find subjects for his camera.

To those who have never searched the woods and fields for the first sign of life awakening from the long winter's sleep of rest and recuperation, I would like to say that you have missed some real pleasure and also much worthwhile information. To search for and find the first wild flower that succeeds in pushing its way through the half-frozen ground; to see the first butterfly flitting in the sunlight; to hear the first peep of that great chorus of frog and toad voices; to search in pools for the first glimpse of pond life — these things carry tremendous thrills to one who is sufficiently interested in nature and her offspring to take a tramp in the out-of-doors at this time of the year. Such a tramp will lead to the discovery of interesting photographic material that may not be found at any other season.

To be a completely successful nature photographer, one must forget, as far as possible, all considerations of personal comfort. Anyone who is afraid of soiling his clothes or getting his shoes muddy, who does not enjoy walking in the snow or wading in ice-cold water, who is too sluggish to move under a blazing summer sun, or too tired to lug a heavy camera outfit under all such conditions, had best forswear nature photography before he starts. For all of these more or less disagreeable incidents, and many more, await him who would conscientiously follow nature's trails and photograph her offspring. In spite of all these drawbacks, or perhaps because of them, a lover of the out-of-doors rarely tires of it, but becomes more and more deeply interested as he progresses. Each picture obtained is something of considerable value gained, and those secured under uncomfortable and sometimes dangerous conditions, or by hardship, exposure, and diligent toil, are the ones that we prize the most, even though they may be far from the best that we have from the point of real excellence.

But to get back to March. For the botany specialist there is considerable to be done, and the subjects increase in numbers as the month advances. March is the month for gathering sap from the sugar-maple trees to boil down into syrup and sugar, for now in all trees the sap has again begun to run freely to awaken the buds into quickened life, although most of the branches remain bare throughout the month. At this time the little gray " pussies," the staminate (male) flowers of the glaucous willow, commonly and more familiarly known as " pussy willow," begin to burst and send forth their stamens thickly coated with the bright yellow pollen, to make the twigs of this particular willow a thing of beauty. They are eagerly sought by the early bees who hover about them, often by the thousands. The pistillate, or female, blossoms are borne on separate trees and have none of the attractive characteristics of the " pussies." They are green and of comparatively little beauty. Nevertheless they should be photographed as well as the more handsome male flowers. The tassels (aments) of the alder and of the hazelnut still hang on the branches. The hazelnut tassels do not remain on the branches

BLOSSOMS OF THE RED BIRCH

nearly as long as do those of the alder and, therefore, should be photographed as soon as they reach maturity, well covered with pollen.

The staminate blossoms of the American aspen, popularly known
as the "trembling aspen" from the fact that its leaves, borne on
long, slender, flat stems, are almost constantly in motion, appear in
the latter half of the month. These are also tassels and remain on
the trees but a day or two after maturing, so we must grasp the opportunity to photograph them as soon as they are fully matured.
Other trees whose staminate flowers borne on aments appear in
March are the yellow, red, and white birches. Both pistillate and

staminate flowers of these trees are borne on the same twig, the former upright from the base of the newly forming leaves, the latter pendent from the tips of the twigs. Thus a photograph of both can be made on the same negative.

By the middle of the month the red, or swamp, maples begin to stand out on the hillsides from the surrounding trees by virtue of their blossoms which appear long before the leaves. The pistillate flowers are bright red, and the staminate red with bright yellow stamens. Both the staminate and pistillate blooms are borne in separate clusters on the same or different trees, but both are equally noticeable from a long distance on account of their vivid coloring. The red maple is well named for both its flowers and its fruit are red. The stems of the fruit, flowers, leaves, and even the smaller twigs have also a ruddy hue. It is the first maple to bloom, and the winged fruit (samaras) follow the flowers very closely so that by the time the leaves have fully expanded they have nearly all left the tree.

One more fairly well-known small tree or large shrub, whose purplish pink flowers clothe its bare branches and sometimes even the trunk itself with loveliness in the latter part of the month, is the redbud, or Judas tree. The tree grows in Judea and it was given its popular name from the legend that it blushed for shame for allowing Judas to hang himself upon its branches. This legend apparently took no thought to the fact that none of the branches of this small tree are capable of bearing the weight of a human being. The pealike blossoms are very lovely and when in full bloom in otherwise drab and more or less dreary surroundings, they are such a delight to the eye that this tree is particularly popular for ornamental purposes. Personally I greatly prefer the name red-bud to the other rather infamous one.

Among the herbaceous plants there is but little in this month to gladden the heart of the botanically inclined photographer, but in the damp meadows, swamps, and low, wet places we will be certain to find that predominant plant of such places, the skunk cabbage, pushing its dark red, horn-like flower through the dark soil, often when it is completely surrounded by ice and snow. It is malodorous and unattractive, and I must confess that as a flower it is not much of a success. Nevertheless it is hailed by the early bees and flies that find in it a source of food that is not attainable elsewhere at this time of

JUDAS TREE, OR RED-BUD BLOSSOMS

year. Also we must give it all the credit due the first flower of spring, which it undoubtedly may be called, for I have frequently found it starting its growth in some sheltered hollow as early as the first part of February. By the end of March it is usually in full bloom and should then be photographed before the large leaves expand and completely hide the flower. A series of photographs can be made of the same plant, begun when it first appears above the earth and continued at intervals until the leaves are fully expanded. Later we may add to it a picture of the fruit. Unsightly and malodorous as it undoubtedly is, nevertheless this lowly flower is a close relative of the little Jack-in-the-pulpit, beloved of all children, which may be found in similar localities a little later in the year, as well as of the white arrow-arum, a lovely swamp plant of the south; and all three are members of the same family as the stately calla lily. At one time in New York City this plant was the principal in a huge hoax perpetrated on the gullible public. Street hucksters gathered the young plants in huge quantities in the Jersey swamps and sold them on the city streets under the various names of Porto Rican, Japanese, Mexican, or Chinese lily as their fancy directed. Many a person brought home with enthusiasm one of the plants and guarded it carefully expecting to see it develop into some kind of gorgeous lily, only to be sadly disappointed when it turned out to be nothing but an ill-smelling skunk cabbage.

One of the daintiest of our woodland flowers, the trailing arbutus, is in bloom in this month. Unfortunately it is rapidly nearing extinction owing to the ruthless manner in which it is pulled up, its flowers made into tight little balls and sold, in a half-faded condition, on our city streets. From many places where it once grew profusely it has now completely disappeared. I have in mind a wooded hillside that I once was in the habit of visiting every spring at arbutus time just to feast my eyes upon the masses of blossoms that fairly covered the ground in every direction as far as one could see. It was there that I made the accompanying photograph, but today, although otherwise the condition of the hillside remains unchanged, the last vestige of the lovely carpet of arbutus has completely disappeared. This is but one of many spots of which the same may be said. Anyone fortunate enough to know where this delightful little flower still blooms, should photograph it at the first opportunity, before he finds it gone. The Pilgrims after their first awful winter in this country, were gladdened by the sight of this plant blooming profusely throughout the woods. They named it mayflower, a name by which it is sometimes still called, but probably more in memory of the ship that brought them over than because of the time of its blooming for, even in New England it may be found in full bloom by the first of April. I have frequently brushed the snows of late February or early March from over its blossoms.

This is the month when we should commence to make a series of frog photographs and, incidentally, these little amphibians make most interesting subjects for photography. It is during this month

MAYFLOWER OR TRAILING ARBUTUS

that the majority of these creatures emerge from hibernation. They have spent the winter in a torpid condition well buried in the mud at the bottom of some ditch or pond or tucked comfortably away beneath an old stump, stone, or other sufficient covering. Nature, in some unknown manner, rings the alarm in their minds when the time has arrived for them to awaken, shake off their drowsiness and leave their snug retreats, and if they are in a dry situation, seek the nearest water. Some of them, as I have said, choose the muddy bottoms of pond or ditch rather than seek a drier location in which to take their winter's snooze. When they emerge in the spring and rise to the surface of the water, they frequently bump their noses against the ice that still covers a part of the pond.

Few people are entirely unacquainted with at least the voice of a frog, especially if they are fortunate enough to be country dwellers, but I fear that with many of us this knowledge is entirely superficial. How many, I wonder, can tell to what class of animals a frog be-

longs? Do we know anything about its life history? Have we even
an approximate idea of the number of species of frogs native to the
United States? These are the simplest of many interesting facts
that can be learned concerning these lowly creatures, but I know
that there are many people who would shudder at the very thought
of having anything to do with " such slimy things."

To begin at the beginning, a frog is a member of the class *Amphibia* (the batrachians), a class of vertebrate animals that occupy
a position between the fishes and the reptiles. Although the terms
amphibian and amphibious have the same derivation, meaning capable of existing both in water and upon land, they are not synonymous.
A number of land animals spend much of their time in the water.
They are truly amphibious but they are not amphibians. The members of the class *Amphibia* are distinguished by having two distinct
forms of life, one aquatic, and the other terrestrial. They undergo a
more or less complete metamorphosis. The eggs, which are comparatively small and without hard shells, are laid in stagnant water or
in very damp places near the water. In the case of a very few, the
young are born alive. The tadpoles are fish-like and spend the first
few months of their lives as entirely aquatic animals, breathing
through external gills exactly as do the fishes, although the formation of the gills is not exactly similar to those of fishes. The second
part of their existence is spent largely upon the land, although they
do return to the water frequently, and occasionally for quite considerable periods of time. In fact, a few species spend by far the
greater part of their lives in water.

There are but two orders in the class *Amphibia:* the *Caudata* composed of tailed batrachians, or salamanders, of which I will tell more
fully in the next chapter; and the *Salientia* comprising the frogs,
toads, tree toads, etc., or tailless batrachians. There can be no con-
fusion in placing an adult batrachian in its right order as a member
of one of these groups. The *Caudata* are always possessed of a tail,
an elongated body nearly, if not quite, as long as the tail itself, and
four legs about equal in size. The members of the *Salientia* all have
a short body, stout and tailless, and have elongated hind legs developed for jumping and swimming. In the immature stages, however,
the young of these two orders may easily be confused by the uninitiated for they are very similar, both being born in the water and both

having tails. The tails of the young of the *Salientia* are gradually absorbed as they grow, until by summer or early fall they have entirely disappeared, except in the cases of a few species whose metamorphosis occupies two or three years.

The frogs and toads can by no possible stretch of imagination be confused with any other class of animal as there are no others that

THE COMMON TREE "TOAD," AN EARLY SPRING SINGER

in general shape and appearance even remotely resemble them, with the possible exception of the horned lizards, more popularly called horned toads. Even here the resemblance is quite superficial. So that, when we see an animal with a short, squat body, no tail, and with hind legs so elongated and developed that it is capable of making a jump of many times its own length, we may be reasonably certain that it is either a frog or a toad.

Frogs and toads, far from being the repulsive, disagreeable creatures that most people imagine them to be, are really gentle, inoffensive animals with no bad qualities and asking only to be allowed to live in peace. They may be handled with impunity, despite the many tales to the contrary, for although the skin is always, to a certain degree, moist and slimy, they secrete no poison that is in any manner injurious to man, nor do they ever attempt to bite. They do, however, exude a somewhat poisonous juice that is extremely irritating to the mouths of animals such as dogs. This is a protection against their enemies. They are not difficult to catch and are easy to handle, all of which makes them ideal subjects for photography. If any of my readers have never photographed these amphibians I would earnestly advise them, on some mild day in early spring, to visit the nearest piece of low meadow, preferably one that borders upon a pond or that has a brook running through it, and catch a few of them. Take them home if you wish, or work with them where they are caught, and see how easy it is to make photographs of them. You will find them interesting as well as fairly docile subjects, and the photographs will be valuable additions to a collection of nature subjects.

The smallest of our frogs, Pickering's hyla, a member of the *Hylidae*, or tree frogs, and only about one inch in length, is the first of our frogs to put in his appearance in the spring. He is more commonly known by the name of " the spring peeper." He must be well known to anyone who has ever spent part of an early spring in the country. I should say, however, that it is his voice with which we are familiar and not the little fellow himself, for I greatly doubt if one out of every fifty persons has ever seen one, and I consider that this is a most conservative estimate. The little fellows usually commence to sing about the first of March, and they are true vocalists. I have, on occasions, heard a lone individual utter his " peep " on some mild day as early as the latter part of January, and frequently a mild day in February will bring out quite a few to join the chorus. They will sing when the thermometer is well below fifty degrees. The entire chorus, however, seldom gets into full swing before the first week in March, and it is by this full-throated chorus that they are generally known. The note of an individual can be heard for only a comparatively short distance, but when a thousand or more of them join forces with their voices, the sound carries more than half a mile and when one is close to the pond or piece of marshy ground where the choir is assembled, the sound is almost deafening.

To one who is not well acquainted with their ways, it might seem as though it should be an easy task among the great throng of creatures that makes up this tremendous chorus, to locate at least one. If any of my readers imagine that this is so, let them try it some day and find out how greatly mistaken they can be. These little fellows are adept at the art of hiding, and their coloring helps them. Also their voices have a ventriloquistic quality that makes it almost impossible to be certain in which direction or how far away the singer may be. The sound may seem to come from directly in front of you when in reality the singer may be some distance away at your side. As you approach the spot where the company of singers is located, the voices gradually cease until there is a dead silence. Stand perfectly still for a few moments and presently one performer will tune up again with a single, rather uncertain, peep, and gradually the others will join in the refrain until the entire company is again in full swing. Start to move, and silence once more descends as completely as though there had never been a single singer within a mile. Progress from tussock to tussock, if you do not mind wetting your feet, until you estimate that you are about in the midst of the assembly of frogs, but you will have seen no evidence that any are there. Stand perfectly still again and soon the singers will be in full voice about you, even at your very feet, but do you see a single individual? No. Have patience, remain motionless or as nearly so as possible, and presently you may be rewarded by seeing a slight ripple in the water and a diminutive creature, not more than an inch in length, climbs out on a floating stick or leaf and you have seen your first peeper. Your first thought is likely to be how it is possible for so small a creature to make such a noise. It is remarkable, for the carrying power of the voice of the spring peeper is much greater than is that of any of the other frogs, not excepting the giant bullfrog. I would advise you not to attempt to catch one of them without a net, for all you will get is a handful of mud and dead leaves and your clothing will be well spattered with muddy water, not to mention the fact that you will have soaking wet feet. Incidentally the spring peeper makes a most acceptable pet to keep in a terrarium. There should be a shallow dish sunk in one end of it, which should be kept filled with water. Despite their small size they are not delicate, they are easily kept, and small worms, flies or any other small insect will be readily accepted by them as food. They remain awake all winter when in the warmth of a house and, although they will climb about on the plants and the inner sides of the glass of their cage, they will seldom attempt to escape but are, seemingly, entirely satisfied to remain in their small world so long as they have a plentiful supply of food, and their habitation is not allowed to dry out too much. They are very pretty little creatures, ranging in color from a light yellowish brown to a distinct reddish tone, and they have the ability, shared with other members of their class, of changing their color to a certain degree, apparently at will, but always within the shades of brown. On their back is an oblong mark in the shape of an oblique cross which makes a distinguishing mark for easy identification of the species. There is also one V-shaped mark between their eyes and another, reversed, back of the cross. Placed in such a cage, these little fellows will very soon become entirely tame and will make excellent subjects for photography. I would advise, however, that the cage be kept as far as possible from the sleeping quarters of the house, else the entire family may suffer from sleeplessness.

A close relative of the spring peeper, about the same size and coming to life in the spring at about the same time to join the frog chorus, is the cricket frog. To call him a tree frog is almost a misnomer, for, although he is a member of the *Hylidae*, he has entirely terrestrial habits. While he has on his fingers and toes the discs of the climbing frogs, they are so minute as to be useless for that purpose, therefore he must spend his life upon the ground. His voice is not nearly as strident as that of the spring peeper, but more nearly resembles the chirping of a cricket from which fact he derives his name.

Another member of the same family, and also of about the same size, is the swamp tree frog. This species has the widest distribution of any member of the *Hylidae*, being found from the Hudson Bay region of Canada to Florida, and from Maine to California, with the exception of a few states. They are early risers also and in the south their chorus is often heard in late January and early February, before the spring peeper has begun to sing. They, also, are more of a terrestrial than an arboreal species. They are found in marshes, swamps, and pools that are well shut in by thick growth of shrubs and vines. Their voices are not so high or penetrating as are those of the spring peeper, but are low pitched, soft, and have been said to have a soothing sound that " swells and recedes like the waves of the seashore." They are slender and almost delicate in appearance. Their color ranges from almost black to a light shade of brown or tan.

GREEN TREE FROG, ANOTHER BEAUTIFUL SPECIES

Among the tree frogs (*Hylidae*) are some of the most beautiful members of the *Salientia*, and when I say beautiful I really mean beautiful. Of these the Anderson's and the green tree frogs are, perhaps, the handsomest. They resemble each other to some extent in their coloring but once known need never be confused. For years the Anderson's frog was considered to be extremely rare. In fact, up to the year 1904, but six specimens of it had been discovered. Since then, however, it has been found in considerable numbers but is still far from being common. This is largely due to its restricted range which is confined to the cedar swamps of southern New Jersey, eastern Pennsylvania, and South Carolina. It received its name from the fact that the first, the type specimen, was found at Anderson, South Carolina. It is not large, averaging a little less than two inches in length, but is fairly robust. The entire upper portion of the body is a bright pea-green, edged everywhere by a line of white below which is another line of black or dark brown. The upper sides of the legs are green, and the feet purplish gray, with the greater part of the undersides bright yellow. The underparts of the body are violet gray, spotted at the posterior portions with bright yellow.

The coloring of the green frog, which is found in the southern states, is quite similar except that the coloring of the back is apt to be a somewhat more metallic green and the stripe separating the color of the back from that of the underparts is usually yellow with a narrow edging of dark brown on each side. The underparts are unspotted bright yellow. This frog is also considerably larger than Anderson's. In fact it is one of our largest members of the *Hylidae* averaging nearly two and one-half inches in length. It also has a much slimmer body. It is extremely difficult to determine which of the two is the handsomer, but they are both very well worth becoming acquainted with.

Another beautiful species is the Pacific coast tree frog. Its range covers an area from Vancouver Island to Cape St. Lucas, and from the islands of the coast to the eastern base of the Cascades and Sierra Nevada. It is small, averaging an inch and a half in length. Ordinarily its color is any shade of gray, brown, green, or red, usually with some elongated dark spots on the back. These frogs have the ability, which is shared to a greater or less extent by all the members of the *Hylidae*, to change color rapidly and at will. Let us see what Miss Dickerson has to say of two that she watched: " They have been in wet moss in a dark place, and are nearly black in color. When looked at more closely, one is seen to be a very dark green, and the other a rich, dark brown. There is no trace of spots; only the light band above the jaw shows. On exposure to bright light, the color immediately lightens; one becomes decidedly green, the other decidedly brown. Soon a pattern of spots and bands shows obscurely on their backs. This pattern becomes more and more distinct as the background grows lighter. When the medium shade of green or brown is at its brightest, the pattern shows most vividly. However, if they still continue to remain in bright light, we could hardly have time to draw the pattern while it is vivid, for as the background continues to grow light, the spots begin to be dulled. They become less and less distinct, the background becomes still more light in tone, and the pattern wholly fades, and leaves one frog metallic fawn color with golden reflections, and the other yellowish green, of a very light tone. This change from a color so dark that there are no spots, to a light unspotted coloration may take place within eight or ten minutes. Putting the frogs into a dark situation again, they reverse the change, becoming vividly spotted, and finally dark and unspotted."

GREEN AND LEOPARD FROGS

The little southern tree frog is also quite pretty. It is small, averaging only about one and one-quarter inches in length, but it is one of the liveliest of all the tree frogs. In color it is extremely variable and again to quote Miss Dickerson: "At any moment *Hyla squirella* may wear any one of the following costumes: unspotted dark chocolate brown or dark brownish olive; light purplish brown with dark brown spots; light yellowish or grayish brown without spots; any medium shade of brown with green spots; olive green unspotted; light yellow green spotted with brown; unspotted light pea-green; light greenish gray; light fawn color, or still lighter shades ranging down to flesh color."

The member of the *Hylidae* with which the majority of us should be more or less well acquainted, at least through the medium of his voice if not by actual sight, is our little common tree frog, miscalled "tree toad" (*Hyla versicolor*). All through the spring and summer months, especially at dusk and on cloudy or rainy days, we may hear his song coming to us from the foliage of the trees. The note is not unlike that of some bird, high and sweet, but it never varies. The little singer is not easily discovered, for his is an excellent example of protective coloring and marking, although these vary greatly at different times and under differing conditions. In bright light and high temperature it may be a yellowish white with very faint markings or no markings at all. In a dark or damp situation it may be stone gray or brownish with distinct markings, but under most ordinary conditions it is a bright greenish gray with the markings dark and well pronounced. There are times also when considerable bright green appears. His color and markings usually harmonize with his surroundings to such a degree as to make him almost invisible to all but the sharpest eyes. I have frequently placed my hand directly upon one without realizing that he was there until I felt him. He is gentle, confiding, and does not seem to mind being handled, all of which makes him an ideal subject for photography. With all of the *Hylidae* one may obtain a series of photographs showing the different phases of color changes, which greatly enhances the interest.

The bullfrog is the largest of our native batrachians belonging to the family *Ranidae*, frequently reaching a length of body of eight or nine inches exclusive of the legs. He it is whose legs, which often measure as much as ten inches in length, furnish us with one of our epicurean delicacies. These same legs, incidentally, are possessed of great strength, making their owners powerful swimmers as well as jumpers. They are capable of covering without great difficulty a distance of six or seven feet in a single leap. Despite the fact that they are our largest species of frog, they are the last to leave hibernation in the spring and it is usually late May or early June before we hear their deep, guttural "jug-o-rum," "jug-o-rum" coming from the swamps, ponds, and watercourses where they make their homes. They are not so common as are some of the other species of frogs, possibly owing to the fact that they are killed so extensively for food. Also they have many natural enemies. Almost any flesh-eating mammal or bird will prey upon the adults, while the tadpoles are food for fishes and other enemies of pond life. Furthermore they are cannibalistic in their tendencies and the larger ones will eat the smaller whenever the opportunity occurs. The tadpoles of the bullfrog do not develop into frogs until the second season and, therefore, fully grown specimens may be found at any time during the spring and summer months. Despite his size the bullfrog is not aggressive, but on the contrary is gentle and extremely docile when handled, and when placed upon a spot will frequently hold the pose for some time without attempting to leave.

BULLFROG, LARGEST OF ALL OUR SPECIES

The green frog is probably our most abundant species and is to be found commonly throughout eastern North America, from Canada to Florida. It may easily be confused with the bullfrog when the latter has not yet attained his full size, as in coloring and shape the two species are somewhat similar. When both have attained their full growth, however, the bullfrog is fully three to four times the size of the green frog. Both species are almost entirely aquatic, more so than any other of our frogs, and will never venture far from water. " Screaming frog " is an old name by which the green frog is known in many parts of the country because they will, when disturbed on the bank of some pond or stream, especially in the spring, make a high jump into the water, at the same time giving utterance to a high-pitched cry, nearly a scream, which has an almost human sound. One is frequently startled to suddenly hear this at his feet as he is walking along the bank of some pool or brook. In the adult frog, the head and about the forward third of the body is a metallic green which merges into a dull olive brown on the rear portions and sides.

Common in similar localities as the green frog, but often much further away from the water, are those two very similar species, the leopard and the pickerel frogs. The two are nearly related and much alike in appearance, both being brown or greenish brown, with numerous dark brown spots distributed over the body. The spots of the leopard frog, however, are irregularly round, while those of the pickerel frog are decidedly square in shape. Also the underparts of the leopard frog are white, or occasionally pale yellow, while those of the pickerel frog are white in front but bright orange yellow posteriorly. Both are found in grassy meadows through which brooks run, and more often some distance from the water rather than on the immediate bank. Both being extremely active and strong jumpers, they are rather difficult to catch. Once caught, however, and after a little handling, they quiet down to a considerable extent and become fairly tractable subjects for photography. Probably the daintiest and prettiest of our native *Ranidae*, with a modestly delicate beauty all his own, is the little wood frog (*Rana sylvatica*). Slim and streamlined, in color generally a light chocolate brown or fawn color with yellowish underparts and a dark brown elongated patch on either side of the head extending from the eyes back to the shoulder, he is really a thing of beauty. Some day when walking through the woods we may catch a glimpse, if we keep our eyes open, of what seems to be nothing more than a streak of brownish light passing over the dead leaves on the ground. If we have the curiosity to go to the spot where the streak ended we will be rewarded by seeing it again, going off at a tangent for five or six feet. If we are wise in the ways of our native *Batrachia* we will at once know that what we have seen is that will-o'-the-wisp of the woods, the little wood frog. We must, however, have exceedingly sharp eyes, even though we have seen just where he has landed in his last leap, in order to detect him

LEOPARD FROG

against his background of dead leaves, so nearly does his coloring match that of his surroundings. Even after we have been successful in finding him, we will discover that it is next to impossible to catch him, so quick and elusive is he in all his movements. As someone with a poetic turn of mind has said, the wood frog " is to the ground what the chickadee is to the trees — a gentle spirit of the woods."

Many frogs lay their eggs in March or early April, preferably in stagnant pools. Some, especially the *Hylidae*, lay them attached to some water plant in small groups or singly. Others, as the green frog, lay them in large masses often containing a thousand or more eggs. These masses usually float free near the surface of the water, but occasionally are attached to the stem of some water plant. They are always much larger than the frog that lays them, sometimes as much as seven or eight times the size. To the novice it must seem almost a miracle that one small frog can possibly lay the mass of eggs that she does. The mystery is explained by the fact that each true egg is surrounded by a jelly-like, transparent substance which expands to several times its original size immediately upon coming into contact with the water. The eggs themselves are small, averaging about one and one-half to two millimeters in diameter. The size varies somewhat with the different species.

This jelly-like mass that surrounds the true eggs serves three very important purposes. It acts as a kind of incubator for the eggs, and as a buoyant support to keep them from sinking, and also as a most efficient protection to them from the attacks of fish, water insects,

TADPOLE OF THE BULLFROG

turtles, etc., for it converts the entire mass into such an altogether slippery and unwieldy object as to make it next to impossible for any such enemy to handle it successfully.

One should collect and photograph these egg masses even though doing so may necessitate wading in icy water. Moreover they must be collected within a day or so of the time they are laid, for they soon commence to change in appearance and in a few days the young tadpoles begin to wriggle out. It is best, of course, to carry them home in a pail and transfer them to the photographic tank, as it is next to impossible to photograph them where they are found. A tank suitable for this purpose is described in the first chapter of this book. In collecting the eggs, never attempt to lift them from the water with your hands, else you will find them slipping through your fingers like so much soft jelly. Always dip them from the water with the pail or dipper. Also in transferring them to the tank do not pour them in, but take them in a dipper and allow it to sink gently in the water until they are floating free.

GREEN FROG TADPOLE SOON TO BECOME
A FROG

In a few days we will see a change taking place in the shape of the eggs. At first this is only a slight elongation of the black center, but by the fifth or sixth day the embryo has become sickle-shaped and the head end is easily discernible. By the seventh day there is a distinct motion in the embryo, and by the eighth or ninth day the young tadpole will work its way through the surrounding jelly, which has in the meantime softened considerably, and cling by a sucker-like arrangement on the underside of its head to the outside or to any

other support which it may be able to find. At this stage the tadpoles are about a quarter of an inch in length, jet black, and with
the transparent tail fin not difficult to see. They are not active, being content to remain attached to their support for the present.
Each day, however, sees a change. The tail gradually lengthens and
there is a corresponding enlargement of the head.

In two weeks, or a little more, they acquire mouths and at the same
time the suckers by which they attached themselves to the support,
have disappeared. They have also developed an amazing appetite
and from now on until fully grown they seem to have but two real
needs: to eat all that they can get, and to escape their enemies of
which there are always a goodly number about. For those living in
your aquarium the latter need is eliminated, but in their native ponds
the danger is very real. Practically everything that lives in water,
from water beetles and the larvae of various insects to fishes and turtles, and even their own kin, attack and eat them. It is a good deal
of a miracle that any survive this onslaught and become frogs, to
turn the tables on some of their erstwhile enemies and devour them
in their turn. In point of fact but a very small percentage do survive, which is perhaps most fortunate, for if all the tadpoles that are
hatched every spring lived to be full grown frogs, the world in a short
time would be overrun by these batrachians and we would have another plague of frogs. It is one of nature's provisions for maintain-
ing a proper balance among her offspring.

Their food consists entirely of the delicate tips of water plants, the
green slime that forms on stones, etc., on the bottoms of the ponds,
and similar vegetable matter. They spend all of their time nibbling
at these or in short periods of swimming about. By the first of May
those fortunate individuals that have thus far managed to elude their
enemies, are between one and two inches in length, of which the tail,
with its broad, partly transparent fin, occupies nearly two thirds.
Shortly thereafter the hind legs appear and grow very rapidly. A
few days later the front ones break through, the left one usually appearing first. The changes in mouth and eye structure begin. The
tail is slowly absorbed until there is nothing left but a stump, and by
the latter part of the month the entire metamorphosis is complete,
and our tadpole has become a frog.

This description is of a species whose metamorphosis is completed within a few months. A series of photographs taken at intervals during the process is of great interest, and the leopard or the pickerel frog is an excellent subject with which to do it. The metamorphosis of both the green and the bullfrog occupies two and sometimes three years. In making a series of photographs of either of these, it would be best to free the tadpoles in the fall, for they need at least six inches of mud in which to hibernate. New ones can always be caught in the spring in any pool.

The full grown frog can also, of course, be photographed in the tank if we desire to do so. When first put in, however, they are almost certain to jump about in their attempts to escape, thus splashing the water on the inside of the glass and forming ugly bubbles that show in the picture. We should wait until they have quieted down and then carefully wipe the inside of the glass with a wad of cotton on the end of a stick before attempting to photograph them.

APRIL

APRIL is apt to be more or less fickle, especially in the early part, with cold and rather cheerless days and snow flurries not at all uncommon in the northern latitudes, but balmy days become more and more frequent as the month advances, and by its end the weather has become fairly well settled. By the middle of the month, in reality, one can take his camera out for a jaunt in search of new subjects with full assurance that he will meet with no really undue unpleasantness in the way of bad weather.

Someone once remarked, in a moment of temporary poetic aberration, that " April showers bring forth May flowers." He could just as truthfully have said that March showers, or even snowstorms, bring forth April flowers, for very nearly as many flowers can be found in April as in May, but probably the rhymester had never taken the trouble to brave the slightly inclement weather of April to discover just how many flowering plants there are that can be found blooming in that month.

It is true that in the early part of the month the trees are still bare although the buds on most of them are ready to burst, the streams still have a fringe of ice along their edges, and one may find some remains of snowdrifts in the secluded hollows. Nevertheless there are already a considerable number of blossoming plants to be found and as the month advances these increase in number until by the first of May there are a great many more than the average person might think possible.

On many of the trees the leaves start to unfold not long after the first of the month, and on the majority they are fairly well open by its end. There are some rather lovely tree flowers to attract the attention of the botany specialist during the month. Many people who should be better informed are totally unaware of the beauty of the flowers of many of our native trees. True, the majority know the apple and cherry blossoms, but it is doubtful if many of them can differentiate between these and the blossoms of the peach, pear and plum. Unfortunately for the good of the tree, the blooms of the dogwood, which open in this month, are too well known especially to those Sunday drivers of automobiles who deck their cars with branches torn from this most beautiful of all our woodland trees, only to throw them on the rubbish heap upon their return home, faded and useless, all their beauty gone. A few years ago I knew a hillside that was literally white in the spring with dogwood. A highway was built along the base of the hill and today not a single dogwood is left there. I wonder how many of my readers know that the lovely white " petals " of the dogwood are not petals at all, but are enormously enlarged bracts of the true flowers which are clustered in the center and are small, greenish yellow and perfect, that is bearing both stamens and pistils in the same flower. This knowledge does not in any way detract from the beauty of the flower.

Aside from the dogwood and the cultivated fruit trees, there are many of our native trees whose blossoms are really handsome and which make artistic and beautiful photographs when properly handled. Photographs of the blossoms of any of our trees, no matter how small and insignificant, are useful from a botanical standpoint and the nature photographer should not pass any of them by. Probably first among the attractive tree blossoms are those of that small tree or large shrub (it rarely exceeds thirty feet in height), with the pure white, five-petalled, starry blossoms, variously called shadblow, service-berry, or June-berry, which is found on hillsides and in moist soil, particularly along river banks. Its range extends from New Brunswick and Manitoba to Florida and Louisiana. The name shadblow, or shadbush, was of New England origin and given to the tree because it blooms at the time when the shad are swarming up the rivers to spawn. At all events, the flowers are lovely and well worth a trip to the damp woods at this time of the year to photograph. In

June, or early July, the blossoms develop into bright red pomes, or drupes, erroneously called " berries." They are somewhat less than half an inch in diameter, and are the reason for the other common names for the tree. They are a favorite fruit of the birds and also the country boys, if they can reach them before the birds have stripped the trees, for they are sweet and palatable. The wood is fairly resilient and, under the erroneous name of lancewood, is sometimes used in the manufacture of fishing rods. The true lancewood, however, is a small West Indian tree. It is also said that the Indians made their bows from the wood of this tree.

The American holly is in bloom in April, although its blossoming season extends well into May. Joseph Illick, in *Tree Habits*, gives an interesting account of the migration of the American holly: " The original range of the tree was restricted to the southern states but for centuries it has been pushing northward. Each forward step meant the sacrifice of many individuals not hardy enough to withstand the cold of the north woods, but among each generation came a few select specimens hardier than the rest. As these grew their seeds were carried still further north by the birds so that each generation became better fitted to endure the cold. After many years of struggle the holly obtained a foothold in southern Pennsylvania and, in time, became rather abundant. The growth of a few generations of trees in this region produced a race of baby holly trees that were quite frost hardy. In time these yielded frost-hardy seeds that were carried even farther northward, and these seeds developed into trees producing seed crops still more frost hardy."

Today the range of the tree extends from Massachusetts southward along the coast to Florida, Texas, and Missouri. In the north it is more or less stunted, the " Baby race " that Mr. Illicks tells about, rarely becoming much more than a glorified shrub, but in the south, especially the foothills of the Carolinas and the bottomlands of southern Arkansas and Texas, it reaches its full beauty and a height of fifty feet or more. The trees are male and female. That is, the pistillate blooms are born on one tree and the staminate on another. These flowers are somewhat insignificant singly, about three-eighths of an inch in expanse and with four greenish-white petals. They grow in close clusters, however, and make a very pretty sight against the dark, shining green of the leaves.

SHADBUSH OR JUNE-BERRY BLOSSOMS

Two maples also choose this month in which to put forth their blossoms. The sugar maple's staminate and pistillate flowers, borne on the same or on different trees, are suspended on long, drooping, filamentous, hairy pedicels, a considerable number in a single tuft. Together with the newly opened leaves they impart to the trees a delicate loveliness and, incidentally, lend themselves particularly well to photography. The ash-leaved maple, or box elder, differs from all the other maples in that its leaves are compound, having from three to five leaflets which closely resemble those of the tree from which it takes its name. It bears its blossoms, somewhat resembling those of the sugar maple, in April. In another respect it also differs from the rest of the maples. While all the rest may bear the staminate and pistillate blossoms on the same or on separate trees, this one never has both flowers on the same tree.

The two hornbeams, both bearing their blossoms in aments, are blooming in April. The American hornbeam, or blue beech as it is sometimes called because of the resemblance of its bark to that of the beech tree, is found from Nova Scotia to Florida and Texas. It is usually a small tree, rarely reaching a height of more than thirty feet, and usually somewhat less. It has a spreading top that helps to distinguish it from any other tree. The hop hornbeam, so-called from the close resemblance which its fruit bears to that of the hop vine, is a slightly taller tree, occasionally attaining a height of fifty feet. Its bark is rough, somewhat similar to that of the elm, and it does not spread in the manner of the American hornbeam. It is found in much the same range and localities. The name ironwood is sometimes given to this tree on account of the hardness of its wood.

The willows and the poplars put forth their tasseled blossoms in this month, and those who may be interested in photographing them will have to be on the lookout as they are more or less short-lived, dropping within a day or two of maturing. The American elm is also one of our trees that blooms in April. Its flowers are perfect, that is they bear both pistils and stamens in the same blossom. These are also rather short-lived and quite insignificant, but they form a necessary part of a tree series and therefore should not be overlooked. Despite their small size and rather indeterminate coloring, they bloom in such considerable numbers as to impart to the tree a distinct feathery appearance at this time of the year.

There are quite a number of herbaceous plants that bloom in April. All of the early spring flowers are low in growth, most not exceeding four or five inches in height, and many even closer to the ground. Also the more delicate colors prevail, light blue, light pink, and white. There is, of course, the purple of the violets, many of which are in bloom in April, although the full army of the blossoms of these plants do not arrive before May. It may surprise some of my readers to learn that there are about thirty species of violets common to the northeastern states, some twelve or fifteen of which may be found in any one locality. Of these the commonest is the meadow violet (*Viola obliqua*) found almost everywhere in the woods, meadows, marshes, and even along the roadsides, from Nova Scotia to Georgia and Kansas. It spreads with great rapidity and is easily transplanted to any garden, but if left undisturbed it will soon overrun the entire place to the detriment of other plants. Undoubtedly the handsomest of all our species is the bird's-foot violet (*Viola pedata*), so called from the fancied resemblance of its palmate leaves, divided into five or more narrow lobes, to the claw of a bird.

MEADOW VIOLET

The flowers are a dark purplish blue with petals one-half to one inch in length. This species is not common but it may be found growing on dry hillsides or fields from Maine to Florida. It is a plant well worth an extended and persistent search to find and photograph. It should not be confused with the early blue violet (*Viola palmata*) which grows in the woods and has somewhat similar palmate leaves, but with a much lighter blue flower. The coast violet (*Viola Atlantica*) which grows in sandy soil near the coast, has similar leaves, as does also the prairie violet (*Viola perdatifida*) found on the prairies of Saskatchewan, Colorado and Arizona.

There are a few yellow blooms at this time of the year. Among these is the hairy yellow violet (*Viola pubescens*) found in the dry woods, and that outstanding plant of the swamps and low marshy meadows, the marsh marigold or American cowslip, which often grows in half a foot or more of water. Both of its names are misnomers, for the plant is neither a marigold nor a cowslip. It is a member of the crowfoot family to which also belong the buttercups, columbines, anemones, meadow rue and many others of our attractive flowering plants. Another plant that has a yellow blossom is the adder's tongue, or dog-tooth violet. The name dog-tooth violet is a complete misnomer, for the plant does not belong to the violet family and there is no resemblance in any part of its growth to a dog's tooth. The early pointed shoots of the plant when it first starts above the ground may have some resemblance to the point of an adder's tongue, but it needs a vivid imagination to see that resemblance. Another name by which it is sometimes known which is much more appropriate is trout lily. It is a member of the lily family and its favorite haunts are along the banks of woodland streams where trout are wont to lurk.

Of course we are all familiar with that commonest of all our wild flowers, the dandelion, but I wonder if all of us know that it is just as familiar to the inhabitants of every part of the civilized world as to us. It is really somewhat of a pest, for no matter how carefully we may extract each smallest plant from our lawns, we will find them completely starred with the little golden buttons again early the next spring. Nor is it only in the spring and summer that dandelions are in evidence, but through every month of the year, even in December and January, its flowers may be found. Its long, stocky root penetrates very deeply into the ground, and in order to eradicate it completely this root must be pulled up in its entirety. If it is broken and even a small part left in the soil, it simply means that it will send up two shoots where before there was but one. Its motto might well be said to be " never say die." Its name is a corruption of the French " dent-de-lion," or lion's tooth, given to it in France because of the serrated edges of its leaves which were thought to resemble the teeth of this animal.

Trailing the skunk cabbage very closely for honors as first flower of spring comes that really delightful little woodland plant, the hepatica, or liver-leaf. In point of fact its blossoms even open in midwinter on some warm day and in some sheltered spot. This is made possible by the fact that this plant, which is an evergreen,

LIVER-LEAF OR HEPATICA

forms its buds in the fall and they lie under the snow all winter, well protected by a close furry coat and by the leaves which lie close to the ground and cover them. Thus they are all prepared to burst into bloom at the first warm breath of spring, or even a warm day in winter. By the first of April they may be found almost anywhere in the woods.

Closely following the hepatica is the delicate little anemone, or wind flower, so fragile that it would seem as though the least breeze might destroy it, and yet it is sufficiently hardy to brave the winds and cold of early April. Owing to the slenderness of its stems the flowers are in almost constant motion, and one needs a very still day, or a very fast lens and emulsion, to photograph them successfully. There probably are few flowers more honored in folklore and legend than this little star-like blossom. In Greek mythology Anemos, the wind, was supposed to employ it to herald his coming. Pliny declared that their buds could not open unless breathed upon by the wind, which statement is difficult to refute as they are almost constantly played with by every passing zephyr. In Germany they are called " windröschen," or little wind roses. Chemists tell us that they secrete a somewhat dangerous juice and yet the ancient Romans picked them with the remark " I gather thee for a remedy from disease " and were, in their belief, protected from illness thereafter. The Chinese plant the flower on their graves and call it Death Flower. In a way the genus *Anemone* is somewhat remarkable for it encircles the earth in its various species, but never steps outside of the temperate zone.

To me one of the loveliest sights of early spring which may often be seen in the latter part of March or throughout April in marshy spots, is the young shoots of the cinnamon fern, commonly called

A " Fairy Ring " of Cinnamon Fern
" Fiddle Heads "

" fiddle-heads " from the fact that their coiled leaves so closely re- semble the head of a violin. They frequently grow in rings called by the imaginative " fairy rings," and they have great possibili- ties for artistic results in photography. The name is given this fern from the fact that its fertile fronds, which we may later see standing above the surrounding sterile fronds, are a distinctly cinnamon color.

Two of the daintiest of our earlier spring flowers are those two dwellers of the dry woods and rocky hillsides, found blooming throughout April, the bloodroot and Dutchman's breeches, both members of the poppy family. The first is well named for, on break- ing the stem or root, a blood-red sap exudes which stains anything with which it comes in contact. The Indians used it as a war paint, hence another name by which it is sometimes called is Indian paint.

BLOODROOT   DUTCHMAN'S BREECHES

The flowers have an evanescent beauty and those of today are gone by tomorrow, so that in order to obtain a photograph of them, we must catch them when they first open. The Dutchman's breeches, or *Dicentra* which, to me, is a much more appropriate name for such a daintily lovely flower, is somewhat sturdier in its growth in that the blossoms will last for several days. Its flowers, and the manner of their attachment to the stem, show it to be a close relative of the bleeding heart of our old-fashioned gardens.

One of our early spring flowers that is found blooming throughout the month of April and well into May is a member of the orchid family, the showy, gay, or spring orchis. It is found in rich woods, especially under hemlocks, from New Brunswick to Ontario and Minnesota, and south to Georgia, Kentucky, and Nebraska. Its four to seven flowers, whose upper petals are a pinkish purple, with the lower one (the lip) white, are borne on a thick spike which rises to a height of from four to eight inches from between two glossy green, broad, fleshy leaves. It is far from common and the finding of one, and photographing it, is quite an event in the life of any nature photographer. It may surprise those whose knowledge of orchids is confined to those exotic species found in this country only in greenhouses and florist's shops, to learn that there are in North America about one hundred native species, more than half of which are to be found growing in the eastern states. While the majority of these cannot compare either in size or beauty with those specimens found in the tropics, we have many that are among the loveliest of our wild flowers.

The trilliums, or wake robins, immortalized by John Burroughs, make their appearance in this month. The first to bloom is the dark red, ill-scented trillium, its flower rising on an erect stem from the center of a whorl of three leaves. It is a rather handsome flower, laboring under the disadvantage of a somewhat disagreeable scent which it uses to attract the early bees and flies. A little later come the large-flowered and painted trilliums, both beautiful blossoms that would grace any garden. The trilliums earn their name from the fact that they govern their lives by the rule of three. They have three sepals, three stamens, three petals, three styles, a three-celled ovary, and the leaves grow in whorls of three, from the center of which rises the flower stem.

In low meadows the spring beauty, a close relative of the gaudy-flowered portulaca of our gardens, and that pest of the farmers the purslane, or " pussley," frequently spreads a carpet of delicate pink over considerable areas, while on the higher, drier hillsides and fields the little bluet (*Houstonia*) covers the ground with a most delightful bluish haze.

The early saxifrage is blooming in April. The cluster of small white flowers tops a six-inch stem rising from a small mat of leaves pressed close to the ground. Not infrequently it grows from some rock crevice, or even from a split rock, where it would seem as though no plant life possibly could exist. Probably the type specimen, from which the plant was named, was found growing in some such situation. At all events, the name given it would indicate as much for it is derived from two Latin words: *saxum*, a rock, and *frango*, I break.

In the brooks the water cress is blossoming. It is probably better known to the majority of people as a salad green than as a blossoming plant, and yet its flowers are not unattractive. Later in the month the wild azalea, or pinxter flower as the Dutch colonists named it, is in bloom in the dry woods. This beautiful flowering shrub is in grave danger of becoming extinct, owing to the ruthless manner in which the flower-gathering vandals destroy the bushes in their endeavor to pick every last flower. In the low woods at this time of the year grows the wild mandrake, putting forth its rather showy white blossoms, one to each plant, beneath its umbrella-like leaves. It usually grows in quite large groups. Later, in July and

WILD AZALEA

August, the yellow, egg-shaped fruit is a delight to the small boy who, despite its sickly sweet taste, considers it decidedly edible.

A strange and rather lovely plant that may be found in bloom in April is the naked, or pale, broomrape. It is a parasitic plant living on the roots of various herbs. As it takes its sustenance from the assimilated juices of other plants it has no need for the green coloring matter, chlorophyl, with which honest plants protect themselves from too strong light. Therefore it stands brown and leafless, although the flowers themselves are a pale violet, sometimes white.

On some rocky hillside, most often growing in the rich, dark loam made by rotting leaves lodged between the rocks, we will probably find what is possibly one of our most peculiar wild flowers, the wild ginger. The aromatic, ginger-like taste of its roots is responsible for its name. Two large heart-shaped leaves, dark green above and lighter beneath, rise conspicuously on six to ten inch downy stems, and the solitary flower on a stem seldom exceeding half an inch in length, sprouts from beneath the leaf stems at their base. It is often lost among the dead leaves on the ground and is so inconspicuous that it is seldom noticed unless looked for. It is a peculiar flower with a deep, cup-shaped calyx terminating in three spreading, sharply pointed, dark purplish-brown lobes. It is said by botanists that this plant produces its flowers thus close to the earth in order to accommodate the earlier flies and gnats that find it not only a source of food, but a snug retreat from the cold of early spring.

A member of the arum family which we will find in bloom at this time is that rather strange inhabitant of the marsh ponds, the golden club. The spadix, or flowering part, corresponds to the " Jack " of Jack-in-the-pulpit and is very similar to that of the calla lily, both of which plants belong to the same family. It lacks, however, the enveloping white cloak, or spathe, of the latter and the greenish and reddish " pulpit " of the former. In order to obtain photographs of this plant, it is often necessary to wade in ice-cold water.

This is the month when we must look for our salamanders if we wish to photograph them. The name salamander probably means but little to the majority of my readers, for unless one knows their habits and just where to look for them, and is willing to spend hours in cold, damp situations hunting them out of their hiding places, it is unlikely that he will ever see one except by some extremely lucky chance. One may tramp the woods and fields frequently, with eyes well on the lookout for anything in the way of wild life, and never see one of these interesting creatures. A few species in certain localities, such as the common newt and dusky salamander, are fairly common, but the great majority are not at all common and some are extremely rare and, owing to their retiring habits, are far from easy to find even by one who knows their ways. On a sunny, warm day of early spring they may be found in the greatest numbers in their chosen haunts, but we must know these haunts in order to find them. A haphazard search will produce no results or, at the best, but meager ones.

Salamanders are very interesting little creatures, and though most of them are more or less dull in coloring, some are quite beautiful and the search for them is never anything but a pleasure, and the finding of each new species an event to be looked forward to with tremendous anticipation. Furthermore they may be handled with impunity as they are all entirely harmless. As they are not extremely rapid in their movements, some being even quite sluggish especially upon a fairly cool day, they do not make very difficult subjects for photography.

But I can hear some of my readers exclaim, " Just what is this elusive creature, the salamander, about which you are talking? " If one can believe the ancient myths, it was once a creature, one of the genii, that was partial to and passed most of its existence in fire. The word, therefore, has come to mean by common usage any person or creature that can easily withstand great heat. Possibly such an animal once existed. Who knows? But if so, and the present salamander is its descendant, then it must have made a material change in its mode of living since its earlier, fire-loving days for in its present existence at least half of its life is spent in water, and the remainder in fairly cool, damp situations. It may be possible that, in the choice of such living quarters, it is endeavoring to eliminate from its body the heat accumulated during its existence in those torrid, prehistoric days.

But to leave fiction and come down to hard facts, the salamanders are cold-blooded vertebrates, intermediate between the fishes and reptiles and belonging to the class *Amphibia*, to which class also belong the frogs and toads. They are called batrachians and belong to the order *Caudata*, or tailed batrachians, as distinctive from the tailless batrachians (the frogs and toads) which belong to the order *Salientia*.

Like the frogs and toads, the young, or tadpoles, of the salamanders are born in and spend the first months of their lives as entirely aquatic animals. With most of them the second half of their lives is spent more on land than in the water, although they return to that element quite frequently, some, in fact, spending most of their lives there.

In both the *Caudata* and the *Salientia*, when the time comes to leave the water, lungs are developed and the gills disappear. Thereafter they breathe through their mouths and nostrils. The main point of difference between the two orders, by which they may always be distinguished, lies in the fact that the young of the frogs and toads, as they approach maturity, gradually absorb their tails. When they leave the water, there is but a short stump left, and even this eventually disappears. The tails of the salamanders, on the other hand, never grow any smaller but increase in size with the growth of the body. In fact in some species, notably the long-tailed salamander, this member increases in length out of all proportion to the growth of the body. The eggs of the two orders are similar, with the exception that those of many of the frogs are usually laid in large masses often consisting of several thousand eggs, while those of the salamanders are laid singly or in twos or threes, or occasionally, as in the case of the spotted salamander, in small masses.

According to most herpetologists, there are nine families and about two hundred and fifty known species of salamander, of which nearly one hundred are found in North America. As I have said, some of these are fairly common in their special haunts, but many of them are not common and are rarely seen by the casual observer. To photograph them one must first learn something of their habits and then hunt them persistently or else but very few of the many species will be found.

When the time arrives for salamanders to leave the water after they have attained their full growth and exchanged gills for lungs, they seek cool, damp situations, for they will soon die if forced to remain for any length of time where it is dry and hot. In fact when using them for photographic subjects one should never allow their skins to become entirely dry. They are to be found under stones, fallen tree trunks, in decaying vegetation, beneath dead leaves and other similar hiding places in low, moist woods. The decaying debris around a stagnant pool or watercourse will generally disclose several. I have frequently found them in damp cellars and old outhouses. Probably one of the most likely spots in which to find them is beneath some half-rotten log, lying partially submerged on the bank of some woodland pool.

The species that are found in this country range in size from the four-toed salamander which is one about two and one-half inches in length, to the hellbender which attains a length of two and one-half feet. It is a water species, spending but little time on land. It is found from western New York and the Ohio River and its tributaries, southward to Georgia and Louisiana. The largest known salamander, the giant salamander of Japan, belongs to the same family as the hellbender and frequently attains a length of five feet or over.

The hellbender is not only the largest of our salamanders but is also by far the ugliest in appearance, but it is entirely harmless. It exudes a quantity of slime which makes it not only difficult but extremely unpleasant to handle, but if one cares to he can do so with complete impunity. It is a dark, muddy brown or gray in color, and is altogether a most unattractive creature, but despite this fact we should photograph it when we have the opportunity.

In some parts of Pennsylvania and New Jersey, and further south, occurs the next largest of our salamanders, the mud puppy or water dog. It has much in common with the hellbender as it is large, reaching a foot and one-half in length, is about the same color and is almost, if not quite, as repulsive in looks. It may be distinguished from the latter, however, by the fact that it has on each side of its neck three bushy, bright red gills. It has been called the " Peter Pan " of salamanders because it " never grows up " but remains in the larval stage all of its life, never leaving the water. During the day it remains quiet among the weeds at the bottoms of the ponds and sluggish watercourses, but at night it wanders about in search of the small fish, worms and water insects upon which it feeds. It has been given the name locally of " mud-eel " on account of its slow, eel-like movements.

Probably the species of salamander that is better known than any other by the majority of people is the common newt. This little fellow really passes through three stages of existence. During the first season it remains in the water in the larval stage, in color dark green above, yellowish below, and with a row of bright red spots along each side. In the fall, after completing its first metamorphosis, it leaves the water and its color changes to a uniform bright vermilion with a series of golden spots along each side. In this stage it is known as the red eft, red lizard, red evet, and other locally common names, and is frequently met in the woods, especially after a shower, shining like a living jewel on the wet leaves. It is one of the loveliest objects of our woods. This land existence lasts until the autumn of the third or the spring of the fourth year. It passes much of its time in rotten logs, beneath stones, or burrowing beneath the fallen leaves, in its search for small worms and small insects. It emerges from its obscurity quite frequently but only after rain or at night. At the end of this period, when it has reached full size and sexual maturity, its color gradually changes back to the original green, its lungs cease to function, and it returns to the water in order to breed. In this stage it may be found in considerable numbers in almost any stagnant pool immediately after the ice melts in the spring. If we wish to photograph these little newts while in their amphibious existence, we must use the tank described in the last chapter. Take them from their native habitat with a net, carry them home in a small pail and transfer them to the tank in which you have first placed some water plants found growing in places that the newts frequent.

Another common member of this class is the dusky salamander, sometimes called brown newt. In many situations it is by far the most abundant of all the species. It is found beneath stones, dead leaves, and similar locations in wooded spots near streams. In some places it is so numerous that nearly every stone will conceal one or more. It is very agile and when uncovered will quickly wriggle out of sight. In color it is a uniform dark dusky brown. The redbacked and the two-lined salamanders, the former with a broad, dark-red band along the length of its back, the latter with a dark streak along each side, are almost equally as common, equally as agile, and are to be found in similar localities.

One of the most brilliant of the species is the red salamander, or red triton as it is also called. As its name implies, it is of a uniform, brilliant, orange red fairly well covered with minute black spots. It is rather robust and measures about four and one-half inches in length when fully matured. Old specimens occasionally become a uniform grayish brown in color. It is almost entirely aquatic, although found occasionally in damp upland woods and fields under wet logs or stones. Cold woodland springs seem to have a special attraction for it. Cope, an authority on reptiles and amphibians, most aptly said of it that " here, beneath stones, it may be always found, occupying, if possible, the fissure from which the limpid water rises, and displaying its beautiful hues through the transpar-

BLOTCHED SALAMANDERS

ent medium with the brilliancy of a strange exotic, rather than the pallor of a dweller in the chilly depths and dark recesses of a cave."

Two other handsome species are the spotted salamander and the marbled salamander. The former is black with a row of yellow spots, often as much as an eighth of an inch in diameter, on either side of the body from the head to the tail. The latter is also black with a series of grayish-white hour-glass shaped markings across its back and tail.

Probably averaging larger than any other of the smaller species, often reaching a length of nine inches, the tiger salamander is also a handsome fellow. With its large, wide head, broad tail, and beautifully mottled yellow and black body, it is most distinctive. It is a southern species rarely, if ever, found north of southern New Jersey. A most remarkable fact concerning this species is that, should conditions under which the young are born and live not be entirely suited to their wants and needs, their development is suspended for a prolonged period, frequently extending over the entire length of their lives. What is still more remarkable is that, while in this immature condition, they are capable of reproduction and the young thus produced may either go through with their complete metamorphosis or, like their parents, remain in the tadpole stage all of their lives. This immature form is called axolotl.

The blue-spotted and the Texas salamanders are very similar in appearance although belonging to different genera, and both rather handsome. They are both black, liberally covered with blue spots, but those on the Texas salamanders are likely to be somewhat paler. It is unfortunate that the blue-spotted salamander is remarkable for the viscous or powerful sticky secretion which it exudes, which makes it unpleasant to handle. From this fact it is also known as the slimy, or sticky, salamander. The Texas salamander is not confined, as its name might imply, to Texas but is found from Kansas and Nebraska to Illinois, North Carolina, Louisiana, and Texas. Another handsome species is the ringed salamander found in Arkansas and Missouri. Probably the species most easily recognized of them all is the long-tailed salamander whose tail is fully twice the length of its body, and tapers to a sharp point.

The photographing of a salamander is not a difficult proceeding, because none of them are very rapid in their movements. It is not easy to photograph them satisfactorily in their actual habitat, although it can be done with a reflex camera. My method is to remove them to some spot specially prepared for the work. After securing my specimen I select a suitable posing place, an old log, stump, stone, or the ground itself. Here I place an object, as nearly as possible the same size and shape as my subject, and on this I focus sharply. I then stop down my lens slightly to be certain of sharp focus over the entire field, set my shutter, remove the object upon which I focused, and place my subject in the same spot. In most cases the salamander at first refuses to stay where it is put, but after being replaced several times it usually decides to remain quiet for the few seconds necessary for the exposure. One must always bear in mind in this work that the handling of these little creatures must be done with care. If one finds that after a time the body of his subject is becoming dry, he should give it a dip in water or place it on a damp piece of moss for a while. A salamander must keep its body moist in order to live.

I once asked a friend how many species of toads there are in North America. His answer, given with an air of supreme surprise, was: " Why, are there more than one? " This man had every reason for knowing better, for he is a well-read man, far above the average in intelligence, and, moreover, he is interested, to a certain extent, in the natural sciences. He has accompanied me on numerous photographic jaunts and helped me in many of my tight places, and yet

RINGED SALAMANDER

he was greatly surprised to learn that the common little friend of our gardens, fields and roadsides, the American toad, was not the only species of toad in North America. But this lack of knowledge on the subject was entirely natural for, after all, unless one is particularly interested in learning of the different species and searching for them, there is only one that will ordinarily be seen. Should one see other species in different parts of the country, he will probably quite naturally class them all as the same animal, so closely do they in many instances resemble each other.

We have in North America some twenty-eight different species and sub-species of toads. The commonest is the American toad (*Bufo americana*), undoubtedly well known to us all. Throughout the Rocky Mountain region its place is taken by the Rocky Mountain toad. In the south the Southern toad is pre-eminent, while the west and southwest can boast of a number of species.

Although the American toad is common, and can be seen on any day throughout the summer, I wonder just how much my readers really know concerning him. He is greatly maligned, for we are constantly hearing stories that tend to give him an unsavory reputation. How many times have I heard someone exclaim when a toad is seen: " Do not touch him or he will give you warts." Of course this is ludicrously untrue, as is also the epithet of " slimy " that is frequently applied to the toad. Under ordinary conditions he is dry, but when roughly handled he has a protective habit of exuding a fluid which is colorless and odorless, but entirely harmless. He will also, when seized in the mouth of an enemy with such a grip as to cause pain, exude a slightly poisonous fluid which has a somewhat disagreeable effect upon the glands of the mouth and will frequently cause his enemies to drop him after having once been seized. Snakes do not appear to be affected by it, as they will devour a toad whenever the opportunity offers, but a dog or other animal will seldom bother one a second time after having experienced one dose, unless driven to it by extreme hunger. This fluid is absolutely harmless to human skin, but one should never rub his eyes after handling a toad, before washing his hands, as it is just possible that he might have some of the secretion on his fingers which would cause his eyes to smart although doing them no real harm. However, the toad rarely, if ever, uses this means of protection unless he is being severely hurt.

It has also been said by superstitiously inclined persons that the toad brings ill luck. Far from this being a fact, the reverse is true, as anyone who owns a garden in which a few toads have made their home will testify. The toad has an insatiable appetite. His entire diet consists of insects and worms, and one or two toads in a garden will do more than almost anything else to keep the plants free of insect pests. The manner in which a toad obtains his food is interesting. He will have nothing but living, moving viands, and his tongue is very well adapted for catching them. Its surface is covered with a glutinous substance to which any small object which it touches will adhere. It is attached to the extreme front of his mouth, instead of the back as in other animals, extending well back into the throat, and is capable of being thrown forward for about two inches, with great rapidity. Let an unfortunate fly, or other insect up to the size of a June bug or fairly large-sized grasshopper, alight within that distance of his nose, and without the least perceptible motion of his head or body the tongue has shot forward, has touched the insect which adheres to its sticky surface, and has been withdrawn with its captive into the toad's throat. All this is done with such incredible speed as to be practically imperceptible. One instant the insect is there, and the next it is gone, and that is all we know about it even though we are watching the operation closely. If the prey is somewhat beyond the reach of the tongue, there is a slight forward movement of the body as the tongue is flipped out, and the result is the same — the instantaneous disappearance of the insect.

The toad is largely nocturnal in its habits. Its eyes are not fitted for seeing in the dark, but there is usually sufficient light even on the darkest nights, for him to see his prey with sufficient clearness to make his catch. The period between daylight and dark is the time that he loves best. He also knows that a light will attract insects, and when possible he will make such an illuminated spot his hunting ground. I knew, with some intimacy, a toad that lived near a street arc light. Every night he would appear shortly after the light was lit and proceed to catch the insects that fluttered to the ground. After some hours of this he would become so completely sated that his return to his retreat seemed more than he could accomplish.

Besides the idea entertained by many people that toads cause warts if handled, there are many other weird traditions surrounding these little, inoffensive creatures. In early writings may be found many allusions to their venomous qualities, medicinal virtues, and many other absurd beliefs. Possibly the most amazingly ludicrous of them all was the tale of the valuable jewel that the toad secreted inside his homely old skull. Up to the present day many such superstitions are firmly believed by otherwise intelligent people. One can still find those who place great reliance in the belief that a toad's breath will poison infants; that good luck will visit a newly built house when a toad takes up his abode in the cellar; that if a toad is killed it will cause cows to give bloody milk; that " ring-bone " can be cured by tying a toad to the ankle of the afflicted horse; and many other absurd and conflicting attributes. Even in poetry the toad was thought ill of and despised, as is evidenced by the couplet from Spenser's " Faerie Queene ":

" The grisly toadstool grown there mought I see,
And loathed paddocks (toads) lording on the same."

Another extravagant story told of the toad is its ability to live
indefinitely without air or food. Every little while we see accounts
in the papers of the finding of a toad imbedded in a rock, where it
must have been for years if not centuries, and still alive. It is entirely improbable that any of these stories can be borne out by
facts. Experiments seem to show conclusively that, while the toad
undoubtedly is capable of remaining in a dormant state for considerable periods of time, there is a limit to his existence under such conditions. Buckland, an eminent zoologist, buried toads both in sand-
stone, where they were dead in thirteen months, and in limestone,
where they survived for two years. Other experiments of similar
nature have been made with similar results. The fact that they are
able to retain life under such conditions for such lengths of time
seems sufficiently remarkable to me, without attempting to stretch
the truth.

We all probably know that in its early stages the toad is an
aquatic animal. The adult constructs a retiring place, wherein he
sleeps and is secure from his enemies during the day, by excavating
a burrow under some stone, board, shrubbery or other place that
will provide a roof. He excavates backward with his hind feet, and
always enters backward so that he may be facing the entrance. In
the fall he pushes his way further in and allows the dirt and debris to
fall over him and enclose him completely, and there he spends the
winter in a torpid state. About the first of May, toads emerge and
seek the nearest pool or stagnant watercourse where the eggs are
deposited by the female. Each female lays from four to twelve
thousand eggs but, unlike the frogs, these are laid in a long string
surrounded by the jelly-like mass, the whole having the appearance
of a rope dotted at regular intervals by small black dots. The tadpoles when first born and until their legs appear, are jet black.
They remain in the water until their tails have been almost completely absorbed, and until all four of their legs are in working order.

Early in July the borders of pools, ditches and ponds are apt
to be literally alive with baby toads averaging about half an inch
in length. They cover the ground and frequently find their way

into our streets and yards, giving rise, should a shower occur at about that time, to another foolish superstition: that they have rained down. Their growth is extremely slow and it is two or three years before they reach complete maturity. During this period the skin is shed a number of times, every few weeks when young, and about four times a year when older. The process of molting is peculiar and well worth watching, if one is so fortunate as to find a toad in the act of changing his dress. In order to understand the process one must know that the toad's skin extends in an unbroken sheath not only over his entire face, but over the lips as well. When the time arrives that his coat has become too tight for comfort, he humps his back and the skin splits down the midline, across the end of his body, and across his chest. The skin, thus loosened, is then drawn into the mouth at the corners until it has entirely disappeared. In other words he literally eats his old suit and appears in a bright new one.

The song of the toad is a sweet, tremulous note very like a bird call, that we may hear almost any evening during late spring and early summer, coming from the edges of ponds and watercourses. It is one of the sweetest sounds of nature, despite the grotesque appearance of the creature that produces it. When the entire toad chorus is in full swing it is something well worth going some distance to hear. It has been likened to the opening movement of Beethoven's " Moonlight Sonata " which may to some seem to be far-fetched but which is, in reality, a not inapt comparison.

I have been speaking in particular of our common species, the American toad, but what I have said is also applicable in most part to almost any of the species. Fowler's toad is almost equally as common in the eastern part of the country as the American toad. The two species may readily be confused by one not well acquainted with both, as they are very similar in appearance, but their voices have no resemblance, for that of the Fowler's toad is decidedly harsh and guttural. The call, often starting on a high note, rapidly descends to a low mournful croak. It may be heard for a considerable distance and when a number of toads are congregated in some pool, as often happens, the resulting sound is weird and most disagreeable.

Although Fowler's toad may easily be mistaken for its American cousin, it may readily be distinguished by the following features: It

is always tan or olive in coloring, never having the richer reddish
tones which are often found on the American toad. The undersides
are immaculate while those of the American toad are spotted or
blotched. Also its upper parts are more uniform in coloring and
pattern and much smoother, never having the large warts so much
in evidence on its cousin. The light vertebral stripe that extends
from the nose down the middle of the back to the tail is distinct in
Fowler's toad, while in the American it is not nearly so pronounced
and often entirely wanting.

Undoubtedly the strangest of all of our native species are the
spadefoot toads (*Scaphiopus*). There are four species in the United
States, the hermit spadefoot of the east, the southern spadefoot, the
western spadefoot, and the spadefoot of the plains. While they are
all more or less sluggish, nocturnal, subterranean creatures that seldom see the light of day, our hermit spadefoot of the east is pre-
eminent in this respect. He spends nearly his entire life in underground burrows, and when he does see fit to leave his subterranean
retreat it is always in the night. He has been found as deep as three
or four feet beneath the surface of the earth with nothing to show
how he got there, or how he could get out if he wished to do so. If
by accident we should happen to turn one up during some digging
operation, we would be very likely to think it nothing but a clod of
earth unless he should open his eyes wide enough to attract our
attention. These eyes are large and of a beautiful golden color with
a vertical slit of black. Placed on the ground these toads will never
attempt to jump or crawl away, but will gradually sink into the
earth until, in a short time, they will have entirely disappeared.
This is accomplished by means of their hind feet which are specially
formed for digging. Once a year they leave their burrows and
seek the nearest pool by the hundreds, in order to lay their eggs.
This occurs in late April or May, always at night, and usually during a rainstorm. They remain but one, possibly two, nights before
again resuming their underground life. During this short period
they can make the nights hideous with their weird, raucous calls.
These have been likened by various writers to " a deafening agoniz-
ing roar, hoarse and woeful," " shrill, ear-piercing groans," " loud
bellowings," etc. Such terms are hardly exaggerations as descriptive
of their calls. At its best the " song " can never, by the wildest

stretch of imagination, be called tuneful. After the eggs are laid, the spadefoots disappear again and thereafter, for another year, the finding of one is entirely a matter of accident.

The smallest known toad, a diminutive, dusky, hopping creature which no doubt has often been mistaken for a young Southern toad, is the dwarf, or oak toad, found from the Carolinas to Alabama,

HERMIT SPADEFOOT TOAD

Florida and Louisiana. It averages only about one and one-quarter inches in length when fully matured. It is an extremely active little fellow, in color a rich, dark brown, and is abroad at all times of the day and night, sunshine or rain.

Another very small species, averaging but slightly larger than the foregoing, found from South Carolina, Georgia, and Florida westward to Texas, is the narrow-mouthed toad. It can never be mistaken for any other species as its head is tiny in comparison to its body, and completely out of all proportion. It narrows almost to a point at the nose, with a small mouth from which it takes its name. Its legs are short but, nevertheless, it is surprisingly active, proceeding in a series of short, quick jumps which makes it exceedingly difficult to catch.

The majority of toads make most desirable subjects for the nature photographer. They object but little to being handled so long as the handling is not done in too rough a manner, and being naturally of a somewhat sluggish nature, they will often remain quiescent in one spot long enough to allow of focusing upon them and making the exposure. Some are more active and with these it is best to use the method of focusing upon some object approximately their size and then substituting them for the object when we are ready to make the photograph. If preferred, the photographic tank without the water can be used as a cage in which to photograph them. Incidentally this is the only kind of cage I ever use in my work.

MAY

MAY has been called the month of flowers, but while it is true that a great many are in bloom in this month, there are just as many, if not really more, in some of the other months. However, there are more trees in bloom in this month than in any other, and many of them are those that bear the finest blossoms. Foremost among these are our so-called fruit trees, the apple, cherry, plum, pear, and peach. These are all cultivated species. But growing in the thickets, open woods, old pastures, waste lands, and often along fence rows and old roads, are " escapes " of both the apple and pear that have reverted to their original state. There is one native species, the crab apple, that may be found quite frequently in similar places. The peach tree is also occasionally found as an escape, as are also the plum and cherry. The wild black cherry, or rum cherry as it is sometimes called, and the choke cherry are very similar in appearance except that the fruit of the choke cherry is at first a bright red turning to dark red when fully matured, while the fruit of the black cherry is a shining black when ripe. These, as well as the sour, or Morello cherry, and the St. Lucie cherry, are native trees.

Then there is that small but lovely tree, the mountain ash. The native species should not be confused with the European whose flowers and fruit are somewhat larger, and which is the one most often found under cultivation. Our mountain ash is found from Newfoundland and southern Labrador to Manitoba, and southward to North Carolina. Its favorite habitat is moist woods, especially by lake shores and along mountain streams. The European species has been naturalized in the northeastern states and Canada where it is frequently found growing wild. It is no less lovely in the fall when hung with bunches of bright red, berry-like fruit (pomes) than in the spring when fairly well covered by the masses of white blossoms.

BLOSSOMS OF THE HAWTHORN

One of the loveliest of our smaller trees, or large shrubs, is the hawthorn. This rarely grows to a height exceeding twenty feet under the most favorable conditions, and its dainty, white, cherry-like blossoms appear toward the end of the month. It is a member of the thorn family (*Crataegus*) which comprises several hundred species, all characterized by the long, exceedingly sharp thorns with which they are armed. The blossoms of them all are white, and the cherry-like fruit is red, and they are nearly all natives of the United

BLOSSOMS OF THE SWEET BAY, ONE OF THE MAGNOLIAS

States or Canada. They are very closely related to one another, and have many characteristics that are practically identical, so that it is often difficult to distinguish them. There are some that are fairly distinctive, however, such as the cockspur thorn, the Washington thorn, the scarlet thorn, the dwarf thorn, and, of course, the lovely hawthorn.

Another tree made beautiful at its blossoming time in the latter part of May or early June, is the common, or black, locust, undoubtedly well known to us all. It is a member of the pea family, as is readily testified to by the sweetly scented, white blossoms, as well as by the seeds which are borne in pods in the fall. At one time the tree was confined to the slopes of the Appalachian range of mountains from Pennsylvania to Georgia, but it gradually extended its range until now it is distributed pretty generally over all those states east of the Rocky Mountains.

As a family the magnolias must rank high among the trees of America for beauty not only of the flowers, but of the foliage as well. The family is composed of some twenty species from which many showy varieties and hybrids have been developed, which are used extensively to beautify our gardens. In this country we have seven native species, all found in the eastern and southern portions. But only two, the sweet bay, or laurel magnolia, the smallest of the species, and the cucumber tree, so named from the shape of its fruit, are found in any numbers except in the southern states. The sweet bay is found from eastern Massachusetts along the coast to Florida, and through Texas to Arkansas. In the north it is hardly more than an overgrown shrub, but in the south it reaches a height of about fifty feet. Its leaves, dark green and glossy, are from three to six inches long and shaped like those of the laurel. Its lovely blossoms are first found in May and continue in bloom until August. They are cup-shaped, satiny in texture, and of a light cream color. They measure about two inches in depth and about the same or possibly a little more in width, and are things of very real beauty. The cucumber tree might be called the poor relation of the family. Its flowers with straggly, ill-shaped petals of a greenish-yellow color, so nearly matching that of the foliage as to make them hardly perceptible, are far from being attractive. These flowers, and the long, cucumber-shaped fruit, turning from green to bright red in the autumn, are sure identifications for this tree. It grows to a height of from fifty to ninety feet, and is found more or less commonly from western New York along the mountains to Virginia and Georgia.

The handsomest of them all is the long-leaved magnolia, a truly magnificent tree whose habitat extends from the foothills of the Alleghenies to North Carolina and Florida. It is not a tall tree, seldom exceeding fifty or sixty feet in height, but the beauty of its enormous blossoms, ordinarily six to eight inches across and frequently as much as a foot, and its leaves, dark glossy green, and from sixteen to thirty-six inches in length, fully recompense for the lack of height in the tree. As far as is known, the magnolias were the first trees to develop flowers, and the blossoms produced by some of them are the largest borne by any tree of the present time. They were given their name in honor of Pierre Magnol, a distinguished French botanist and professor of botany at Montpelier, in the seventeenth century.

The tulip tree, the closest relative of the magnolias, is one of the largest trees of the eastern states. In the southern states it ordinarily grows to a height of one hundred and fifty feet and has been known to reach a height of two hundred feet. In the north it seldom exceeds one hundred feet, but is still one of our finest trees. Its peculiar square-shaped leaves and its handsome, yellow, tulip-like flowers, which give to it the name by which it is commonly known, are easy identifications for the tree. The flowers appear late in May or early in June.

A tree producing handsome, pale bluish purple, bell-like flowers in tall upright racemes in May, is the Paulownia, or Princess Tree. It is a native of Japan and China and named for a Russian princess — Anna Paulownia. It was introduced into this country many years ago for the beauty of its blossoms and leaves, which are large and heartshaped. It was extensively planted for ornamental purposes and has since escaped from cultivation and is found, not too commonly, from southern New York southward to Florida and Texas. It is a close relative of our native catalpa, or Indian bean, as may easily be seen by the similarity between both the flowers and the leaves, although the flowers of the catalpa are white strongly veined inside with purple and do not appear before June or July.

There are many other trees whose blossoms appear in this month which make beautiful photographs. The oaks all put forth their tasseled blooms (aments). The sassafras, from the roots and bark of which is derived the oil used in flavoring candies and scenting soap and liniment, bears its flowers in pendent, yellowish-green racemes. The ash trees bear both staminate and pistillate flowers on the same tree, the former in dark purplish clusters, the latter in elongated, rather open panicles. The sycamore, buttonwood, or plane tree, also bears both flowers on the same tree, the staminate being a small, dark red ball pendent on a long woolly peduncle, or stem, while the pistillate pendant is on a similar stem but somewhat larger, green and hairy. The American linden, or basswood, used extensively for street and other ornamental planting, has sweet-smelling, yellowish-white blossoms which are a boon to the bees that visit them in swarms for the nectar which they carry to their hives to turn into the finest grade of honey. Then there is the ailanthus, Chinese sumac, or tree of Heaven, an immigrant from China brought to this country for ornamental purposes in the latter part of the eighteenth century.

It was also hoped that the caterpillar of the ailanthus moth (*Samia cynthia*) which feeds exclusively on its leaves and was imported from its original habitat with the tree, might prove to be a good silk-producing species and help establish an industry in the production of raw silk, since the Chinese had been able to obtain a fair quality of coarse silk from its cocoons. This venture was never a success, but the tree quickly established itself in its new surroundings and became thoroughly naturalized so that now it is widely distributed as a " weed " tree in the northeastern states and Ontario. Its large clusters of both the staminate and pistillate flowers, borne on separate trees, are not unlovely. Unfortunately, however, the former gives forth a very unpleasant odor which is attractive to carrion-loving flies and bees, but which has gained for it, in many localities, the rather uncouth name of " stink tree." A good quality which it possesses is the ability to take root and flourish in the poorest soil, and therefore it is found in many waste places and city back yards. Its clusters of red and yellow winged fruit (samaras) which mature in August, are most attractive.

A word as to the methods of photographing these blossoms. Branches bearing first-class specimens of the flowers can, of course, be cut and carried home where they may be arranged and photographed indoors against a white background. By this method the possible change of movement in some vagrant breath of air is eliminated, and it is sometimes advantageous to do this, but I do not advocate the method as there is always the chance of serious wilting to the subject before reaching its destination. When it is possible to pull a branch down to the level of the camera and fasten it there, this should be done. When this is not possible, a branch bearing perfect examples of the blooms should be cut, arranged immediately by fastening it to the top of a stake driven into the ground, and photographed there. By this method one can not only obtain a natural background, but also make the picture before the subject has had an opportunity to wilt.

Among the herbaceous plants there are quite a large number that are May bloomers. The fields are beginning to turn yellow with the innumerable blossoms of the meadow buttercup, while in the marshy meadows, especially along streams, the larger and somewhat more showy but not so tall swamp buttercup makes bright yellow patches.

In the genus *Ranunculus* (the buttercups) there are some two hundred species widely distributed in both hemispheres. About seventy of them are natives of North America, fairly well distributed over the entire continent. The commonest of the lot, however, the meadow buttercup, is a naturalized species brought to us from Europe. If we are lucky we will find in the low meadows another member of the crowfoot family (*Ranunculaceae*) to which the but-

AMERICAN GLOBE FLOWER

tercups belong. This is the American globe flower, a low growing, profusely flowered plant, with blossoms and leaves quite similar to those of the buttercups, although the flowers average considerably larger and are of a much paler yellow color. The two baneberries, white and red, both members also of the crowfoot family, are in bloom during this month on dry rocky hillsides or open woods. The feathery cluster of white flowers, topping a bushy stem from one to two feet tall, are similar in both species, but a little later the white baneberry will produce a spike of rather curious white berries with dark spots which have been called, and rather aptly, " doll's eyes," while the berries of the other variety are red. The plants have been named " baneberry " because these berries are somewhat poisonous.

In late May we may find, if we are particularly fortunate, two of our most beautiful orchids, the pink and the large yellow lady's-slippers, both also known by the equally suggestive names of whippoorwill's shoes, and moccasin flowers. Their preferred habitat is the deep woods, the latter rather leaning toward rocky hillsides. They are perennial and will be found blooming in the same place year after year, gradually increasing in numbers if left alone. These are flowers well worth searching out to photograph, for they are growing scarcer each year owing to the ruthless way in which they are pulled up by most people who happen to find them.

In the more northern woods, especially common throughout the Adirondacks, a lowly but lovely little relative of the flowering dogwood, the low or dwarf cornel, or bunchberry, comes into bloom this month. It is a really exquisite little plant, rarely exceeding a height of more than six to eight inches. From the center of a whorl of four to six leaves arises the white flower on a short stem, an exact miniature of the blossom of the flowering dogwood. As in that plant, the white " petals " are really petal-like bracts surrounding the true, but insignificant, yellowish-green flowers. The name bunchberry has been given this attractive little plant from the fact that when the flowers fade they are replaced by tight bunches of berries that turn to a bright red in the autumn. They are almost as attractive as the flowers themselves.

In late May and early June throughout the damper woodlands we will find considerable troops of that great favorite of the children, the Jack-in-the-pulpit, or Indian turnip. It is a poor relation of the stately calla lily, as one glance at the striped spathe surrounding the erect yellow spadix will show. The staminate and pistillate flowers, which are found at the base of the yellow spadix, are borne on separate plants so that it is not every Jack that will become studded in July with green berries which will later turn to a bright red. In the south, from southern Virginia to Florida, usually growing directly in the water of bogs and springs, we may find another relative, the white arrow-arum, which bears an even closer resemblance to the calla lily, as its three to four inch spathe is pure white.

Many of our marshes and low meadows in the latter part of the

BLOSSOMS OF THE BUNCHBERRY

month are made purple by the masses of blue flag, or fleur-de-lis, which grow there in great profusion. When Louis VII, the crusader, adopted a near relative of our native wild iris as the emblem of his house, the flower was called fleur-de-Louis which later was corrupted to the present spelling. The slender blue flag is found growing at the same time and in the same situations, the two often commingling. It may be identified, however, by its much narrower, grass-like leaves, and by its smaller, bluer flowers.

The Solomon's seal, with its long, drooping stem from which swing the dull yellow or whitish bell-like blooms, is a familiar sight along our roadsides and throughout our fields, woods, and thickets, from the latter part of May throughout June. The flowers grow in clusters of from one to four from the axils of the leaves, and are rather insignificant, but the entire plant, with its large light green leaves, is not unattractive. Possibly it is even more attractive in the fall when its flowers have given place to the dark blue berries. The plant springs from a thick, jointed root stock. A single stem appears from this root each year. This stem fruits and then withers away, leaving a round scar on the root which, to the imaginative, resembles the mark of a seal.

In the same localities, often directly beside it, and blossoming at the same time as the species just spoken of, is its half brother, the wild spikenard, or false Solomon's seal. Its single stem with its alternate leaves very closely resembles that of the true species, hence the name. But here the resemblance stops, for its cluster of white blossoms occurs in a feathery plume at the tip of the stalk and is very conspicuous instead of being hidden beneath the leaves as is the case with the true Solomon's seal. Later its branching clusters of berries are pale red.

Another close relative is the diminutive false lily-of-the-valley, or two-leaved Solomon's seal. It is very common in the moist woods and on the shaded hillsides of May, where its shining, rather heart-shaped leaves often form a dense carpet covering a considerable area to almost the exclusion of any other vegetation. These plants are frequently sterile and some patches will show no signs of flowers, while others will be crowded with the short spikes of entirely white flowers rising above the leaves on short stems. The plants usually have two leaves each, hence one of its common names. Occasionally but not often, they have three, and many of the sterile plants have but a solitary, long-petioled leaf. In the autumn, the fertile plants bear spikes of pale red, speckled berries, similar to but somewhat smaller than those of the false Solomon's seal.

In rocky woods, sprouting from clefts in the rocks themselves, and on barren hilltops where one would hardly search for much plant life, grows that elfin-like flower the wild columbine, a member of the crowfoot family to which belong the buttercups. Its flowers, blooming in early May, are almost constantly in motion on the tips of their long, slender, almost black stems. The least breath of air sets them dancing, and it would seem as though a strong wind might destroy them entirely. And yet I have seen large colonies of them growing upon hilltops where the wind was blowing strongly most of the time, causing them to bow almost flat upon the earth with each fresh onslaught, but from which they would quickly recover and spring upright again when a momentary lull occurred, none the worse for the battering. The generic name of this plant, *Aquilegia*, is derived from the Latin, meaning eagle, and was given to this genus because of a fancied resemblance between the flower spurs and the talons of an eagle.

That strange, ghost-like plant the Indian pipe, or corpse-plant may be found from late May until August in partially shaded, somewhat damp woods almost throughout entire temperate North America. Despite its cold, pallid beauty it is a degenerate parasite, a

INDIAN PIPES

ghoulish saprophyte that, because it lives entirely upon the juices of living plants or the decaying matter of dead ones, needs no leaves or the green coloring matter (chlorophyl) of honest, upright plants and, therefore, has dispensed with both. The nodding flower is usually solitary, bell-shaped, wax-like, scentless, and has from four to six scale-like petals and from two to four white sepals which fall early. It has the peculiar character of turning black when bruised or roughly handled which fact, together with its deathly whiteness, is responsible for several suggestive names which have been given it such as, ghost-plant, ice-plant, corpse-plant, etc.

In making photographs of the herbaceous plants one should always place his camera as nearly on a level with them as possible, for if it is pointed downward at the plant, the result will be a rather distorted image with the lower part of the plant likely to be out of focus. Make the image of the flower as nearly life-size as possible and stop down the lens to obtain sharp focus over the entire plant. A breeze, no matter how slight, is always a great obstacle in this work, so choose a day, if possible, when there is little air stirring. Use a panchromatic film and a color filter if necessary. See instructions in the chapter on " Equipment." Many flowers have yellow stamens and pistils or the perfect flowers are yellow surrounded by white rays, as in the case of the common daisy, and yellow always photographs dark if we do not use color-corrected emulsions.

May is the month when the majority of birds commence their housekeeping arrangements. There are, however, notable exceptions to the rule that May is the month for nest building. Undoubtedly the earliest of all birds to breed is the great horned owl. Nests of this bird have been found containing eggs as early as January, and it is not unusual for a pair to raise their young in a nest half-covered with snow. Most of the owls are early breeders and their nests will usually be found to contain young in May. One is very likely, however, to find eggs in the nest of the little saw-whet owl and the screech owl in the early part of the month. Both of these little raptores raise their young in hollows in trees or stumps, and they are particularly partial to old excavations of woodpeckers. If you explore one of these cavities when the occupant is at home, wear a heavy glove, for the hooked bill and talons of either one of these birds are sharp and strong, and they know how to use them to good effect.

Hawks are fairly early breeders, many of them having eggs in their nests in April, while others wait until May before depositing eggs. Should any of my readers wish to visit a hawk's nest, they need not be frightened by the sudden dashes of the parent birds. They, apparently, are made merely as an attempt to scare the intruder away, and seldom culminate in a direct attack.

Crows have eggs in their nests by the early part of May, and among the smaller birds the robin and the blue bird are notable examples of early breeders. I have frequently found eggs in the nests of both these birds as early as the latter part of March or the first of April.

They both raise two and sometimes three broods in a season, so one may well expect to find eggs, and later young, of their second brood in May.

When a boy, I collected eggs as many another boy has done, taking one egg from each nest found, with the mistaken idea that the bird would never miss it and would return to the nest and hatch the remaining eggs and rear its young as if nothing had happened. When I grew a little older I learned two things: that few birds will return to nests that have been disturbed in any way, and that my collection had no value, either scientific or otherwise. Whatever happened to it I do not recollect. Probably all the eggs became broken and were, eventually, thrown out. Later, as a young man, I made a really worth-while collection of eggs in full series with nests and complete data. It contained some thousands of eggs, and finally became part of one of the largest collections in the country.

The first camera I ever owned, a four by five tripod outfit, was purchased solely with the idea of making a series of photographs of nests in situ as an adjunct to my collection. I very soon discovered that, while I had always derived great pleasure from tramping the woods and fields in my quest for new egg specimens, the enjoyment which I found in searching for and making photographs of the nests and eggs so far surpassed that of hunting them merely to take them from their rightful owner, that I very soon gave up my collecting entirely. Since that time I have never taken an egg from a nest, although I have found and photographed many hundreds of them.

The use of the camera helped me to realize how well the birds deserved the right to be undisturbed with their nest and eggs when I began to study not the nest itself so much as the manner in which it was built, and the infinite patience with which the little workers labored to accomplish their ends. In my photographic work it has always been my first endeavor to disturb as little as possible any nest upon which I happened to work, so that the owner might return and, finding it in the same condition as when she left, not desert it.

Anyone who cares at all for the out-of-doors and its lesser inhabitants, cannot fail to find the keenest pleasure in photographing birds' nests, and a series of them has a real scientific value, besides making a most interesting collection. To be successful in this work one must first acquaint himself somewhat with the habits of the birds.

Should he go out nest hunting with no knowledge concerning the situations in which the various species elect to build their nests, he would be more than likely to return greatly disappointed in the results of his search, for each species has its own particular choice of a general situation in which to build, and they rarely deviate to any great extent. Moreover, many of our birds are adepts at the art of hiding their abodes, which often makes it difficult even for one well versed in their ways to locate them, while a novice would have no chance at all.

NEST AND EGGS OF THE KILLDEER PLOVER

The greatest difficulty in the quest for nests to photograph is often the finding of the nest itself, even when one is certain that he is within a short distance of it. The quest is well-nigh hopeless if one has no knowledge of the manner in which that particular bird breeds. As an example of this I would like to tell an experience of mine. I was passing a piece of wasteland not far from my home when I thought I heard the unmistakable note of the killdeer plover. At first I thought I must be mistaken, as I had never before found the bird breeding in that vicinity, but presently the note was repeated so

clearly that there could be no doubt about it and I was sure that her
nest must be somewhere in that piece of wasteland. The killdeer is
one of those ground-breeding birds that builds no nest at all, simply
laying her eggs in a slight hollow on the bare ground. The eggs,
which are white, speckled and blotched with black, so nearly resemble their surroundings as to make them almost invisible, which would
not be possible if a nest were built. Sure as I was that the nest must
be somewhere within this barren field, to start searching for it over
this piece of sandy waste ground which covered several acres well be-
sprinkled with pebbles and small stones would, I knew, be like searching for the proverbial needle in the haystack. I could not even see
the bird, only hear its voice, and this had a sort of ventriloquistic
quality that made it impossible to determine from just which direction it came. I knew that I must first locate the bird before I could
hope to find the nest, and that is what I proceeded to do. A short
distance away from me was a rather thick clump of bushes on a little
rise of the ground, from which a comprehensive view of the entire
field might be had. Into this thicket I crawled and, lying flat on my
stomach, began my vigil. From this vantage point, well screened
from the prying eyes of the bird, I searched with my eyes every inch
of the ground in front of me for some time, to no avail. Had I had
my binoculars with me, the search would have been simplified but,
unfortunately, they were at home. Finally, however, on the far side
of the field I caught a movement and realized that I had found my
object. Now began a long, intensive, nerve-wracking, and eye-
straining vigil, for I did not dare let my eyes wander from the bird
for a single instant for fear of losing her entirely. Once I inadvertently did so and it was some time before I was able to pick her up
again, some distance from where I had last seen her. For two full
hours she zigzagged back and forth about the field, running for a
few feet, then remaining motionless for several minutes, only to be
up and off again. Several times she rose to her wings and flew for a
short distance, and on a number of occasions she disappeared completely in some dip in the ground. Two or three times the disappearance lasted so long that I was on the point of investigating,
when she suddenly appeared again. At long last, however, when
my patience and eyes were both about exhausted, she disappeared
again. This time, after waiting for about ten minutes for her re-

appearance, I determined that she had at last reached the end of her wanderings. I therefore rose and, keeping my eyes fastened directly upon the spot where I had last seen her, walked quickly toward it. When I was still some forty or fifty feet away, the bird rose and commenced to circle overhead, giving voice to distressed cries. But when I reached the spot I saw no signs of the eggs. Had I not been well acquainted with the habits of this bird never to rise directly from her nest but to scuttle over the ground for some distance before doing so, I might have then and there given up my search. As it was, I stood perfectly still that I might not step on the eggs, and began an inch-by-inch search of the surrounding territory and it was not long before I discovered them as they lay, in a slight depression in the ground, about ten feet from where I stood. I could never have found the nest had I not forced the bird to lead me to it and this is a method that must frequently be used on ground-breeding birds and also on low bush breeders.

Birds are by no means the only creatures that build nests, but they are beyond doubt the only class of animals from which the term nest is inseparable, at least in the minds of the majority of people. It is true that many birds build no nests at all, merely laying their eggs on the bare ground, as in the case of the killdeer, or on flat rocks or fallen leaves, as the case may be. The majority, however, are such wonderful architects, and the styles of their dwellings, if such a term may be applied to a structure that is used only to hold and protect the eggs and young, are so many and diversified that we have come to consider the birds as the nest builders pre-eminent in nature's realm.

The nests of birds may be found almost everywhere and in nearly every conceivable locality and situation. They are to be found on the ground and even beneath its surface; in low bushes and tangled herbage and in the topmost branches of the tallest trees; on the sands of the seashore and prairie and on the inaccessible ledges of the highest most formidable cliffs; in chimneys, caves and hollow trees; under bridges and the eaves of our houses; in barns and other outbuildings; from the miasmic depths of the lowest, most dismal swamps and morasses to the limit of vegetation on the highest mountains; from the sun-scorched deserts and treeless plains to the deepest forests where the sun's rays seldom penetrate; and from the equator nearly to the poles or, at least, to the outskirts of the region of eternal ice and snow. Therefore one can hardly go amiss in looking for them, but unless he knows just where to look he may easily pass within a foot or so of them without ever suspecting their proximity.

YOUNG NIGHT HERON READY FOR A MEAL

No one who has ever examined a bird's nest with anything more than a mere superficial scrutiny, can help but be struck with the beauty of symmetry and the intricacy of its structure, perfectly adapted, as each one is, to its special uses. When we stop to consider that all the tools which the little builders have for use in its construction are their feet and their bills, the wonder is not only that the finished article is so perfect a thing of beauty, but that they are able at all to accomplish the building of it. No human being, with all the tools which he has available, could hope to reproduce it.

Some years ago I had the desire to make a photographic record of the building of a bird's nest. This I discovered, after repeated unsuccessful attempts, was not so easy of accomplishment as I had thought it might be. A bird has been made a most suspicious creature by years of persecution, and its main endeavor in selecting the site for its nest is to have it as well hidden from prying eyes as possible. After the nest has been started, if the bird learns that it has not been altogether successful in its attempt at secrecy it will almost always leave its unfinished job and start again in some other spot where it hopes for better luck.

In the latter part of May I once discovered that a pair of vireos were starting to build on a low-hanging limb of an apple tree not far from my house. As the site chosen by the birds was in easy view from my front porch, as the nest was hung at just about the right height from the ground for easy photographic work, and as the foliage failed to hide the nest to any great extent (I eliminated two leaves in order to obtain an unobstructed view), I concluded that here was an ideal subject for another attempt at the series.

The nest of the red-eyed vireo is rather a small affair, averaging about two and one-half inches in diameter. It is cup-shaped, pendent from some small crotch of a horizontal limb, and never at any great distance from the ground. It is generally near the end of a branch, and is built of dead grasses, strips of grapevine and other barks, woody fiber from dead weed stalks and other sources, and similar material that is pliable. Small bits of paper, spiders' webs, small cocoons, pieces of lichen, etc., are often added to the outside in an attempt at a kind of camouflage and also, probably, to satisfy the artistic sense of the birds. Altogether it is really a rather remarkable bit of symmetrical construction.

When I first saw the birds at work, they had only just started the nest, with a very few strands of material. I realized that I must begin my operations immediately, and also if I lingered about any length of time my series would end, as did all of my others, with the first photograph.

I decided that a tripod would be needed and I chose a four by five view camera as being more easily handled than any other. This outfit I set up in the house, lengthening the legs of the tripod to the height that I judged would be about correct. I set the focus as near as I could guess the distance at which I would want to operate, and stopped the lens down so that I would not be forced to do this after setting up my outfit at the nest. Then, after covering the camera with the focusing cloth, with the forward corners fastened down so that it could be quickly pulled over my head without dislodging it, I carried the outfit as it stood to a point about fifty feet from the nest, where I could watch it without being seen by the birds.

Here I waited for nearly an hour while the birds repeatedly visited the nest but always alternately, never arriving or leaving together, until I began to fear that what I had hoped for would never come to pass. Finally I was rewarded by seeing them come one immediately after the other, and depart simultaneously. I waited until both birds were out of sight and then ran with my outfit to the nest. Once there, the camera was set up, the little adjustments of focus and distance made, the plateholder inserted, and in almost less time than it takes to tell, I had my first picture. Before leaving I took pains to press the legs of my tripod well into the earth in order to make marks in which to set them the next day. I also left my camera attached to the tripod exactly as it was when I made the exposure, so that all that would be necessary to obtain the remaining pictures would be to place the tripod legs in the marks and make the exposure without stopping to focus. This I did on each of the four succeeding days which, fortunately for me, were all bright and clear, with the sun shining. In all that time I am quite sure that the birds had no idea of what was going on at their nest while they were away. If they had, I am certain that they would have deserted it and I would not have obtained my series, for the vireo is a very shy bird and objects most strenuously if anyone even looks at its nest. I have actually known a pair, not only once but on several different occasions, to desert a nest containing eggs merely because they knew that I had found it, although I had not disturbed it at all.

The fifth day found the nest completed, and five days later it held a full complement of four eggs, and after making this last picture of it I felt that my task had been carried to a very successful ending.

One is apt to consider the life of a bird to be one of absolute care-free happiness, with no labor, cares, or worries. Had anyone been with me during the five days that I watched the building of this nest he might have found reason to change his ideas. From morning until night these two birds worked indefatigably. Each piece of material was brought to the nest separately and woven into the fabric with the bill and feet while the body was used to press the pieces into shape. Frequently they were forced to carry this material some distance, and more pieces go into the construction of a nest than one would ever think. After this nest had been deserted I took the pains to carefully dissect it and count the pieces. There were one thousand, one hundred and eighty-six of them. Quite a number for two

ENTRANCE HOLE TO NESTING BURROW OF THE KINGFISHER

little creatures to carry one at a time and weave into the structure of the nest in five working days.

But, after all, nest building by a bird is a matter of business and necessity. The nest is, primarily, a utilitarian affair and if in the making it is formed in such shape and constructed of such material as to give it beauty in the eyes of the beholder, it is a matter more of accident than design. The one and only object for which the birds strive, is to erect a structure in which may be combined the greatest amount of security from their enemies with the greatest amount of comfort for their young. The use, in its building, of materials that often tend to add beauty to the finished structure is, in most cases, only an attempt to make it conform more closely with its surroundings in order to make it as secure as possible from the prying eyes of those foes who are ever on the lookout for such tempting morsels of food as young birds and eggs.

Birds may well be said to represent, in their nest-building activities, many of the different vocations of mankind. The miners are well represented by such birds as the kingfishers, bank swallows, burrowing owls, and others who excavate more or less extensive tunnels

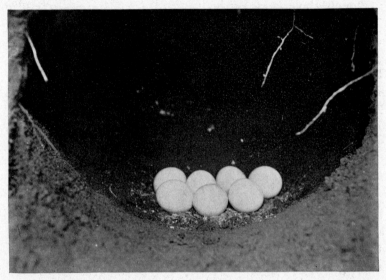

KINGFISHER NESTING BURROW OPENED TO SHOW EGGS

in the earth, at the ends of which they construct an enlarged chamber in which the eggs are deposited and the young raised. These abodes are almost impregnable fortresses in which the young are fairly secure, for very few of their enemies are able to penetrate to this inner chamber. The entire tribe of woodpeckers are fairly efficient woodworkers. Using their bills as chisels, they make deep excavations in the limbs and trunks of dead and often even living trees in which to rear their young. Some birds are good masons. The thrushes use clayey mud in the construction of their nests, and so does the flamingo, whose tall nest is almost entirely composed of this material. The male hornbill of South America, when the female is ready to incubate the single egg which she lays, seals her in the hollow tree, where she has made her nest, by closing the opening with clay, leaving only a small hole through which to feed her. The orioles of our country and South America, or the weaver birds of India and Africa, some of whom make nests of pliable material in the shape of closely woven bags twelve or fifteen inches long, may surely be termed most dextrous weavers. Probably, however, the most wonderful of all the birds that might be included in this type are the cassiques of tropical America. Their nests are pendulous bags suspended from the ends of the limbs of tall trees by thick cords woven by the birds from vegetable fibers. The entire structure is often as much as six feet in length. The tailor bird of India is small, not much larger than our wren, but his specialty is the sewing together of several of the large leaves of certain trees to form a bag in which to build his nest. His bill is the needle with which he pierces holes in the edges of the leaves. The pliable fiber of different plants forms the thread which he carefully passes through each hole, drawing the leaves closely together, and actually making a knot in the end so that it will not slip through and allow the bag to open. The fantails of Europe and Africa may well be called the tent makers of the avian tribe, for they build their nests in tall grass the tops of which they draw together and fasten with threads of their nesting material to form perfect tents over their abodes, often of sufficient density to shed the rain. These serve the twofold purpose of keeping the nest dry and preserving its inmates from the too ardent rays of the sun. Our little marsh wren is an accomplished plaiter of reeds. His nest is a compact, round, or egg-shaped ball of plaited rush leaves and grasses, warmly lined with cattail pappus. So closely woven is it that it is impervious to the worst driving storm, and the entrance, a small hole in one side, is so placed on the lower slant and inclined upward that no rain can drive in.

Few basket makers can surpass the skill of our vireos whose cup-shaped nests, woven of grasses, strips of the inner bark of cedar, grapevine, etc., are marvels of symmetry and beauty. Barn swallows were the original brick makers who learned, long before mankind, that clay will not hold together successfully without straw. Cliff swallows were the first pottery makers. Their nests, placed in colonies on the faces of cliffs or, in later years, under the eaves of our barns and outhouses, are made of clay lined with straw and feathers, and are in shape perfect models for an earthenware jug turned upside down. The entrance here also points downward to prevent the rain from entering. The chimney swifts are joiners who use a glue of their own secreting to join together the small twigs of which their nests are built and to fasten the entire structure, originally to the inside of hollow trees or to the walls of caves, but in later years, to the inside of chimneys when houses were provided with them. There are several species of swifts inhabiting the Andamen and Mo-

NEST AND EGGS OF THE CHIMNEY SWIFT

lucca groups of islands, whose nests are composed entirely of a glutinous secretion of the salivary gland which quickly hardens upon coming into contact with the air. These are the nests from which is made the famous bird's nest soup so highly prized by epicures of the East. I am tempted, even at the risk of being considered somewhat facetious, to call them the original noodle makers.

The brush turkeys and mound birds of Australia and various Pacific islands actually build incubators in which to hatch their eggs, for they do no incubating themselves. These are huge mounds of decaying vegetable matter in which the eggs are buried and left to be hatched by the heat generated by the fermentation. They are frequently very large, often as much as ten or eleven feet tall by twenty to twenty-five feet in circumference, and are built and used by several pairs of birds.

In the photography of nests, the prime consideration should be to disturb the nest and its surroundings as little as possible. This is not only out of consideration for the birds, but also in order that the

NEST AND EGGS OF THE KINGBIRD

actual conditions of the nest and its environments should be portrayed in the photograph with absolute truthfulness. Therefore I am opposed to the so-called "control of the nesting site" which is advocated by some nature photographers. By this is meant the removal of the nest from its original site to set it up somewhere else where it may be more easily photographed. I have never believed, nor can I be convinced, that this can ever be done with entire success, leaving out of the question all consideration for the birds themselves.

With the tree builders it is sometimes fairly difficult to obtain the photograph in situ, but with the aid of a camera clamp or by lashing the legs of the tripod to the limbs and branches and by the use of the tilting top, it can usually be accomplished after the exercise of some agility and considerable patience. When it is completely impossible, then one should wait until another more accessible nest of the species is found.

NEST AND EGGS OF THE PEWEE

It was only after a wait of several years and the examination of scores of nests of the Baltimore oriole that I finally found one that I could photograph. This was built at the extreme tip of an over-hanging branch of an elm. It was some twenty feet above the ground, but by throwing a rope over the branch I succeeded in pulling it down sufficiently far so that, by lengthening the legs of my tripod with additional sticks lashed to them, I was able to make an excellent picture of the nest without disturbing it in the least. In fact, I cut a small window in one side of the nest to show the eggs, and when I was through with it I fastened the piece I had removed back in again with some pieces of string so successfully that the parent bird was not alarmed by my handiwork and returned to hatch her eggs and rear her young.

The same method was used in making the accompanying photograph of the nest of the kingbird. This member of the flycatcher family likes to build in old orchards, any one of which is more than likely to harbor one or more pairs of these birds during the breeding season. They usually place their nests well toward the end of one of the topmost branches of an apple tree, an almost impossible place to reach with a camera. After many years of searching I finally found a nest on the lower branch of an apple tree so close to the ground that by pulling it down a little more and fastening it by a rope to a stake driven into the ground, I brought it within easy reach of my camera.

Another bird that is a frequenter of old orchards is the pewee, also a member of the flycatcher family. Its nest, always saddled on the horizontal branch of a tree, is a miracle of camouflage. It is so covered with bits of lichen as to closely resemble, when viewed from beneath, a knot or other excrescence of the tree itself. I have frequently been uncertain if what I saw was really a nest until I had climbed the tree to view it from the top. It is difficult to find one of these nests in a situation easy of access with a camera, and the one in the photograph shown here was no exception to the rule. It was a beautifully built and situated nest fastened to the top of the crotch on a horizontal limb of an apple tree and I was extremely desirous to obtain a photograph of it. As it was nearly twelve feet from the ground I realized that without some help and accessories, which I did not have with me, it would be utterly impossible to do so. The next day I returned accompanied by my brother. We lashed a stout stick about nine feet long to each leg of my tripod. This brought the camera to a level with the nest, and the focusing and making of the picture I accomplished by standing on the shoulders of my brother. I would like to add that my brother has aided me in like manner upon a number of occasions, notably in photographing the nest of a ruby-throat which I never could have managed in any other way without removing the branch upon which it was built. I have always considered, as did he, although his was the hardest part of the job, that the results justified the means.

Probably the most difficult piece of nest photography which I ever attempted was making a photograph of the nest of a crow. For several years I had searched in vain for a nest of this bird so situated that it could be photographed. This one was built in the upper branches of a hemlock about sixty feet above the ground. To photograph it from the same tree was out of the question, but I thought I saw possibilities in another tree which stood some ten feet away. Climbing it to a level somewhat above that of the nest, I found much to my delight that I could obtain an excellent view of the nest from this vantage point, after bending back a couple of branches that came between the camera and the nest. When these were tied back so as to be out of

NEST AND EGGS OF THE PIED-BILLED GREBE

the picture, there was a clear view of the nest. I secured my camera and tripod to a heavy piece of cord and drew them up to the spot from which I wished to make my photograph, and lashed the tripod to two limbs of the tree in such a manner that the camera would point properly at the nest. This was not so easy as it may sound and the lashing had to be changed several times before it was just right. I then focused and made the exposure, and lowered my outfit again to the ground. All this was accomplished successfully without having disturbed or even touched the nest, and I left, happy in the thought that at last I had a photograph of a crow's nest actually in situ.

A few years ago a friend told me that about twenty feet from the shore of a certain pond not far from my home a pair of pied-billed grebes had made a nest. Naturally, I took the first opportunity to visit the pond. The grebe builds a floating nest composed entirely of dead and decaying vegetation on the surface of some pond or small lake. It rarely is attached to anything stationary and, therefore, its position is frequently changed by the action of the water.

I searched the edges of the pond diligently for about an hour without seeing anything that in the remotest degree resembled a nest. I was about to leave, thoroughly disgusted and thinking my friend had sent me on a wild goose chase, when I caught a glimpse through a thick screen of bushes growing in the shallow water of what appeared to be nothing more than a mass of dead leaves caught among the stems of the bushes. From where I stood at the edge of the pond it had not the least resemblance to a nest, but knowing that when the grebe leaves its eggs it covers them with some of the same material of which the nest is made, I decided that I would be wise to investigate. When I reached the spot and lifted away the top layer of dead vegetation from the mass of debris, I disclosed eight eggs which had been completely hidden by it. The great difficulty in photographing the nest of a grebe is that, floating on the surface of the water as it does, it moves with every little movement of the water. In this instance the wind was blowing fairly strongly across the pond, causing miniature wavelets which made the nest continually rise and fall. I waited for nearly half an hour before the time arrived when the movement ceased long enough for the two-second exposure which I gave it.

The photography itself of a bird's nest, presents no difficulty. The nest will not depart while you are operating the camera, and it is usually still unless it happens to be built near the end of a small branch that is easily swayed by any breeze. But it must be remembered that for a photograph of a bird's nest to have any real value, scientific or otherwise, it must comply with the following rules: It must be made in situ; it must show enough of the immediate surroundings to give a clear idea of the situation in which the nest is built; it must not show where any herbage has been cleared away; it must show clearly the detail of construction and the manner of attachment of the nest to its support; it must also show the eggs, or at least some of them. Do not make the mistake of pointing the camera directly downward at the nest to show the eggs. This is bound to give a distorted view of the nest and surroundings.

JUNE

JUNE is the month of roses, but it might with even greater appropriateness be called the month of birds. In May the birds return, in the greatest numbers, from their wintering in warmer climates. By the end of the month all those whose nesting range is farther north have passed through on their journey home, leaving with us only those summer residents who make their homes with us, the majority of whom are busily engaged in their homemaking and parental duties during the month of June. It is true that some early arrivals from the south, such as the bluebirds, robins and phoebes, already have young in their nests to engross their attention, but as soon as this first brood is launched upon the world they build another nest and prepare to raise another family. June, therefore, is preeminently the month of the greatest domesticity among the birds, so that it should also be the month of greatest activity for the nature photographer who specializes in bird pictures or even includes them among his other subjects. At no other time will he find it so easy to obtain pictures of them. While it is often possible to make photographs of birds at other times of the year, especially by enticing them to a feeding station, the breeding season is indisputably the best season of the year for bird photography.

Not only are the birds at this time restricted to a limited range surrounding their nests, but there is a most decided attraction in their nests and young that invariably draws them to one particular spot, and sooner or later one is absolutely certain of finding one or both of the birds there. Moreover, at this time of the year, the birds are wearing their best and fullest plumage. In some cases the males wear special nuptial adornments. The best examples of this are the egrets and snowy herons of the south who grow from the middle of their backs tufts of long, beautiful, snow-white plumes called aigrettes, which are discarded after the breeding season. These plumes are so beautiful that the birds were nearly made extinct by hunters who shot them for the plumes for millinery purposes, before that traffic was stopped. The fact that these plumes are worn only during the breeding season caused the birds to be killed only at that time, which left the young to die of starvation in the nests.

In the east two outstanding examples of a special breeding and summer costume are shown in the males of the bobolink and of the goldfinch. The former in June and July wears a striking costume of black and white, while at other times he is garbed like the female in buff, having a close resemblance to a sparrow. The goldfinch, during the fall and winter, wears a dress of dull olive brown, but after the spring molt he appears in an outfit of brilliant yellow, with wings, tail, and a cap on his head, of jet black. As this bird is one of our latest breeders, not nesting until late August or early September, this costume is not discarded until October.

Birds are more easily photographed in the breeding season, because then the fear for their own safety is largely overshadowed by their parental love and protective instinct. This protective instinct is well exemplified by many of the smaller birds who will fight viciously in defense of their nests and young. I well remember standing beneath a small maple tree whose lowest branch was only about a foot above my head. Suddenly something darted past my head so close as to almost touch me. At first I was a little startled as I did not immediately recognize what it was, but after several repetitions I realized that I was being attacked by a pair of ruby-throats. They drove so directly at my head in such a vicious manner that I involuntarily ducked each time one came, although I knew they would not actually hit me as that would cause them more damage than it would me. Knowing that there must be some reason for this attack, I investigated and found that the cause of the sudden onslaught was their diminutive nest occupied by two young, which was saddled on the limb directly above my head.

The fear of mankind is inherent in all birds, but by careful treatment this can be temporarily, to a considerable extent, allayed although very seldom completely overcome. Birds, however, have their idiosyncrasies the same as human beings, and these frequently form one of the most insurmountable objects to success in trying to photograph them. One individual of a species may be quite amenable to our advances and perfectly willing to pose for us, while the

SONG SPARROW AND YOUNG

very next individual of the same species which we try to photograph may be so wary and difficult of approach that we may have no success at all. Moreover the disposition of a bird may change completely within twenty-four hours and whereas it may allow its photograph to be taken with comparative ease on one day, upon the next, under exactly the same conditions, it may refuse to come within any reasonable distance of the camera.

As an illustration of this I have in mind a pair of house wrens whose nest, in an old willow stump, I found one June day a few years ago. It contained nearly full-fledged young and I wished to get some pictures of the old birds at the nesting hole. I feared the worst, for but a short time before I had unsuccessfully attempted to photograph another pair of house wrens, and from that experience I fully expected that it would take this pair some time to overcome the fear of the camera, if they did so at all. But my fears were needless, for while I was focusing with my head still underneath the cloth, I was surprised to see one of the birds fly down and enter the hole with food in its bill. It seemed so fearless that instead of attaching my remote control to the shutter and retiring to a distance, I stood by the side of my camera with the shutter release in my hand, hoping that the visit might soon be repeated. Nor were my hopes doomed to disappointment. I had waited but a few minutes when either the same bird, or its mate, alighted upon the stub of a dead branch that protruded from the stump a few inches from the nesting hole, and after eyeing me and the camera for a moment as much as to say " what's the big idea," calmly entered the hole. I made my first exposure while the bird was perched upon the stub. Thereafter one or the other of the birds visited the nest every few minutes, keeping to their regular routine and ignoring my presence entirely, as something of no consequence in their lives. The only thing that mattered to them was the necessity of keeping up the steady flow of food to their offspring. Occasionally one would arrive while the other was still in the hole and would wait patiently its turn to enter, paying no attention to me, and at least once both birds entered the hole practically together. Frequently my camera was used by the birds as a perch before entering the hole, and once one of the birds actually lit upon my shoulder. Within an hour I had made twelve perfect exposures, which I think must be a record.

Two days later I again visited the nest with the intention of removing the young to some near-by perch, where I felt sure I could get some pictures of the old birds feeding them. But they had already left the nest and I was able to find only two of them in the surrounding bushes. These I succeeded in inducing to sit quietly upon a branch, after they had tired of hopping off for a while as fast as I placed them upon it, and after arranging my camera I confidently awaited the approach of the old birds. My confidence was completely misplaced, however. Although the birds would repeatedly alight with food upon the same branch with the young, it was always at a distance of a foot or more from them, and they always tried to induce the young to come to them, never going to the young. After some three hours of this kind of disheartening performance, I finally succeeded in getting two rather indifferent pictures, with which I was forced to be content.

Not long ago I came across an article on photographing birds in which the author stated " as a matter of fact I have found that the majority of birds, after a little preliminary excitement, accept the camera even when set up within a few feet of their nest, and without camouflaging, as a part of the landscape and pay no at-

Robin Feeding Young in Nest   House Wren About to Enter Nesting Hole

tention to it." He further stated specifically that such birds as the chickadee and red-eyed vireo are tame and confiding, and that the veriest tyro of a nature photographer should have no difficulty in dealing successfully with them.

Twenty-five years' experience as a nature photographer, during which time I have photographed most of our more common eastern species of birds, forces me to take exception to these statements. Had he said that some birds are fairly tractable and easily approached and photographed, I would have felt more inclined to agree with him. More than half the species of birds are difficult of approach within photographic distance. Photographs of them can be made only after the exercise of the greatest caution and patience. We must possess more than a modicum of both these qualities if we would be successful in this line of work, or, indeed, in work with any of the wild things. Moreover it is utterly impossible to state positively that any one species of bird is more easily made friends with than any other. With all the avifauna this is entirely a matter of the idiosyncrasy of the individual.

The same author made another statement with which I find it very much easier to agree. He goes on to say that " a good deal of the so-called ' fear of the camera ' is really due to the injudicious behavior of the photographer who either fails to remain motionless while waiting to make the exposure or else does not exercise due caution as to the time and manner of his approach to the nest to change his plateholders."

This is especially true of beginners who are only too apt to make their presence evident by constant motion and noise. It is not always necessary to remain hidden during the wait for the return of the subject to the nest, although with very many subjects this is necessary, and with nearly all it helps to reduce the length of the wait. Nor is it always imperative to retire to a distance from the camera. Many of my photographs of birds were made while standing by the side of my camera within a few feet of the nest. It is essential not to move any more than necessary, because a bird is much more easily frightened by a moving object than by a stationary one. It is also well to have nothing about the camera that can move. I have known a bird to refuse to return to its nest and young because a loose corner of the focusing cloth was moving in the breeze, but the bird approached without evidence of fear soon after this was stopped. Furthermore, after having made an exposure, it is well to wait until the bird has departed on another trip for food before approaching the camera. Even after the bird has passed out of sight, approach with due caution and remain by the nest as short a time as possible while making the required changes.

Many devices have been used by nature workers to camouflage the camera. I have failed to find that they improved the situation much. A bird that is naturally unusually shy will object just as much to a tent or other covering to the camera as it will to the camera itself without covering. I have found that birds may be roughly divided into three classes as photographic subjects: those that are practically fearless and will approach the nest when the camera and photographer are standing close to it; those that are somewhat fearful of any unusual object suddenly appearing near their nest, but who may always be photographed by the exercise of care and discretion; and those that look upon everything which they do not fully understand as a potential enemy, to be completely and forever shunned. Photographs of any of the last class are extremely difficult to obtain.

But birds cannot be grouped by species into such classes. One individual of a species may be fearless and easily approached, while another individual of the same species may be very suspicious. One can never be certain, until he has tried to photograph it, just how any particular individual bird will react to his presence. Therefore the best procedure is to work on the supposition that your subject is timid, and act accordingly. If the bird should approach the nest almost immediately after you have set up and adjusted your camera and retired to a hiding place, you are justified in taking a chance and going boldly to your camera and waiting there. In about nine cases out of ten the bird will continue its parental duties, paying little attention to your presence. If, however, you are forced to wait for some time before the bird makes it first appearance at the nest, then you had better make all your exposures from the spot where you are hidden, and when going to the camera do so with caution.

The statement that the chickadee and red-eyed vireo were two species always easy to approach, made by the same author, particularly caught my attention. It so happens that I have had a great deal of experience with both of these species and am in a position to speak from knowledge. While the idiosyncrasies of every species of bird are considerable, I do not know of any other species with greater individual idiosyncrasies. The red-eyed vireo has always been considered to have rather a shy and suspicious nature. On a number of occasions I have known a pair to desert their nest, even when it contained eggs partially incubated, if it had been in any way disturbed, or even looked at. I have been both successful and unsuccessful in photographing this bird both at the nest and feeding its young on a branch, and my successes or failures depended entirely upon the individuality of the birds themselves, and not upon anything that I did or did not do. I have in mind particularly two pairs of vireos that were as completely different in their actions as it is possible for two birds to be. The first pair, whose nest containing half-fledged young I found hanging at the end of a drooping apple branch, made no objection to my appearance and did not even utter a note of protest. For more than an hour, they continued to attend to their duties of feeding the young as if I were not there, despite the fact that my camera and myself were within a few feet of the nest.

YOUNG KINGFISHERS JUST TAKEN FROM THE NEST

The second pair, whose nest containing young I found the following day, looked upon me and my camera with the gravest suspicion. While arranging the camera and even when I had retired to a distance at the end of my shutter release, both birds persistently scolded me from near-by trees, but were very particular to keep themselves out of sight in the thick foliage. After my experience of the previous day I had expected little trouble with this pair, but despite my utmost precautions I was forced after a wait of more than three hours, to retire from the field beaten.

I could relate a number of similar experiences both with these birds and with chickadees. Possibly the latter are even more temperamental. At all events on numerous occasions they have come directly to the nesting hole with no apparent fear while I stood within a few feet of it, while on other equally numerous occasions they have refused absolutely to approach it even while I was at a considerable distance, and well hidden.

The actions of a pair of robins once surprised me considerably. These birds, as a rule, are extremely suspicious of the actions of any-one near their nests. I have, on numerous occasions, waited in my hiding place for several hours while a pair of them gave utterance continually to their particularly unmusical danger note from the near-by shrubbery, and on most of these occasions have been forced to leave without any pictures. The pair of which I am speaking, however, were quite different. The nest was placed on a rafter that was raised some four or five feet above ground beneath a farm build-ing and contained half-fledged young. The old birds did not seem to be particularly suspicious of me and it occurred to me that I might possibly get some pictures if the nest were only in some place where I could photograph it. I therefore took a chance and removed it from the rafter to the crotch of a small cherry tree a short distance away. After having focused upon it and arranged my camera, I re-tired to the interior of the building where I was out of sight. I soon discovered, much to my delighted surprise, that I need not have gone to even this trouble, for one of the birds almost immediately visited the nest with food, and during the next hour one or the other of them was in almost constant attention at the nest while I sat at ease on a chair not more than eight feet away.

With one exception this is the only time that I have ever removed a nest from its original site in order to photograph it. This excep-tion was when I took a nest full of young phoebes from a strut under a small bridge over a brook, where it was impossible to photograph it, and placed it on top of a post near by. I did not know how the birds would respond to this sudden and radical change in their household arrangements, but I was agreeably surprised to find them resuming their ministrations to their young almost immediately, as though this moving of their home was not an unusual occurrence.

The brown thrasher is rather a timid bird, rarely allowing one to approach it closely, contenting itself with remaining in the denser shrubbery or perched on the topmost branch of some tree where it gives voice to its very lovely song. I had two experiences several

years ago with two different pairs on successive days. The first pair
had young in the nest and I waited, well hidden, about seventy-five
feet from the nest, holding my shutter release for about four hours
before giving up in disgust. During this time I had caught sight of
the birds only two or three times, in quick glimpses, but they had
made their presence known all the time by continuous utterance of
their rather raucous scolding note from the surrounding bushes.

BROWN THRASHER WITH FOOD FOR YOUNG

The next day, while exploring a field covered with small bushes and
second growth, I came upon a young brown thrasher apparently out
of the nest but a short time. I placed him upon a branch of a dead
sapling, where he settled himself quite contentedly. I thought to
make a photograph of him and was actually in the process of focusing upon him, when one of the old birds flew to the branch with food
for him, seemingly entirely oblivious of the fact that I was within a
few feet. It was with no trouble during the next half hour that I
made several fine photographs of the pair without moving from my
camera.

Screech owls are subject to what is known as dichromatism. That is they are found in two distinct color phases of plumage — gray, and bright reddish brown. These color phases are attributable to neither age, sex, nor conditions, nor are they hereditary. A bird of each color may mate and their offspring be all of one or the other phase or a mixture of both, or the same thing may happen when both birds are of the same phase. This distinct difference of plumage in these birds has never been entirely satisfactorily explained, but it has been determined that a bird of the gray phase can change to reddish brown without change of plumage.

Posing young birds and trying to induce them to remain posed, in order to photograph them by themselves or with the old bird in attendance, is apt to try the patience of anyone to the fullest extent, even though he may be possessed of as much of that admirable quality as was Job.

If you are hoping to get a picture of the old bird feeding the young, your troubles will be about doubled. You have the young all posed and sitting quietly. The moment the adult appears on the scene, if she has not already caused most of them to leave their perch by calling to them from some near-by branch, it is about a ten-to-one shot that the excitement of seeing her approach will cause half of the brood to lose their balance and topple from the perch. However, with patience and perseverance the seemingly impossible can be accomplished.

Young birds are most tractable when secured a day or two before they would, in the natural course of events, leave the nest. They can then be removed from the nest without the least discomfort or danger to them. They appear to be glad to be out of their crowded, and usually vermin-infested, quarters, and it is utterly impossible to induce them to return once they have tasted this freedom. The period of time occupied by the young in their nests varies greatly with different species. The young of the precocials, the quail, plover, woodcock, sandpipers, grouse, etc., leave within a very short time of being hatched and are then able to care for themselves. Every egg in these nests will hatch and the young desert the nests within the course of two or three hours. Swallows always remain in their nests until they are able to fly at least for a short distance, and the young of none of the birds whose nests are built in trees will leave them until they are very close to that stage, and are able to perch with safety on the branches. The young of ground breeders, on the contrary, and even those species which build in shrubs and low herbage, frequently desert their nests as soon as they are able to struggle out, and once gone it is extremely difficult to find them among the long grass and weeds, for they are adepts at the art of hiding.

I am not trying to discourage anyone from entering this field of photographic endeavor, for it is one of the most fascinating branches of nature work. Birds make a strong appeal to anyone who is interested in the natural sciences, and they are probably the first subjects one is likely to experiment upon when he ventures into the field of nature photography. Such was the case with me, and if the first few subjects which I tackled had not proved to be fairly tractable, I might have forsworn that branch of nature photography entirely, and taken up the picturing of something that would remain reasonably still. But no matter how discouraging it may seem at first, and despite the many failures that you are bound to have, those pictures that you obtain will fully repay you for all the time and patience spent.

June is also probably the best time of the year for exploring ponds, ditches, and watercourses for photographic material. How many of my readers, I wonder, have ever done this? By this I mean thoroughly examining the bottoms as well as the surfaces in order to discover something about the inhabitants of these places. Many of us are acquainted with the batrachians, the frogs, toads, and salamanders and their young the tadpoles, that are common dwellers of every pond, puddle, and ditch. I wonder, though, how many of us have any considerable knowledge of the great throng of living creatures, aside from the batrachians, that swarm in these places. The very first animals were water dwellers, and many of their descendants still cling to their original residing place because they find there more properties that help them to live and multiply than they could find anywhere else. Those shallow ponds whose greatest depth is not more than two or three feet no matter how much ground they may cover, fairly teem with animal life, and it is to these that I would like to call attention.

Water is seven hundred and seventy times as heavy as air, and so it supports objects much too heavy to float in the air. It also has a surface film capable of supporting creatures that would otherwise sink. All fluids have this surface film, but that of water is stronger than that of any other except mercury. Watch a water strider, one of those long-legged insects that stride on the surface of ponds and brooks, for a while. With every movement of the insect, each of its feet makes a slight indentation in the surface of the water, actually bending down this film, but it does not sink as it inevitably would do

SPOTTED SANDPIPER AT NEST

if the film was not there. There also are insects that cling to, and hang from, the underside of this surface film. The commonest example is the larvae of the mosquitoes, the " wigglers " that one sees in any stagnant water. They swim up from the bottom, thrust their air tubes through this film and hang from it head downward until they have sucked in enough air to last them while they make another trip to the bottom where they feed.

We remember the dragonflies, the " darning needles " of our childhood which we were told would sew up our lips if we talked naughty. There are many people well beyond childhood age who, if they do not literally believe this fairy tale, do believe that these insects carry a needle or a sting at the end of their tails that is capable of inflicting a

dire injury. The fact of the matter is that not only do they possess
no sting but they are absolutely harmless and may be handled with
complete impunity. Moreover they are of considerable value to mankind as they destroy countless numbers of mosquitoes, gnats, and
other small insect pests, on which they subsist. There are a large
number of species of these graceful and interesting insects, and many
of them are very beautiful. They are to be found in the greatest
numbers flying back and forth over any small piece of water, for it
is here that they find the abundance of insects that form their food.
They make most interesting subjects for photography. Their larvae, or nymphs as they are called, are aquatic, spending their lives
up to the time of the metamorphosis, at the bottoms of ponds and
watercourses. They are predatory animals living entirely upon water insects, small fish, etc. They are of diversified forms and are, in
their way, almost as interesting as are the adults. They vary in size
from those scarcely an inch in length to large ones two or three inches
long. They may easily be captured by means of a net made of some
stout material through which the water will easily drain, and attached to a ring that will not bend. Each time this is dragged along
the bottom it is likely to bring up several specimens. They must, of
course, be taken home and photographed in the tank described in the
chapter on " Equipment." In such a tank any kind of water creature
may be photographed.

Many people cannot tell the damsel flies from their cousins the
dragonflies. They may easily be distinguished because damsel flies
always rest with their wings closed over their backs, while dragonflies
always rest with their wings spread at right angles to the body.
Moreover the damsel flies are much smaller and more delicate in
appearance.

Probably the commonest forms, at least those most readily seen,
are the " black-wings," those familiar ones that flutter about the un-
dergrowth that borders some woodland or meadow stream with all the
nonchalance of a butterfly, and with much the same motions. The
commonest species is the *Agrion maculatum*. The body of the male
insect is a beautiful metallic, or blue-green, with jet black wings.
The female is similar, but near the tip of each forewing is a small
white spot. They are not difficult to photograph, as they sometimes
rest for considerable periods of time on some leaf or twig, and it

FLICKER AT NESTING HOLE

seems to make little difference to them whether they rest upright on the top of the leaf or hanging downward from the underside. The nymphs of the damsel flies can be found in the same ponds with those of the dragonflies but can always be distinguished by their smaller size and the fact that their tapering bodies always bear three leaf-like gills at the posterior end, which are entirely lacking in the dragonflies.

Probably the largest of the many water insects is the giant water bug, sometimes called " electric light bug " from the fact that it is a strong flier, leaves the water at night, and is attracted by electric lights to such a degree that considerable numbers of them will congregate about one. It is a true bug, belonging to the order *Hemiptera* and suborder *Heteroptera,* to which order belong also the bedbugs, squash bugs, etc. It is the largest of the order. There are two species so similar in appearance that for a long time they were considered to be identical. They are both large, flat, grayish-brown insects, about one and a half to two inches in length. They are predatory and extremely aggressive, seizing with their powerful front legs anything in the way of animal life up to the size of small fishes two or three inches long. They may be photographed either in the tank or clinging to some support, for while their natural habitat is water, they are often found at considerable distances from the nearest pond.

Another, and rather peculiar, member of the same order is the " back-swimmer." These insects are so named because they always swim upon their backs, using their elongated hind legs much as one would a pair of oars. This fact, if nothing else, tends to distinguish them from all other water insects. They are also predaceous, feeding upon other insects and small fishes up to the size of a minnow, which they are capable of mastering. They carry with them beneath the water such a considerable air film that they are forced when not in motion to cling with their forelegs to some support, usually a water plant, to prevent themselves from rising to the surface, and from this they hang head downward. They are extremely strong and rapid swimmers, and dash through the water with great rapidity. They are rather pretty little creatures. Their backs are convex, rising to a sharp ridge along the middle, and are white with a decided opalescence reminding one of mother-of-pearl. In handling them, one should be a little careful, as they are possessed of a sucking beak with which they can inflict a wound almost as painful as the sting of a bee.

Many of the water insects are beetles. In fact it is probably safe to say that beetles are in the majority. Of the more common species, the one best known to the casual observer is the " whirligig beetle." All through the spring and summer they may be seen in groups of from two or three to several hundred, lying almost motionless upon the surface of the water, or circling about in an apparently aimless manner. These, with the water striders, those long-legged insects which are not beetles but true bugs belonging to the same group as the water bug, are undoubtedly the two best known of all the water insects, owing to the fact that they spend their time constantly upon the surface where they may be easily seen.

Then there are the diving beetles of which there are a great many species ranging from those that are only a few hundredths of an inch in length to those that are as much as one and a half inches long. They are in the habit of hanging head downward from some plant or even from the surface film of the water and, if placed in a tank and allowed to remain there quietly for a while, will assume these postures. They are called diving beetles on account of the rapidity with which they dive to the bottom when disturbed.

Another large shining black beetle that inhabits the same water with the diving beetles, is the water scavenger, of which there are several species, all fairly large. They are quite similar to the diving beetles but may always be distinguished because they hang from any support with their heads upward instead of downward as do the diving beetles. They are active on land as well as in the water and so may be photographed in or out of the tank, as one chooses.

Besides these, there are the crawling water beetles that live in the decaying vegetation that covers much of the bottom of every pond, and another family of small beetles called " riffle beetles " from the fact that they live in the riffles of rapidly running water rather than in stagnant water.

Did you ever in the spring follow the course of some woodland brook? This is the loveliest time of the year to do so. If you know a brook, with pebbly bottom that emerges into a meadow with deep pools where the water seems motionless, with reeds here and there along its course, you will find it a prolific source of subjects for the nature photographer, to say nothing of its scenic beauty.

Many of the same subjects that we have found in the ponds, chief among them the dragon and damsel flies and their larvae, particularly the " black-wings," are more at home here than about the ponds, and in greater variety of species.

The dobson fly (*Corydalis cornutus*) is a large flying insect that is not uncommon, but because it is a night flier it is not often seen by the casual observer. Its larvae, which are commonly known among anglers, who use them extensively for bait, as " hellgrammites," " crawlers," " bass-bait," etc., are to be found quite commonly along any such brook as I have described. They live under stones in the swiftest running water. They are fiercely predatory, equaling the nymphs of the dragonfly in this respect. When full grown, they are about two and one half inches in length, dark brown in color, and have large, strong jaws. They avoid light, and are rarely seen unless the stone under which they are hiding is turned over. They exist as aquatic insects for three years, emerging in the spring of the third year to find a log, piece of wood, stone, or anything else of like nature under which they can crawl to pupate. In about ten days the perfect insects emerge.

These, as I have said, are night fliers and may frequently be seen circling about street lights. Despite the fact that their wings are considerably longer than their bodies, having an expanse of from four to five inches while their bodies are only about one and one-half inches in length, they are not strong fliers and will frequently fall to the ground after a few circlings of the light, where they may be easily captured. Their bodies are reddish brown and their wings a rather dirty white, thickly spotted with brown. The female is provided with short, stubby mandibles, while the male has a caliper-like pair that measures a full inch in length. These are not used to capture prey, as one might suppose, but to hold the female during mating. In fact, the dobson fly eats nothing during its short life of but a few days. The best way to obtain photographs of these interesting insects is to collect specimens of the larvae when they leave the water to pupate. This may be done by searching the banks of the streams and turning over anything under which they might crawl. Take them home, place them in a box with some damp earth, dead leaves, etc., and a couple of pieces of wood for them to crawl under, and allow them to complete their metamorphoses. By this method excellent photographs of the three stages in the life of this insect, larval, pupal and the perfect insect, may be made with no difficulty, and all within the space of about two weeks.

Another flying insect that greatly resembles the dobson fly is the fish-fly (*Chauliodes pectinicornis*). It may easily be distinguished, however, from the fact that its antennae are feathered while those of the dobson fly are not. Its larva is very similar also to the hellgrammite, but only about half the size when full grown. They are found in streams or clinging to submerged trash in quiet back waters.

There are many other forms of insect life that one may find during a jaunt along a brook but possibly the most interesting is the little caddis fly. The flies themselves have very much the appearance of

MALE DOBSON FLY

small moths. Their wings, covered with silky hairs and scales, are usually soft brown or gray in color, and folded over their backs when at rest. They are seen in most abundance about the margins of streams and swarming over the water at dusk, and are also attracted by light near the streams or ponds. The larvae are the most interesting, living in every brook and creeping over the bottom almost constantly. They build cases for themselves in which they spend their entire time during the larval stage. They hold themselves in these cases by hooks at the hind end of their bodies, but the fore parts of their bodies are extended from the case, allowing them to crawl about the bottom of the streams carrying it with them. When danger approaches they can quickly withdraw completely within the case, thus protecting themselves from their predatory enemies. These cases are built of small pieces of leaves, bits of sticks, small stones, grains of sand, or even minute water snails' shells. These materials are fastened together by a viscous silk spun by the larvae. As the creature grows, it enlarges the case to fit its body or, occasionally, crawls out and builds a new one.

As we stroll along the brook we are very apt to see, on some sandy spot at the edge of the water, usually at the foot of an overhanging bank, a small chimney-like structure, about an inch to an inch and a half tall. This is the entrance to the burrow of the chimney crawfish. The crawfish, or crayfish as it is also called, is a small cousin to the lobster. There are several species distributed over North America. They are small, averaging from two to five inches in length. The chimney crawfish is brown, or olive-brown, in color and is rarely more than two inches in length, and its principal characteristic is that it invariably builds these chimneys at the entrance to its burrow, although the mountain, or brook, crawfish also occasionally does so. This latter species is more apt, however, to be found in the rough, rocky highland streams, for it seems to prefer the cold water of these brooks, often making its burrow close to a mountain spring. All crawfish burrow into the ground and these burrows are frequently as much as two or three feet long, although occasionally they go in but a few inches. In them the makers spend their days, emerging only at night to seek their food. In order to obtain one of these little crustaceans it must be dug from its burrow, and this should be done with great care to avoid injury to the little dweller. Once he is evicted, it is easy to photograph him. Place him on the ground with some slight obstruction immediately behind him over which it is difficult for him to back, and he will immediately assume a fighting attitude and hold it long enough to be photographed. These little fellows are often quite numerous along the lower reaches of the brook. I have found the burrows of at least a dozen in less than a hundred yards. Unless one knows their habit of constructing these chimneys, and searches for them, he might never suspect their presence.

There are innumerable snails also to be found in the brooks. Many of these are minute, but some are large enough to be worth photographing. Prominent among these latter is the white-lipped snail which may be found not uncommonly in the lush herbage bordering the brook in the meadows. Usually it may be seen crawling along the stems or branches of some plant, and here it may be easily photographed. The picture should show the snail itself and not simply the shell. We should have the animal extended to the point where it commences to progress. This is easily accomplished, for a snail is a docile animal. It can be picked up, the opening of the shell held against a plant stem or branch, and the animal will very shortly emerge and extend itself. Therefore if we focus upon that part of the plant upon which we wish our subject to pose, then place the snail there and make the exposure only when he has fully extended his body, we are practically certain of obtaining a satisfactory result.

HELLGRAMMITES, LARVAE OF THE DOBSON FLY

JULY

JULY, the midsummer month, might truthfully be called the month of insects, for it is the month of greatest activity in their lives and they are everywhere in evidence. Therefore it is the month when the nature photographer should plan to get their pictures. He need never be at a loss for a sufficient number of subjects. Insects are to be found nearly everywhere outdoors and sometimes, to our discomfort, indoors. Even those who confine their attention to the *Lepidoptera* (butterflies and moths) will find plenty of subjects during this month. The majority of people are more interested in the members of the *Lepidoptera* than in any of the other orders of the great class of insects. This is but natural because among the species are some of the most beautiful as well as the largest of known insects, one tropical species reaching nearly a foot in expanse of wings. The order is composed of but two sub-orders: the *Rhopalocera*, or butterflies, which fly by day, and the *Heterocera*, or moths, which fly by night.

To aid in distinguishing a moth from a butterfly, there is one striking difference which is constant through the entire order with the exception of a few obscure tropical and sub-tropical genera. The antennae, or feelers, of the butterflies are swollen at the tips into club-like forms, while those of the moths are not. The antennae of the moths are in most cases beautifully and often heavily feathered, while those of the butterflies are not. Also the scales on the bodies and wings of the moths are much softer and heavier than are those of

the butterflies. There are other anatomical differences which would
be of little interest to the ordinary person. Those who are interested
in these insects need not hesitate to use the antennae method in separating members of the two sub-orders, for it holds good throughout
the United States and Canada with the single exception of one ob-

ANTENNAE OF THE MALE POLYPHEMUS MOTH (ENLARGED)

scure genus of small fliers which is seldom seen. The majority of the
caterpillars (larvae) of moths spin some sort of cocoon in which to
pupate. Some of these are quite rudimentary, consisting of only a
few strands of silk loosely woven together. Those of the silkworm
and of some of our native larger species, such as the *cynthia, cecropia, polyphemus*, and others, are quite elaborate. A number of species burrow into the ground to pupate. This is true of the majority
of the family of hawkmoths (*Sphingidae*) but even then they spin a
slight lining to the earthy cell in which they accomplish their metamorphoses. On the other hand, the caterpillars of butterflies spin no

cocoon. Many of them attach themselves by their anal extremity
with the aid of a small wad of silk to the underside of a leaf, branch,
fence rail, stone, or other surface, where they may hang pendent and
there change to chrysalids without the benefit of any covering. Others attach themselves in the same manner to upright surfaces, but in
addition to the wad of silk they also spin a silken girdle about their
middle, both ends of which are attached to the support. While the
other larvae hang head-downward, these are attached to the support with their heads upward, held in this position by the girdle of
silk. Some suspend themselves in this manner to the underside of a
leaf or other horizontal support. These chrysalids vary greatly in
shape. No two are exactly alike, although those of the members of
a family have a general resemblance.

With the majority of butterflies the transition stage between the
caterpillar and the perfect insect occupies but a few weeks, and with
these species there are usually two or three broods in a season, the
last brood passing the winter in the chrysalid stage and emerging in
the spring in the perfect, or imago, form to lay their eggs for the first
brood of the season. A number of species also hibernate through the
winter in the perfect form. In the United States there are many
species that have three broods in a season, and some that have two.
Of the former the monarch (*Danaus plexippus*), that large reddish-
brown and black species that is so common, is an excellent example.
It is often called the milkweed butterfly because its larvae feed entirely upon the milkweeds. It is a vigorous but rather slow flier, and
seems to be particularly fond of flying along the seacoast, even
against a strong wind. Frequently considerable numbers will alight
upon the sands of the shore. It has commonly been seen flying over
the ocean far out of sight of land, and has been reported hundreds of
miles out on the Atlantic. It is especially remarkable for its habit
of gathering in enormous, straggling swarms in late summer and
early fall, and migrating to the south where it spends the winter.
During these flights the swarms will alight on bare trees and bushes
in such numbers as to make them appear to be covered with a new
growth of reddish leaves. Many authors have described these flights,
and some years ago I witnessed one in the latter part of September
along the Connecticut coast of Long Island Sound. The swarm was
some two or three hundred feet in the air and appeared as a large

cloud whose shadow was distinctly apparent upon the ground. It passed steadily southward from about nine o'clock in the morning, when I first observed it, until nearly four in the afternoon when it gradually dwindled and finally disappeared.

These swarms are always fall flights. The return flight in the spring is accomplished by individuals or small groups, and not by swarms. It is probable that a large percentage of those composing

LARVA OF THE CECROPIA MOTH

the great swarms in the fall perish during the winter, but a sufficient number survive and return in the spring to perpetuate the species.

A series of photographs showing all the different stages in the metamorphosis of a butterfly or moth is both interesting and instructive. For several very good reasons the best subject for making such a series is the monarch butterfly. It is one of our commonest species and its larvae are easy to find and once found they are kept in captivity with no difficulty. The entire metamorphosis occupies but a few weeks from the egg to the perfect insect. The full series may be made in that time without any long tiresome wait between changes, which is a great advantage. Also the insect invariably gives some hint of what is about to happen just before each change and so, if one keeps a fairly close watch, the chances of missing any of these changes is small. All of this makes the monarch a most satisfactory subject.

If possible it is well to start this series with the egg, the image of which should be enlarged. I imagine that I hear someone asking how he is going to find such tiny things as insect eggs. These are sometimes laid in masses, either on the leaves or on the twigs of the food plant. This is particularly true of the moths. The butterflies, in many cases, lay them singly, which makes them more difficult to find, but many also lay them in small clusters, or in a mass of a considerable number. They may be attached to a leaf, leaf stem, or twig, but always on the food plant of the insect. During the years in which I have been using the wild things as photographic subjects, I have found many by simply watching any butterfly that comes flying along. If it is making a more or less steady, sustained flight without any stop, it has no interest for me. But if it is flitting from one bush to another, if these happen to be its food plant, alighting for a second on a leaf and then going to another to repeat the operation, I mark well the leaf upon which it alights and examine it carefully. Almost invariably I find an egg or two attached to it, usually on the underside. These eggs, if taken home, will hatch in a few days, but always be sure to have a fresh supply of the leaves of the plant upon which they were found ready for the young caterpillars, or else they will soon die.

The egg of the monarch is pale green in color, about one thirty-second of an inch in length, and is ovate conical in shape, distinctly ribbed longitudinally, and with numerous cross lines between the ribs. It is usually deposited on, or close to, the midrib of the underside of the leaf. The caterpillar occupies from ten days to two weeks in attaining full growth, during which period he molts, or changes his skin, several times. When full grown and of normal size, he measures from two to two and one-half inches in length. He is really quite handsome, being banded throughout his entire length with transverse alternate stripes of black, yellow and white. During this time he must be kept supplied with fresh leaves of the species of milk-weed on which the egg was found. Some morning, when you visit your captive, you will find him restlessly crawling over the plant, oc-

THE PARSNIP SWALLOWTAIL

casionally stopping to raise his head and look about before continuing his peregrinations. His actions seem to indicate that he is searching for something which he is unable to locate. This is really the
secret of his actions, for he is looking for a suitable part of the plant
on which to pass the next period of his existence, the pupal, or chrysalid, stage.

This restlessness usually lasts for about a day, but he finally se-
lects a leaf and hangs himself by his tail from the midrib of its underside, attaching himself to it by a small quantity of an adhesive, silky
substance. In this position, curled into the shape of a hook, he hangs
for another twenty-four hours or so. At the end of this period a kind
of convulsion seizes him and his body commences to contract and expand longitudinally, the convulsions running over him in waves from
his head to his tail. These last for about an hour, the body gradually straightening until it hangs completely perpendicular. The

head and upper parts then begin to swell until the skin, given a greater pressure than it can stand, suddenly splits between the eyes and for a short distance up the back, and the chrysalis emerges from its now useless covering, working it backward by a continuation of the convulsive movements until it is contracted into a small, tight wad at the upper end, or tail. This is held tightly between the last

FEMALE SILKWORM MOTH LAYING EGGS

two segments of the chrysalis while the extreme tip of the upper end, armed with a hard, black, barbed point, is withdrawn and the point extended upward and worked deeply into the silky substance until a tight connection has been established. Then with a last convulsive jerk the now entirely superfluous skin is cast off, and the chrysalis hangs entirely denuded of any covering.

During the better part of the next two hours the chrysalis changes its shape, but this is done so gradually that one cannot follow the process. But at the end of that time it hangs, a veritable pendent gem, of an exquisite emerald green with a row of brilliant golden spots near the top, and several scattered ones near the bottom. It is by far the handsomest chrysalis of the many thousand forms from which our butterflies emerge. It is well deserving the name which is commonly given it, of milkweed jewel.

During the ensuing ten days to two weeks there is no apparent change in the chrysalis. At the end of this time, however, the green color fades and turns brownish until, through the now transparent shell, the outline of the wings and their markings can distinctly be seen. We now know that the next change is about to take place and we must consequently be ready and on the alert, for suddenly, and without any further warning, the shell bursts open at the lowest

EGGS OF SILKWORM (ENLARGED)

extremity and the butterfly pulls himself out by his forelegs, and hangs from the empty shell, the process not occupying more than two or three seconds.

At this stage it is a most bedraggled and imperfect appearing insect. The body is swollen and huge in comparison to the pair of crumpled wings that have little resemblance to the things of beauty which they will become in a short space of time. Gradually the juices from the body are pumped into the wings until they become smooth and perfect, and the body shrinks until it has become reduced to the size of a normal butterfly's body. The wings, however, while appearing to be perfect, are still very damp and limp and totally inadequate to fulfill their function as a means of locomotion for their owner. Gradually in the next four or five hours they dry and stiffen until, when they are finally capable of sustaining him in flight, he leaves his perch and flutters away. There is a butterfly (*Basilarchia archippus*) that takes its name, the viceroy, from the fact that it imitates the monarch. It is found all over the United States. Its mimicry of the monarch is so close that it is almost impossible to tell them apart except for the fact that the viceroy is considerably the smaller of the two. It is one of the most striking examples of protection by imitation because the monarch

The " Worm " That Spins the Silk

secretes a juice that is disagreeable to birds which therefore never eat them. By its close imitation the little viceroy also avoids being eaten.

It may help some, in the search for butterfly subjects, to know where they are most likely to be found. Many butterflies have a decided preference for certain localities in which to roam and some of these are so prejudiced in favor of their chosen haunts that they are seldom seen elsewhere. Orchards are the chosen haunts of the anglewings (*Polygonia*). These little fellows are among the best examples of protective markings and coloring in the insect world. Their flight is very rapid and jerky, and it needs a quick eye to follow them when they are on the wing. When at rest on the trunk or limb of an apple or other rough-barked tree, where they delight to alight, with their wings folded tightly together over their backs showing only the undersides, their indefinite grayish brown wings so nearly match the color of the bark upon which they have alighted that at a distance of a few feet it is almost impossible to distinguish them. In the fall they feed upon the decaying fruit that has fallen to the ground. I have seen as many as half a dozen feeding upon one half-rotten apple.

A member of the wood nymphs, the goggle-eye, that dark-brown

Cocoons of the Silkworm

butterfly with a yellow patch on the forward part of the forewings enclosing two dark eye-like spots, should be familiar to us all. It is partial to the woods, and is found in most abundance along old wood roads where it flits along ahead of us with an odd jerky flight, never allowing us to approach within dangerous closeness. It is frequently found in company with its close relative the grass nymph, in grassy meadows and pastures or old fields that adjoin woodlands. Its cousin, the true wood nymph, on the contrary, is found only in low woods where it is often very common. It need not be confused with the goggle-eye for it is smaller, of a lighter brown, and instead of the two large eyes on the forewings it has two smaller ones on both front and back wings. These two butterflies are often seen together.

The blue swallowtail (*Papilio philenor*) is found almost exclusively in the open woods, especially where there is an abundance of flowering plants. The yellow, or tiger, swallowtail (*Papilio glaucus*) is more partial to dry woods, the borders of woods, and orchards.

SILKWORM COCOON CUT OPEN TO SHOW PUPA

The parsnip swallowtail (*Papilio polyxenes*) is rarely found in the woods but is particularly common in fields where there is an abundance of the wild parsnip which, together with its cultivated species, is its food plant. On the other hand the spicebush swallowtail (*Papilio troilus*), whose food plant is the spicebush, is found in most abundance where this bush abounds, in low damp woods, particularly in marshy spots along the borders of streams.

The genus *Argynnis* (the fritillaries) is one of the largest genera of our butterflies. Any of the many species is easily recognizable by the fact that the undersides of the wings are always marked, more or less profusely, with silvery spots. All of them are partial to the open fields or marshy meadows, where they fly from flowering plant to flowering plant and are always the commonest butterflies to be found there.

And so it goes, each species has its chosen habitat from which it may occasionally roam, but where it may always be found in greatest abundance. The mourning cloak butterfly, or Camberwell beauty (*Vanessa antiope*) is found in dry, open, deciduous woods, especially on hillsides; the painted lady (*Pyrameis cardui*), along dusty

ADULT MOTHS OF THE SILKWORM

roadsides, and in dry fields and wastelands, while its nearest relative, the red admiral (*Pyrameis atalanta*), is found in greatest abundance in open woodlands and moist meadows.

The metamorphosis of a moth is similar in every respect to that of a butterfly. It is not so easily followed, however, because the caterpillar shuts itself up in a cocoon when it is ready to pupate and only emerges as a perfect insect. The best way to make such a series is by finding the eggs, rearing the caterpillar by keeping it supplied with fresh leaves of its food plant until it spins its cocoon, then keeping the cocoon through the winter in some cool spot until the moth emerges in the spring. During this time the cocoon may be opened by cutting it very carefully with a sharp knife in order to make a photograph of the enclosed pupa. In this manner all the changes from the egg to the perfect insect can be shown, and the moth is always a perfect specimen with immaculate wings, which is not always the case with specimens caught in the open.

One of the best species with which to make this series is the polyphemus moth (*Telea polyphemus*), which is sometimes called the American silk moth. It is quite a common species, ranging across the entire continent, and south into Mexico, but, as it flies only at night, it is totally unknown to the great majority of people. In the southern states there are generally two broods in a season, but elsewhere it is single-brooded, laying its eggs in the spring, which hatch in a few days, the larva living through the summer to spin its cocoon and pupate in the fall. The cocoon remains hanging from the tree until another spring, when the moth emerges to again lay its eggs and commences another cycle. The caterpillar, or larva, is a really beautiful object. It is about four inches long when fully grown, of an exquisite shade of green with silvery lines on each side, and ornamented with blue spots and small red protuberances. It feeds upon the leaves of a great variety of trees, but is probably found most plentifully on the maples, oaks, and hickories. The cocoon is a substantial affair spun among the leaves and usually firmly attached to a twig. Its maker injects into it a fluid which penetrates the fibers, making them completely waterproof, and which precipitates a white chalky matter when dried. Efforts have been made to reel silk from these cocoons, but they have never been entirely successful. The mature moth emerges under ordinary conditions in late May or early June, and is one of our largest as well as most beautiful species. It quite frequently has a wing expanse of five inches or more. Its general coloring is a lovely soft shade of tan with an eye-like semi-transparent spot on each hind wing, and a smaller one on each of the forewings, of blue and yellow, outlined with dark purple.

The larvae of the *Sphingidae*, or hawkmoths, burrow into the ground for some inches in order to pupate. This family deserves particular attention. Their principal time of flight is at dusk, and they are strong, rapid fliers. Except by breeding, the only way in which they may be photographed is by finding them resting during the daytime. They are partial to tree trunks as a resting place, where the indeterminate coloring of their upper wings, which when closed completely cover the lower ones, blends so well with the bark of the tree as to make their detection difficult. There is a genus of this family the center of whose wings are entirely devoid of scales, and are transparent. They are called "clearwings" and also

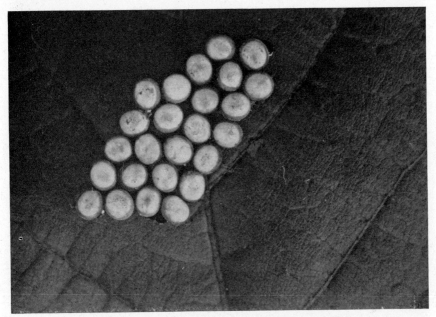

EGGS OF THE POLYPHEMUS MOTH (ENLARGED)

"hummingbird moths," the latter on account of their manner of flight, which greatly resembles that of hummingbirds in its swiftness and in the manner in which they dart from flower to flower and hover over them without alighting, while sucking the nectar. There are but a few species in this genus and they are the only ones of the more conspicuous members of the family that ever fly in the daytime. The more or less famous "death's-head moth" is a member of this family. It takes its name from the fact that the markings on the thorax closely resemble a skull.

The name hawkmoth was given to the members of this family because of the shape of their wings, which are long and narrow, and on account of the rapidity of their flight. The larvae of all of them extend themselves while eating or when in motion, but when disturbed or at rest the forward part of the body is drawn backward and upward with the head bowed down. This position was thought to somewhat resemble that of the Egyptian sphinx, which caused the name sphinx moths also to be given them. Many of these larvae, when ready to pupate, do so in a cell deep under the soil, but some others spin a loose cocoon among damp leaves on the ground.

When the time comes in the spring for the moth to emerge, nature has provided the means by which the escape from this underground cell is accomplished. The abdomen of the pupa is composed of a series of rings, called somites, which it is able to move in a spiral manner thus forcing itself upward along the same path by which it descended in the fall, until it again reaches the surface. Many moths besides the hawkmoths pupate in the ground, but the members of this family are the largest that do so. It is well, if you are proposing to rear moths from the larvae, to have your breeding cage covered with earth on the bottom to a depth of five or six inches so that your captives may burrow into the earth if they want to.

Few people have any conception of the enormous number of insects there are in the world. I am not speaking of individuals but of species. Insects constitute by far the largest group of living creatures. With them are not included the *Arachnida* (the spiders and their kin), or the *Myriapoda* (the centipedes, millepedes, etc.), for these are not insects at all but belong to entirely different classes. It is safe to go still farther and say that in number of species insects are much more numerous than all of the other groups of land animals put together. A most conservative estimate of the number of species in existence places it at five million, while Riley, one of our greatest entomologists, puts it at about twice that number. This, of course, covers the entire world. While insect life is much more abundant in tropical climates, nevertheless North America still has a high enough percentage of the grand total to give any man sufficient work for a lifetime if he attempts to picture only the more noticeable forms.

In this work it is, naturally, best that one should have some slight idea of the habits of the subjects for which he is searching. Also he should be able to distinguish the specimens which he finds and photographs, and at least place them in their right order, even though he

may not be able to name them specifically. He should be able to differentiate between a bee and a fly; a moth and a butterfly; a locust
and a cicada; or a beetle and a bug. There are many people who
know so little about these creatures that they call a moth a butterfly,
or vice versa, and to whom all crawling things are just " bugs." It
is a common error with the majority of people to misname the cicada,
calling it a locust, while to them the universal term for the latter is
" grasshopper." And there are flies that so nearly resemble a bee
that it is not easy to distinguish them apart until they are examined
closely.

There is a group of insects, instrumentalists we might call them,
which forms an immense orchestra. The members are beginning in
this month their greatest activity which will be continued until well
into October. Upon the individuals of this group the nature photographer will find it very interesting to use his camera, and he need
never fear being without subjects. The members of this orchestra
are legion, and they may be found any and everywhere throughout
the fields and meadows and along the roadsides. They are the members of three families of the order *Orthoptera:* the *Acridiidae*, the
short-horned grasshoppers or true locusts; the *Locustidae*, the
long-horned grasshoppers (katydids, etc.); and the *Gryllidae*,
crickets.

What vibrant, whirring " music " they make over the meadows
and fields throughout the summer and fall, more at night than in
the daytime! Instrumentalists is a most appropriate name for them.
There are no insects that possess vocal organs, and therefore they
can do no singing. This music is in every instance produced by the
rubbing, or beating, of some portion of their bodies against some
other portion, these parts being specially modified to produce the
sound, which is made by the males alone. With the crickets the
sound is made by rubbing the upper pair of wing covers together.
Some of the grasshoppers might well be called the violinists of the
orchestra. Their forewings constitute the violin, against the edge of
which they press their hind thigh as the bow, raising and lowering it
to produce the music. This is so veined and grooved that the sounds
made by the different species vary considerably.

Among the members of the family *Locustidae* are some of the most
pretentious musicians. This family comprises the green grasshop-

pers, those species whose antennae are much longer then their bodies. The females have long, curving, sword-like ovipositors, composed of six pieces instead of four as with the *Acridiidae*. The musical apparatus of the males is situated at the base of the wing covers and consists of a curiously developed membrane. These are the aspiring soloists of the insect orchestra, and one need search but a short time before hearing the performance of one of the more common of them. As we walk through the fields, especially where the grass is thick and high, we will be sure to hear, rising clearly above the undertone of the myriads of smaller insects, a certain note, or rather series of notes, that is familiar and yet to which we may never have paid any particular attention. Let us follow it up this time and see if we can discover what is producing it. The tune — *tzip-tzip-tzip-tzip-tzee-e-e-e-e-e-e-e* — seems to come from but a short distance away. But as we approach the spot from which we think it comes, it advances in front of us until we find we have covered several times the estimated distance before we can feel reasonably certain that the performer is but a few feet in front of us. Just as we think we have found him, the performance abruptly ceases and, search as we may, we fail to find any least trace of the performer.

Let us remain perfectly quiet for a few minutes. It will not be more than that before we again hear the notes, this time from a spot very close to us and, if we search carefully the tall grasses surrounding the spot from which the sound comes, using only our eyes and not moving more than is absolutely necessary, we will surely soon discover the little musician. Clinging close to some grass stem, in color exactly matching that of his perch, it is little wonder that our eyes failed to find him sooner. He is about an inch in length, with transparent wings through which the outline of his green body may easily be seen. His hind legs are long and exceedingly fragile, as indeed are those of all his family, causing one to wonder why they do not break on some of his long and seemingly reckless jumps.

This is the common meadow grasshopper (*Orchelimum vulgare*). Now let us approach as close to him as possible without causing him to leave his perch. We can get very near, if we move slowly and carefully, and watch for a repetition of his performance. At the base of his wings, directly back of the thorax, or collar, by looking closely we can see a small glassy spot. This might be called his

THE IO MOTH, MALE

tambourine. He makes his wings vibrate with such rapidity as to cause them to appear only as a blur and by a few convulsive movements he so beats, or scratches, on this spot as to produce the rasping strain already described, which we may hear with endless repetition throughout the fields and meadows during summer and autumn. It is probably the most omnipresent note of the entire winged orchestra.

Another meadow musician, belonging to the *Locustidae,* whose harsh, grating, file-like music can hardly be overlooked even among the multitude of other insect notes, is the cone-headed grasshopper (*Conocephalus ensiger*). His attempt at producing musical notes is a very poor imitation of the first three notes of the meadow grasshopper, " *zip-zip-zip-zip-zip-zip-zip,*" in a continuous rasping string of sound, monotonous in the extreme. Its author, or possibly I might say composer, is a comical-looking fellow and might well be called the clown of the minstrel group of grasshoppers. He is long and attenuated, with pointed head and narrow wings twice the length of his body and in color a shade of green that so nearly matches that of the high grasses among which he is at home, that it is often extremely difficult to distinguish him from his surroundings when he is at rest. The ovipositor of the female is as long as her body, and sword-shaped, which has given to her the name of " sword-bearer." A close relative (*Conocephalus triops*) is similar in appearance, but with shorter wings. In the female of this species the wings do not reach the end of the ovipositor, while in the *ensiger* they do. Both of these insects are found in two phases of color, green and light brown, but the brown phase is much more common in *triops* than in *ensiger*.

There is another member of the long-horn family with whose musical performance we must all be familiar even though we may not know the performer himself. This is the katydid. He is a day as well as a night performer, but it is with his night-time music that we are most familiar, for his stridulations make the nights of late summer and early autumn resonant. There are several species of these insects in three genera, that are commonly known under the name of " katydid " (derived from the notes that they produce). One of our commonest species is the oblong-leaf-winged katydid (*Amblycorypha oblongifolia*). Another, somewhat less common, belonging to the same genus, is the round-winged katydid (*Amblycorypha rotundifolia*). The katydids, throughout the evening and night, are almost entirely arboreal, often climbing to the tops of the tallest trees. During the day, however, they will frequently condescend to mix with their more lowly relatives, and may be found in considerable numbers in the tall weeds and grass of the meadows.

There is one member of the *Gryllidae* (the crickets) whose music might almost be called a song, it is so much more softly melodious than is that of any other member of the entire order. We hear it coming to us from the mysterious darkness of the shrubbery on every side. It is seldom heard as an absolute solo, but rather in a continuous united chorus that forms an underlying cadence, an accompaniment to the multitudinous other sounds of the night, for the author is a night performer. Moreover it possesses a pulsating rhythmical beat that is peculiar to itself alone and which forms as much a com-

LONG-HORN LOCUST, SHOWING OVIPOSITOR

ponent part of the late summer and fall evenings as does the music
of the katydids.

The player is as delicate as his note. Less than an inch in length,
with a pale green body, white, diaphanous wings and long and extremely fragile legs, the snowy tree cricket (*Oecanthus niveus*), for
this is the name of our little muscian, appears to be almost too frail
for this earth. Yet he survives the storms and cold of late autumn
and is one of the last of his tribe to perform, his cheerful tune often
being heard as late as mid-November, after all other insect music is
stilled.

The *Gryllidae* take the name cricket, by which they are commonly known, from the French popular name " cri-cri," a translation to words of the sound made by the common cricket of Europe, the house cricket, the " cricket on the hearth " of song and story (*Gryllus domesticus*). It inhabits America to any extent only in Canada. The common field cricket (*Gryllus neglectus*) takes its place with us most effectively, often finding its way into our houses, supposedly bringing good luck with it but carrying it away should we drive it out. The music of the male is familiar to all of us and neither it nor its maker need any description.

The *Gryllidae* can be separated into three distinct types. Of the true crickets, the commonest and most typical representative in this country is the field cricket. The mole crickets are curious creatures that spend nearly their entire lives in subterranean burrows. They are wingless, or with mere rudimentary wings, and their fore legs are modified into digging appliances with which they excavate their burrows. These legs somewhat resemble the forelegs of a mole, and from this fact and their subterranean habits, they derive their name. The third type, the tree crickets, is the group to which belong the little fellow I have just described.

The musical efforts of the locusts, or short-horn grasshoppers (*Acridiidae*) are much more crude than are those of their long-horn cousins. The sound made by a single individual of this family is lost among the various sounds of nature, but what they lack in this direction individually they more than make up collectively. They often congregate in immense swarms which cause great damage to vegetation, frequently destroying all crops over a considerable area. The sound produced by such a swarm has been likened to " the roar of a wild ocean." Probably the most destructive is the western grasshopper, or migratory locust (*Melanoplus spretus*), which has caused tremendous damage to western crops. In the east the American locust (*Schistocerca americana*) has also done much damage, especially in the south where it is most common.

Two of our more common species are the Carolina locust (*Dissosteira carolina*), and the leather-colored locust (*Schistocerca alutacea*). The former is distributed all over the United States and Canada except on the highest elevations. He is drab in color, with the outer wings thickly sprinkled with dark brown spots. His inner wings are black, or nearly so, with the outer borders pale greenish yellow. He should be familiar to all as he is one of our commonest grasshoppers, occuring along roadsides, in cultivated fields, and especially in places where there is more or less bare ground. He is a strong flier and will suddenly rise from the ground in front of one and fly for a short distance, only to be immediately lost to sight again the minute he alights, even though it be on the bare earth. His drab wing covers so exactly match the color of the dusty weeds and bare ground that, when he alights and closes them, he becomes practically invisible until, with a jump, he again leaps into activity from the very spot at which we may be looking. The leather-colored locust is somewhat less common but is found in considerable numbers in underbrush, coarse grass and weeds, especially in moist meadows and marshes. Both species are among our most conspicuous members of this family, because of their abundance and their large size.

The members of the *Orthoptera* do not pass through three phases in their metamorphosis as do the members of the *Lepidoptera* and *Coleoptera*. The young, when hatched, resemble the mature insect in every respect except the lack of wings which are gradually acquired through a succession of molts which finally leaves the insect possessed of a double pair. The forward, or outer, pair are tough and horny, for use only as a measure of protection for the body and for the much more delicate under pair that are used for flying. These are thin and fragile, usually semi-transparent, and often showy. They have radiating veins that allow the insect, when in repose, to fold them like a fan while they are completely covered and protected by the upper pair.

The actual photographing of the members of the *Orthoptera* is not as difficult as one might surmise considering their ability to suddenly and without warning start from any spot in long jumps and flight. Should one attempt to photograph them where found, he will almost certainly get nothing for his pains. The subjects must first be caught, and great care must be observed in handling them. While the back legs of a grasshopper are extremely useful to him as instruments of propulsion, they are not essential to his welfare for he can crawl about very well without them. Therefore he does not seem to be greatly averse to losing them if it comes to a choice between keeping them and freedom. If you should try holding a grasshopper by these legs you are very apt shortly to find yourself grasping one or two legs with no body attached. The best method for obtaining their pictures is to find a spot upon which they can be suitably posed. Focus upon this spot and arrange your camera for an exposure, then carefully place your subject upon this spot, holding him between thumb and finger at the base of the wing covers. The minute your hold is loosened, he will in all probability jump away. Perhaps not, but you must be prepared for this eventuality and catch him again, immediately replacing him upon the perch. You will need some patience in this work for it is probable that you will be forced to repeat this performance a number of times before your subject will agree to remain quietly on the perch for a few seconds. This he will eventually do and, if you are ready to make the exposure, you will have your picture.

Are all of my readers acquainted with that peculiarly odd and rather ridiculous appearing insect, the praying mantis? It belongs to the same order as the grasshoppers (*Orthoptera*) and is an insect eater, for which reason it should be given every protection. It earns its name from the attitude it assumes when resting or while awaiting the approach of a victim. The front portion of its body is held erect with its strong front legs, built for grasping and holding, raised and bent as in an attitude of prayer. In England it is known as the " soothsayer." It is cannibalistic in its tendencies and will frequently fight with another of its own species, the victor devouring the vanquished. In the south, where it is most abundant, it is known under the names of " rearhorse " and " mule-killer," the latter from an absurd superstition, particularly rife among the Negroes, that the brownish liquid which occasionally exudes from its mouth when handled, similar to the " molasses " of the grasshoppers, is fatal to mules. Mantes are easily photographed as they will remain motionless for considerable periods of time, and also because they are very heavy fliers, using their wings but seldom and then only for short, awkward flights seldom covering more than a few yards. Two foreign species have been introduced into the country within the past few years — the European and the Japanese mantis. Both are rapidly spreading throughout the eastern states.

We all know the insect that is commonly, but erroneously, known by the name " locust." Its proper name is cicada, and it is known by various popular names such as harvest-man, harvest-fly, lyre-man, etc. The cicadas include the periodical cicada, or so-called " seventeen-year locust," which visits certain portions of the country in the north every seventeen years but in the southern states every thirteen years. They spend the remainder of their lives, between these visitations, in larval form far beneath the surface of the earth. They are fairly large insects belonging to the sub-order *Homoptera*, and the family *Cicadidae*, of the order *Hemiptera*. They are characterized by semi-transparent wings considerably longer than the body, which when at rest are held in a slanting, roof-like position over their backs. Their bodies are large, with wide, blunt heads, having very prominent eyes on the outer angles. All of the cicadas are great " singers," and from this fact alone are undoubtedly well known to all of us who spend any time in the country during midsummer. Their " song," which resembles as closely as one sound can be said to resemble another, the noise made by a frying pan in full swing over a hot fire, is as much a component part of the heat of a July or August day, as the green of the grass or foliage, or the white-flecked blue of the sky. It is, of course, no song at all but should be more properly called instrumental music, as is that of the grasshoppers. It is produced by the males alone by means of a specially constructed apparatus that somewhat resembles a drum-head, and which is situated at the base of the underside of the abdomen. This is vibrated with gradually increasing force and rapidity, causing the sound to start on a low note and slowly increase in pitch and volume until it terminates on a note that may readily be heard for a considerable distance. It is no exaggeration to say that on a very still day the sound will carry for a distance of half a mile or more. Very strong muscles control these timbals and when the " song " is at its height the whole body of the performer vibrates with the exertion of producing it.

It is supposed that with the exception of the periodical cicadas, all the other species are annual, with the larvae spending some nine or ten months in the ground. It is conceded, however, that it may very well be that the larval period is longer than this, and that the annual appearance of the adult insect is accounted for by the fact of their great abundance and the intermingling of generations. The eggs are laid in twigs at the ends of tree branches. The larvae, which are very small ant-like creatures when first born, drop to the ground and immediately burrow into it. Here they remain until the time has arrived for the change to the adult insect, when they leave the ground in the pupal form, crawl up some near-by tree trunk, or other erect object, and there complete their change. This is accomplished by the skin of the pupa splitting between the eyes and down the back, and the cicada gradually emerging. This operation is an interesting one to photograph.

There is a large and extremely ferocious wasp that is the nemesis of the cicada. Its name is digger wasp (*Sphecius speciosus*), owing to the fact that it excavates tunnels in the ground in which to rear its young. Its prey is the cicada which it hunts assiduously from tree to tree. Therefore if, on some sultry day in August, we should be listening to the whirring music of the cicada and should hear it suddenly end in a discordant, distressful note, we may know that one of these wasps has found its victim. It pounces upon its unsuspecting prey before it can make a start to fly away. A quick stab of its stinger and the unlucky victim is paralyzed and thrown into a comatose condition in which state it remains, without dying, for ten days or two weeks, which is fully long enough to answer the purpose for which the wasp needs it. Having once stung and subdued it, the real work of the wasp begins, for she (it is the female of the species that plays the part of villain in this melodrama) must carry it to her burrow which has already been prepared to receive her unconscious guest which is considerably larger and heavier than herself. Straddling it, always with its head to the front, and grasping it firmly with her long legs, she starts on her slow and laborious flight with her burden. Gradually the weight of the cicada forces her downward until, if the burrow is some distance from the capture, she is forced to land and must finish the journey by dragging her victim. Once having reached her journey's end, she pulls the cicada down the burrow to the chamber at its end, lays an egg upon its body, and completes her task by filling in the hole completely with the sand. In two or three days the egg hatches and the young grub finds a plentiful supply of food that will last it in perfect condition during the short period of its life as a larva. At the end of this time, it spins a rough cocoon on what remains of the unfortunate cicada. In this it stays until the following summer when it transforms to the pupa, only a short time before the perfect wasp emerges to dig her way to the surface of the ground and start the cycle again by searching out another foredoomed cicada.

While many of our insects are large enough for easy photographing, many others of them are small. The majority of them are so minute as to be almost invisible to the naked eye. Thousands of species that swarm on all sides of us are so insignificant that they are

TREE HOPPER (ENLARGED)

never suspected by the casual observer, yet their name is legion. The class in which is found the largest species is the *Lepidoptera* and these are naturally the ones best known. But only a comparative few of these larger species are known to the majority of us. The species whose expanse of wings measures half an inch or less by far outnumber those that are larger.

Of course it is utterly useless to try photographing these minute insects with the ordinary camera, and yet many of them are well worth photographing. Even a life-size photograph of any of the *Tineidae*, for instance, that great family of moths to which the clothes moth belongs, and which comprises a large number of minute but very beautiful species, would be practically worthless, but if we enlarged the image to eight or ten times the original size, the result would be well worth while for it would then show plainly all the markings and detail.

Of course for the very minute species we must use a micro-photographic camera, for nothing else would enlarge them to a desirable size, but there are many between those that must be photographed in this manner and those that are sufficiently large to photograph successfully in the ordinary manner. These species may be easily photographed to a size that will show all details clearly with the ordinary view camera with twenty-inch extension. When only a moderate enlargement is wished, it can be made with a seven or eight inch lens by extending the bellows to full length. Should greater enlargements be desired, they can readily be obtained by using a little supplementary enlarging lens that fits over the regular lens. There are a number of these useful little gadgets on the market, and the cost is small. No nature photographer should be without one.

Among other subjects upon which this little auxiliary lens may be used to great advantage, is the family of small insects, belonging to the same sub-order as the cicadas, known as tree hoppers. There are a number of species of these little fellows that comprise some of the most grotesque insects that nature has ever evolved. Comstock, the entomologist, once remarked that " Nature must have been in a joking mood when tree hoppers were developed." These grotesque shapes are due to a curious modification of the prothorax. The majority of these modifications have been brought about in order to provide protective resemblances for their possessors, since by them many of the insects are made to resemble different parts of plant structures, and excrescences. They are all small, none exceeding a third of an inch in length, and are extremely active, being able to jump great distances in comparison to their size. In photographing them one must be more than just ordinarily careful not to give the branch or twig upon which the subject is resting the least jar, else he will suddenly discover that he no longer has a subject.

A member of a closely allied family is the little frosted lightning hopper. In color it varies from a light gray to a beautiful light green, dusted with a fine, white powder which imparts to it the appearance of being frosted, hence its name. It jumps with great alacrity when disturbed, but its jump ends in a moth-like flight which frequently carries it for considerable distances. While the tree hoppers are more or less solitary in their habits, rarely becoming in the least gregarious, these little fellows seem to like the company of others of their species. They are often quite common on the foliage of many different trees and shrubs, and are not difficult to photograph if one uses even ordinary care not to disturb them by jarring the branch upon which they are grouped. If this happens they are very likely to all leave at once, and with exceeding promptness, and we will find ourselves looking at nothing but a bare twig. Another family, the leaf hoppers, are also close relatives of the members of both these families. It is an extensive group, whose members have a great variety of forms and colors. They are usually slender insects, and are often found in considerable numbers on the foliage of different plants.

MALE OF THE PROMETHEA MOTH

AUGUST

N O doubt many of my readers spend at least part of August at the seashore, for this is the month when the shore is most enjoyable. Here the nature photographer can obtain pictures of subjects that are not only seldom photographed but which can be obtained in no other place, subjects that are very well worth an effort to get for that very reason, if for no other. Naturally, when the tide is at its lowest ebb is the best time to search for these subjects. Then sand flats and rocks that are covered to a considerable depth at high tide are completely exposed or but a short distance below the surface of the water, and easily reached.

If anyone has the idea that a sea beach consists of nothing but sand and water, rocks and seaweeds, let him don a bathing suit and wade about on some sandy flat at low tide, when there is a foot or less of water covering it, and watch the bottom carefully. It needs a clear, calm day when there is little or no wind blowing to ruffle the water, so that he can see the bottom clearly enough to detect whatever may be there. Or let him explore a rocky promontory after the water has receded and left the rocks at least partially bare. When he has done either of these things, and has used his eyes to good advantage, he will discover many things that he never suspected were in existence.

There are many subjects along any sandy beach but the casual observer will see only a few of the many subjects which are there to be found by one who will search for them intelligently. They are on the beach itself, in the grass and herbage back of the beach, among the rocks and attached to them, on the sand flats and even in holes dug into the sand banks. If the beach borders a salt marsh it adds considerably to the number of subjects one may find, and is very well worth exploring, even at the expense of wet feet. One such beach, where I have spent many happy and lucrative hours, stretches for about a mile as a purely sand beach with sand flats off shore that are bare at low tide. This gradually merges into a beach covered with small rocks and stones and finally ends in a point that stretches well into the water and is covered with beach grass and low bushes on which shores large rocks and boulders predominate. I have visited this beach many times and never without obtaining a number of new and interesting photographs.

Such a marsh, as the one which borders this beach, is often traversed by narrow watercourses whose precipitous banks are of more or less hardened sand. In these banks the peculiar and interesting fiddler crabs make their burrows. The male is possessed of one claw that is very large in comparison to its body, and one so small as to be insignificant, giving the crab the appearance of being deformed. The claws of the female are both the same size and but little larger than the small one of the male. They live in burrows which they dig in the sand, sometimes directly on the beach, but more often in sandy banks, always, however, where the sand is compact and hardened. In the " Crustacea of New Jersey," by H. W. Fowler, an interesting account of them is given: " The holes are dug by carrying little pellets of moist sand and running several feet before depositing them. Before going back to their burrow they usually pause a short time as if to apprehend danger, then run back to their burrow and, after giving a last look around, disappear in the hole. Their work is carried on at all favorable hours of the day or night according to the weather, and as the tide is out. The colonies of these animals are quite interesting, the little creatures moving about actively over the sand sideways, suddenly halting and retreating their steps as any disturbance may require. Others may be seen looking cautiously from their burrows. Sometimes these communities extend for several acres. The diameter of the burrow itself is usually small, just large enough to admit the body of the crab. It extends down a foot or more in a vertical direction and becomes more or less horizontal, with an excavation at the lower end. Often, if the under strata of soil, or that below the sand, is dark or black, the pellets carried up from the burrows form a contrast to the general pale surroundings. When leaving the burrow the male usually emerges with the large cheliped (claw) folded and forward. The males use only the small claw in feeding, picking up bits of algae very daintily. The females use either of their small claws indifferently for this purpose."

There are three species of marine mussels that are more or less common along the Atlantic coast wherever there are rocks or beaches covered with stones at low tide. The edible mussel occurs in large masses, and while grown in Europe for food, it is used more extensively in this country by fishermen as bait and by coastal farmers as fertilizer. The horse mussel when full grown is usually considerably larger than the foregoing. The ribbed mussel is about the size of the edible, but narrow, black, and ribbed lengthwise of the shell. There is also a large group of fresh-water mussels. Of these there are more than a thousand species, many of which are found in the United States where they are widely distributed in rivers and small streams. They are valueless as food, but frequently produce pearls, some of which have a considerable value. Strangely enough, pearls have never been found in any of the sea species.

Probably the most numerous of all the creatures that we shall find in shallow water and clinging to the uncovered or half-submerged rocks, are the periwinkles. These are small gastropod mollusks with top-shaped shells that vary greatly in color from a pure olive green, sometimes almost black, to yellow, and even occasionally red. They must be familiar objects to everyone who has ever visited a sea beach on the Atlantic coast, for every pool left by the receding tide abounds with them, and the rocks and even the sea bottom in places are literally covered with them as with a heavy carpet. It is no exaggeration to say that in some places they occur by the millions. They are easily photographed, as their movements are very slow when they move at all, and groups of them will remain absolutely quiescent, attached to some rock, for long periods of time.

Undoubtedly the next most numerous subject that we will find is the little hermit crab that mingles in large numbers with the periwinkles, usurping their empty shells as homes. When they are stationary, which is not very often, they cannot be distinguished from the periwinkles themselves, but if we watch a group of the mollusks for a few minutes we will be certain to see several of them traveling around at quite a speed, and we may be certain that these are the hermit crabs. They are small crustaceans, common along the coast, especially in rocky pools. They grow no shell of their own, but live in the deserted shells of different mollusks which they carry around with them as portable shelters. Their bodies are specialized and

HERMIT CRAB IN OLD CONCH SHELL

adapted to this unusual mode of life. The abdomen is soft, with no protecting shell as on the lobster, and their fan-like tails take the form of a hook for holding them in their shells. The tail performs its duties so well that should anyone attempt to remove the crab from the shell, it will more often than not come away piecemeal. They can move about with great celerity and ease on the sea bottom, carrying their houses with them, but when alarmed will withdraw into their borrowed shell with such speed that their movements are almost impossible to follow with the eye, and block the entrance securely with their right claw, which is somewhat larger than the left.

The little fellows that we see in the shells of the periwinkles and other small mollusks are the smallest species of the hermit crabs, and owing to their extreme activity are very difficult to photograph.

There are a number of other species of these crabs, however, that are much larger, inhabiting the shells of the larger snails, whelks, conchs, and other mollusks. The largest that are found along our shores inhabit the shells of the conchs. While not very common, they may frequently be seen crawling along over the sand flats at low tide. These fellows are not at all difficult to photograph provided it is done in the tank, about which I have already written.

After the periwinkles and hermit crabs, in point of abundance, come the true crabs. There are twelve or fifteen species of these that may be found more or less commonly at low tide along almost any of our beaches. Probably the commonest of them all is the lady crab. It occurs in considerable numbers on all sandy flats below low water mark, and its empty shells are washed up by the waves all along the beaches. It has the habit of burying itself completely in the sand, with only its stalk-like eyes protruding, and there awaiting the approach of a meal. When disturbed it will emerge from its sandy covering, scuttle along over the sand for a short distance, and bury itself again. So quickly can it do this that we see it one minute, but the next it has completely disappeared. The color of its carapace, or upper shell, is a dull tan thickly mottled, spotted and reticulated with pink, which so conforms to the color of the sandy bottom on which this crab lives, as to make it difficult to detect it until it moves.

Next in abundance is probably the common edible variety, the blue crab, although it prefers the deeper water, especially where there is a good growth of eel grass in which it can hide. It is the largest of our crabs and also the strongest swimmer, being often seen at the surface of the water. During the period between the shedding of one shell and the hardening of another, which usually occurs in July or August, it becomes that epicurean delicacy, the " soft-shell crab." It will ascend any tidal river as far as salt water extends.

The rock crab, another common species ranging the Atlantic coast from Labrador to the Gulf of Mexico, is a much smaller species than the blue, but also edible. It is a somewhat secretive species, preferring to remain on rocky or stony bottoms, although it sometimes is to be found on sandy shores. It is reddish brown in color, speckled and blotched with darker brown.

Probably the most peculiar of all our species of crabs is the spider crab that is extremely common all along the coast from Maine to

Florida. It is the " sea-spider " which is so annoying to anglers because it will attack any bait and cling tightly even after being lifted
from the water. It is an expert at camouflage, for the hooked hairs
with which its upper shell is covered collect bits of seaweed and other
marine growths, which in turn become covered with the mud and
sand of the bottom until it more closely resembles an algae-covered
stone or small wad of matted seaweed moving sluggishly over the bot-

BLUE CRAB

tom, than a living creature. There are a large number of species of
spider crabs to be found in different parts of the world, besides the
common one that is numerous along our shores. This group contains not only the largest crab known, but the largest of all crustaceans, the giant spider crab of Japan which attains a leg spread of
as much as twelve feet.

Commonly found along any sandy beach is that strange creature,
a leftover from a prehistoric age, whose relatives are almost entirely
extinct, the king, horseshoe, or helmet crab. Its name " crab " is a
misnomer since it is not only not a crab but is not even a member of
the *Crustacea*, to which class the crabs belong. Its proper name is
Limulus and it belongs to a class of its own between the insects and
the spiders, which is composed almost entirely of extinct forms.

There is but one order in this class in which there are any living representatives, and in this there are only a few known species, of which ours is the only one in this part of the world. Despite the fact that our *Limulus* belongs to an almost extinct class of creatures, the number of individuals is really immense. It is common along the coast from Maine to Yucatan, and in places it occurs in great numbers. As many as half a million have been collected in one season on the

HORSESHOE CRAB

Maryland shore where they are dried, ground, and used as fertilizer. When fully grown it sometimes attains a length of two and one-half feet including its spiny tail which occupies fully half its length. As the creatures grow, they shed their shells and these empty shells are frequently found in large numbers washed up on the shore.

Among the mollusks the number of photographic subjects that one may find along a sea beach is almost legion. In that class known as bivalves, those having two shells connected at the back, there are a great many species. Probably the commonest, or at all events the best known, are the hard clam, or quahog (commercially known as little-necks, cherry-stones, and chowder clams according to size), the soft, or long clam, known as steamers, the piddock, or angel-wing clam, the scallop, and the oyster. On the Pacific coast there is a rather remarkable species commonly called the geoduck, whose syphon, or neck, when fully extended, reaches a length of nearly three feet. When in its native element its mouth protrudes above the sand and is usually open ready to engulf any small crab or other sea animal that is unfortunate enough to crawl into it. The body of the clam is usually two or three feet beneath the surface. The giant clam of the East Indies is the greatest of living mollusks. Its soft parts

SCALLOPS

amount to twenty pounds or more of edible flesh, and its shells often reach a weight of five hundred pounds. Divers have inadvertently had their feet caught between the open shells and been held until they drowned. Scallops, so called because their shells are so beautifully fluted, do not bury themselves in the mud and sand as do the clams, but lie upon the surface of the bottom and are capable of swimming. They are often cast upon the shore in storms.

Bivalves should always be photographed in the tank. Perfectly clean sand should be placed on the bottom to a depth of three or four inches, and the tank then filled nearly to the top with clean sea water. Imbed the clams partially in the sand with that portion of the shell through which the syphon is extended, in the case of those species that possess a syphon, pointing upward. They should then be left undisturbed until they have extended their syphons, or opened their shells; in other words until they have arrived at the condition which they usually maintain when in their natural habitat. You will find that if you approach the tank even with the utmost care, your approach will be known by the mollusks, probably from the slight jar which your footsteps make, and they will withdraw their syphons, or close their shells. Therefore it is well to arrange your camera when you first fix the tank, and when ready to make the exposure approach it as cautiously as possible. This is particularly necessary with the soft-shell clams. They seem to be sensitive to a jar made by the lightest tread. In photographing them I have been forced, after several unsuccessful attempts at leaving my camera and returning to it, to remain seated by it, as motionless as possible, until the syphons were extended.

Among the univalves, next to the little periwinkles already spoken of, the giant whelks, or conchs, as they are commonly called, are probably the commonest species. There are two species that occur quite commonly on the sand flats along our shores. They are often cast up on the beaches during storms. One species has a spiral row of short horns defining the whorls of the shell, while the other may be distinguished by the squarish channels between the whorls. The former is commonest southward, while the latter is more or less confined to the region between Cape Cod and New Jersey. Both are found about Long Island and along the southern New England coast. They should be photographed in the tank, as they will not extend from the shell except in water. The sea-necklaces, consisting of parchment-like discs seemingly strung on a cord, which we frequently find on summer beaches, are the egg cases of these mollusks which have been torn from their attachment on some rock or growth of seaweed by the action of the water and washed ashore. Another univalve which we may find on the mud and sand flats frequently enough to make it worth searching for, is the large sea snail. Its shell is exactly similar in shape to many of the small land snails, although much larger. The hermit crabs find refuge in them as often as they can find one that is unoccupied by its original owner.

In the waters anywhere along the coast, different species of jellyfish occur, often in considerable numbers. Many of these are so large as to make it impossible to remove them to any ordinary tank for photographic purposes. Most of them have long tentacles extending downward often for a yard or more, and these have nettle cells that cause a stinging rash when they come into contact with any part of the body. There is one class of these animals, however, that may be easily collected and photographed in the tank. These are the cteno-phores, commonly called comb-jellies and known to the uninitiated seashore visitor as jellyfish eggs. They are small, oval-shaped, and almost transparent and have no tentacles or nettle cells. Therefore they may be handled with impunity, although this must be done with great care if we would have them remain entire. Like the substance

STARFISH

for which they are named, they disintegrate very readily and if held in the hand will slip through the fingers before one is aware of it. The best way to catch them is by the use of a small dipper, freeing them in the tank by immersing the entire dipper until they float free. There are more than one hundred species of ctenophores, all of them marine. They are all fairly small, the largest only about three or four inches long.

Barnacles are, of course, anywhere. The two most common spe-cies and those of which we become unfortunately aware when we in-advertently rub an arm or leg against a rock or post while swimming, are the rock barnacle and the ivory barnacle. These two species are to be found attached in masses to every rock, piece of submerged wood, dock piers, shells, bottoms of boats, old wrecks, in fact anywhere that they can find a place to attach themselves that is covered, at least part of the time, by water.

Slowly crawling along the bottom or over the rocks at low tide we are bound to find a number of specimens of that curious creature, the starfish. Of course this name is a misnomer, for the animal is not a fish but a member of the *Echinodermata*, one of the great branches of invertebrate animals, while the fish are vertebrates. Starfish have

BEACH PEA IN BLOOM

on each arm from two to four rows of slender, tubular processes, or feet, with a sucker at the end of each, by means of which they can glide over the rocks and stony bottoms. They are extremely destructive to oysters, clams, and other bivalve mollusks, for by encompassing them with their bodies and exerting a steady strain, they can separate the two shells and feed upon the soft bodies of the inmates.

Let none of my readers who specialize in botanical photography get the idea that there is nothing of interest to them along a sea beach. There are a considerable number of flowering plants that are to be found not only on the beach itself but also in the herbage back of it, especially if it happens at any part of its length to border on a salt marsh. What is more, the botanical subjects which are to be found here cannot be found in any other situation. Bayberry bushes,

with their decorative white berries, are common all along the back
edge of the beach, and interspersed among them are the scrubby, low
bushes of the beach plum. In May these are made beautiful by their
covering of lovely little white blossoms, miniatures of those of the
cultivated plum. Toward the end of August the fruit has reached
its full size and is turning purple, ready to be photographed if one
can find a bush with sufficient fruit on it before the birds eat it all

BEACH PEA FRUIT

up. This fruit, when fully ripe in September, is sweetly palatable
and is used quite extensively by those living near the shore for preserving. The vines of the beach pea are everywhere in evidence, covered rather copiously with clusters of fairly large purple blossoms.
A name often applied to this plant is seaside everlasting pea because
it blooms throughout the summer and again in the late fall. The
seed pods are matured in late August and one is likely to find fruit
and flowers on the same vine. Blossoming among the beach grasses,
sometimes fairly well hidden, are quantities of those lovely little
flowers the beach, or sea, pink (*Sabatia*), and the starry, white flowers of the sandwort. In the more marshy spots, often growing directly in water, the perennial salt marsh aster blooms in late August
and early September. From late July until October the salt marshes

in many places have the appearance of being covered by a purplish mist from the myriad blossoms of the sea lavender, or marsh rosemary, that grows in profusion there. In late August one of our handsomest goldenrods, the beach or sea goldenrod, comes into bloom. These are by no means all the flowering plants that one may find in bloom along the beach in August. There are enough to keep the wild-flower enthusiast busy with his camera for some time.

Then there are those two members of the *algae* that are extremely common along any beach, the rockweed, and the kelp. Rocks that are covered at high tide but that are partially or entirely exposed at low tide are nearly always fairly well covered with rockweed which hangs from them in olive-brown clusters when the tide is out, but floats free when the rock is covered by water, being supported by the many air vessels, bubble-like swellings on their branches, with which they are provided. Floating at full length in the water are the long streamers of kelp, our principal source of iodine, secured by their lower ends to stones on the bottom.

The sea and beach birds, terns, gulls, plovers, sandpipers, etc., breed more or less commonly all along our coast, but their nesting activities are usually, but not always, over by August.

Most persons think and speak of a spider as an insect unless they have made some study of nature. This mistake is not unnatural, for they have a decided superficial resemblance to insects, but there are three main points of difference which anyone may discover for himself. The body of an insect is composed of three distinct parts — the head, the thorax and the abdomen — while in the spider the head and thorax are joined together, forming what is known as the cephalothorax. Spiders lack the pair of antennae, commonly known as feelers, which project forward from the heads of all insects. An insect is provided with three pairs of legs, while a spider has four. These are perhaps the most noticeable differences in these two classes of animals, by which they may always be differentiated at a glance.

Spiders, scorpions, harvestmen (commonly called " daddy-long-legs "), mites, and a few other more obscure forms, constitute a group of animals known scientifically as *Arachnida*. This is one of several classes of animals having segmented bodies, furnished with jointed legs, which are classed together under the name *Arthropoda*, one of the chief divisions of the animal kingdom. In fact it is by far the largest of these divisions, comprising many more species than are found in all the others combined.

The principal classes of this group are the *Crustacea*, including the crabs, lobsters, crawfish, etc.; the *Diplodoca*, the millepedes; the *Chilopoda*, the centipedes (these two classes were formerly grouped together under the name *Myriapoda*); the *Hexapoda*, which contains the various orders of insects; the *Palaestracha*, composed almost entirely of extinct forms, the genus *Limulus* being the only one remaining, which is represented in this country by but one species, the horseshoe, or king crab, of which I have already spoken; and the *Arachnida*, the spiders.

It is entirely probable that, next to the snakes, there are no living creatures that are more universally hated and feared than the spiders, but with no very real cause. There is a belief pretty generally held that all spiders are very dangerous, in the habit of biting if given the chance, and that the bite is more than likely to result in grave danger to the person bitten, even frequently causing death. Some of this is true, for there are a large number of species of spiders, and many of those that inhabit tropical or semi-tropical countries are more or less poisonous, especially the larger forms. In their feeding habits they are carnivorous. Insects form the principal part of their diet, but they will eat any kind of animal life that they are capable of overcoming. In South America a tarantula known as the bird spider will capture and devour small birds; while others of the larger species often prey upon mice, small snakes, and other small animals which they enmesh in their webs. Spiders are also cannibalistic in their tendencies and will capture and eat any smaller species of their own class, not excepting weaker members of their own species. In some species the females habitually kill and eat their mates as soon as the mating is over. When making a capture, spiders bite their victims and inject into the wound thus made a small amount of venom sufficient to kill or paralyze their prey. Spiders that inhabit the northeastern part of the United States seldom bite a human being, and the amount of venom which one of them could inject would have no worse effect than to cause a small red spot or swelling on the skin, possibly accompanied by a slight itching sensation, but not so much to be feared nor so troublesome as the sting of a mosquito.

One possible exception to this statement is the spider known as the black widow. Its bite is generally supposed to be dangerous, but some people claim that this is not true, that the creature is much maligned, and that it is not more dangerous than any other species. I do not know if this point has ever been conclusively settled. The species is easily recognized, however, and may be avoided. The male is certainly harmless. The female, which is the one that bites, is jet black, about half an inch in length, and with a spot on the under side of her abdomen, roughly shaped like an hourglass, which is bright red outlined with yellow. I have never heard of an actual case of death resulting from the bite of this spider, but there have been some supposedly authentic cases of severe illness following. However, spiders are exceedingly shy creatures, undoubtedly fearing man more than he fears them, and if left alone they will mind their own business, and they never attempt to bite unless roughly handled.

Spiders are to be found almost literally any and everywhere. There are about twenty-five thousand known species and although, in common with most other forms of animal life, they are more abundant in the tropics than elsewhere, some species are found in the arctic and antarctic regions. Also they are undoubtedly the world's loftiest inhabitants, for they have been found living among the snow-covered rocks twenty-two thousand feet up on Mount Everest, well above the limit of plant life. The most widely distributed of them all is the common domestic, or house, spider which is found abundantly all over the world.

The members of the *Arachnida* vary greatly in size from the mites and other minute forms, some of them almost too small to be seen by the naked eye, to the enormous tropical species of tarantula whose bodies are often three or four inches in length, and with legs as much as nine or ten inches long. Tarantulas are covered with a dense growth of stiff hairs causing them to look even larger than they are, and imparting to them a truly ferocious and horrible appearance. Many of them are poisonous, although the species found in the southern part of this country are considered by authorities to be harmless. Frequently one hears of a tarantula being found in a bunch of bananas. These are rarely true tarantulas, but more often the giant crab spider, a large but harmless species.

Many spiders, rather than being the repulsive creatures that many people consider them to be, are strikingly beautiful. This is particularly true of the common orange garden spider (*Miranda aurantia*). This species probably attracts more attention than almost any other on account of its large size, brilliant coloring, and the beauty of its web.

After the orange garden spider, one of the next handsomest species is probably the shamrock spider (*Aranea trifolium*). The females are rather large, measuring about three-quarters of an inch in length, the greater part of which is taken up by the abdomen which looks as though it might be inflated. In color they range from a very light yellow, almost white, through all the shades of yellow to a dark reddish orange. The markings are variable but frequently there occurs near the base of the abdomen a three-lobed spot somewhat resembling a shamrock leaf, from which the spider takes its name. This is an orb weaver, preferring to spin its web in the rank herbaceous growth of marshy places in the autumn. The spinner is rarely seen in the web itself. When we find a web of this species, if we look closely we shall see that a fine line of silk leads from the web to a bunch of leaves, or goldenrod heads, drawn closely together, forming a retreat. In this we will find our spider awaiting the ensnarement of some victim in its web. Incidentally the spider, once ensconced in this retreat, does not allow itself readily to be disturbed. In fact I have frequently cut off the small branch containing one and carried it home with me without having its occupant leave. It is entirely possible, if the retreat is in a position where it cannot easily be photographed, to move it in its entirety to some other more accessible situation without disturbing the occupant, provided all pieces of herbage that are attached in any way to the retreat and the line connecting it with the web, are carefully cut.

The web-building spiders may be roughly divided into (*a*) those that make irregular nests, a mass of threads extending in all directions without order or system, of which that pest of the housekeeper, the domestic spider (*Theridion tepidariorum*), is a good example; (*b*) the makers of sheet webs which consist of a mass of more or less closely-woven threads extending in all directions in a level plane with no regularity of arrangement, but making a sheet or hammock-like web in low herbage or bushes; (*c*) the funnel-web makers whose webs consist of a funnel-like aperture extending backward from a closely woven platform and which serves as a retreat for the maker from which she rushes forth whenever an insect is entangled in the web. The common grass spider (*Agelena naevia*) is an excellent example of this type; and (*d*) the orb-web weavers. The webs of *Miranda aurantia* and *Aranea frondosa* are probably the finest examples of this type.

These orb-webs, early in the morning when each individual thread is strung with beads of dew, are beautiful objects for photography. One must rise early, however, before the sun has had the opportunity to drink up this moisture. In order to obtain the best results, the web should be photographed against the sun and with a dark background. The lens must be shaded from the direct rays of the sun and a quick exposure made when there is no breeze blowing.

The jumping spiders (*Attidae*) are of medium size and robust body, with short, stout legs. They are common on plants, fences, stonewalls, sides of buildings, tree trunks, and other elevated positions, but are seldom seen on the ground. They weave no web, but construct a sac-like nest among the leaves, which they occupy only when molting or laying their eggs. They are hunters, pursuing their prey or lying in wait for it and catching it by a sudden spring when it approaches near enough. They can move forward, sideways, or backwards with equal ease, and can jump many times their length. Before making their jump they always attach a thread of silk to the support upon which they happen to be, a sort of drag-line, by which they can return to the spot from which they jumped, instead of falling to the ground as they otherwise might do. They are strong and capable of attacking and subduing an insect several times their own size. Among these spiders are many cases of mimicry, usually the imitating of ants, in their external appearance, and this is often so perfect that it will fool even those well versed in the ways of these creatures.

The wolf spiders (*Lycosidae*) are also hunting spiders that catch their prey by hunting and springing upon them, usually upon the ground. Many species excavate burrows in the earth similar to those of the trap-door spider of the west but without the hinged covering which tightly closes the entrance of the latter. They frequently erect turrets about the entrance to their burrows. They may be seen at almost any time running through the grass or along woodland paths or roads. The females carry their egg-sacs with them wherever they go, attached to the posterior portion of the abdomen. When the young are hatched they are carried in a mass clinging to their mother's back, for several days before they disperse.

The nursery-web weavers (*Pisauridae*) seem to have the maternal instinct more highly developed than do any other of the spiders.

WEB OF THE TEGENARIA DERHAMI UNDER ROCK

The egg-sac is carried constantly by the female from the time the eggs are laid until the young hatch. It is held beneath the body and is so large that the mother is compelled, in many instances, to run on the tips of her legs in order that it may clear the ground. When the young hatch and are ready to leave the sac, she attaches it to the leaves of some herbaceous plant and makes a sort of nursery by drawing the leaves together with a network of silken threads. She then remains in close proximity until the young are ready to fare forth into the world and care for themselves. The members of one genus of this family (*Dolomedes*) are known as the divers, from the fact that they can run easily over the surface of the water and even dive beneath its surface and remain there, hidden beneath some floating object for some time. They are fairly large spiders, some species measuring nearly an inch in length, and are not uncommon.

Of the funnel-web builders (*Agelenidae*), the common grass spider, as I have said, is the best type and also the commonest. She it is who builds the blanket-like webs that cover the grass of our lawns and meadows which are particularly noticeable in the mornings, when covered with dew. She also builds in the corners of buildings, bridges, and other suitable places, but the sheet of webbing is always extended into a more or less perfect funnel in which the maker hides. She can be enticed from it, however, by a slight tap on the web, and should one wish to photograph her in front of the funnel it is easily accomplished by first focusing upon the web and then calling her forth by gently tapping upon it. When she emerges from her retreat she will almost always remain quiet for a few moments, probably trying to determine what called her forth. During this period even a short time-exposure is possible, if necessary. Her egg-sacs are not placed near the web, but are usually to be found beneath the loose bark of tree trunks, or in other similar situations.

The crab spiders (*Thomisidae*) are peculiar little creatures, taking their name from the form of their bodies which are broad and flat with legs which are crab-like in shape and attitude, and the fact that they can more easily progress sideways or backwards than forward. They spin no web. Some species pursue their prey, while others depend upon their concealing coloration and wait for their prey to approach them. Probably the commonest member of the family, and the best type of this concealing coloration, is the common yellow crab spider (*Misumena vatia*). It is remarkable from the fact that it can change its color from white to yellow, apparently at will, to match the flower upon which it happens to be resting. It is most commonly found on goldenrod, where its yellow color so closely matches that of the flower as to make its detection extremely difficult unless it moves.

No doubt many of my readers have experienced the rather unpleasant sensation of striking a spider's web with their faces when walking along a path between trees and have wondered how it was possible for the spider to spin a web between two trees often as much as ten or fifteen feet apart. When the spider has selected the spot where it wishes to spin its web, it climbs the support to which it has chosen to attach one end of its first line. When it has reached a sufficient height, it raises its abdomen and spins out a thread, always being sure that the direction of what current of air is stirring is toward the support upon which it wishes to attach the other end of the line. The thread is then carried by the wind until it reaches and sticks to some part of the second support, when the spider pulls it tight, fastens it to the support upon which it is standing, and the first line, or bridge, is formed. A second bridge is then made by attach-

DOLOMEDES WITH EGG-SAC STARTING NURSERY

ing one end of the line of silk to the first support a short distance below the one already laid, and climbing to and along the first bridge, spinning as it goes, until the second support is reached, when it descends to the right point, tightens and fastens the line, and a second bridge has been constructed. Between these two the web is easily fashioned.

There are also spiders that, long before the invention of the balloon, had solved the problem of aerial navigation. Let me quote from Comstock: " It is usually, but not invariably, very young spiders that exhibit this aeronautic habit; and exhibitions of it are most often observed on warm and comparatively still autumn days. At this time great numbers of young spiders, of many different species, climb each to the top of some object. Here the spider lifts up its abdomen and spins out a thread which, if there is a mild upward cur-

rent of air, is carried away by it. The spinning process is continued
until the friction of the air upon the silk is sufficient to buoy up the
spider. It then lets go its hold with its feet and is carried off by the
wind. That these ballooning spiders are carried long distances in
this way is shown by the fact that they have been met by ships at sea
hundreds of miles from land."

GROUP OF NORTH AMERICAN LOTUS WITH ONE JUST GONE
TO SLEEP

The first part of August is the flowering season of one of our rare
aquatic plants, the American lotus. It must not be confused with the
Indian lotus, sometimes erroneously called the Egyptian lotus, which
is shaped like a water lily and is found in this country only under
cultivation. Our native lotus is light yellow in color and cup-shaped.
It is one of our largest native flowers, with an expanse when fully
open of from five to ten inches. It does not lie flat on the water like
the water lily, but stands erect on its long stem from one to three feet
above the water, and this same stem may extend below the water for
a distance varying from three to ten feet. The leaves resemble in
shape those of the water lily and are round, with the stem attached
on the underside at almost the exact center. They are very large,
frequently a foot or more in diameter. Some of them lie flat upon the
water, while others are raised well above the surface. The flowers,
however, invariably tower well above them.

The Indians are said to have cultivated this plant and used it as an article of food. The large seeds were boiled like beans, and the tuberous root was used in the same manner as we use a potato, for it contains a large amount of both starch and sugar. Its distribution is extremely local, for it will thrive only in fairly deep water and where the bottom is an extremely soft mud. This the Indians undoubtedly knew and took advantage of.

On account of the depth of mud and water in which this plant grows, it must always be photographed from a boat, which can seldom be held still long enough for the necessary exposure unless the fastest films are used. Failing this the camera may be set on a tripod whose legs have been sufficiently lengthened by tying poles or small saplings to them, often to a length of ten feet or more.

SEPTEMBER

SEPTEMBER is an excellent month to photograph our reptiles — the snakes, lizards and turtles. I am well aware that to the great majority of people a snake is one of the most repulsive of all living creatures, to be shunned, or killed if possible, wherever met, and no matter what the species. Many people think that all snakes bite, and that their bite is always extremely dangerous and very often fatal. The very name " snake " has been anathema from time immemorial. It has been the synonym for all that is vile and loathsome. Anyone who knows and understands snakes finds it hard to understand why this should be so. Probably a few poisonous ones have given a bad name to the entire class, or their stealthy, gliding manner of progress makes them seem somewhat repulsive to the average person.

The fact of the matter is that out of the more than two hundred species and sub-species of snakes found in this country, there are to all intents and purposes but four that are poisonous. These are the rattlesnake, the copperhead, the moccasin (sometimes called cottonmouth), and a small snake found in the far south, known as the coral snake. To be sure the two genera of rattlesnake (*Sistrurus* and *Crotalus*) are divided into twenty-three species and sub-species. However, as they all have rattles, they come under the general classification of rattlesnake. The little coral snake is found from North Carolina to Florida, in the Gulf States, and in the Mississippi Valley states north to Ohio and Indiana. With the exception of a variety found in extreme southern Florida and a species found in Mexico and occasionally in New Mexico and Arizona which are commonly called by the same name, it is the only member in this country of a family of extremely poisonous snakes which are mostly found in tropical countries. Other members of this family are the cobras, of Asia and Africa, the death adder of Australia, and the Egyptian cobra or "asp," made famous by its alleged use by Cleopatra when spurned by Anthony. Instead of having movable fangs in the front of their jaws, their fangs are located at the back and are fixed. They do not strike, but bite, taking hold and hanging on while the poison is pumped into the wound. For this reason they should be considered one of our most dangerous snakes. There is a member of the family of king snakes which closely resembles the coral snake but is entirely harmless. Both snakes are marked throughout their bodies by rings of scarlet, yellow, and black. The difference is that the coral snake has broad bands of red and black, the black bordered by narrow bands of yellow, while the red and yellow bands of the king snake are broad with the yellow bordered with narrow bands of black. Furthermore, the snout of the coral snake is blunt and black while that of the king snake is pointed and red. One should be careful not to confuse these two species. All other snakes found in this country are harmless and may be handled with impunity. Some may strike and even bite, but they have no poison fangs, and although their teeth are needle sharp, occasionally causing a pin prick injury to the skin, this injury is less to be feared than is the sting of a mosquito.

Snakes may be roughly divided into two types. Some are viviparous, giving birth to living young; and others are oviparous, laying eggs from which the young are hatched. Rattlesnakes bear their young alive, which fact has doubtless given rise to the oft-repeated myth that in time of danger they will swallow their young in order to protect them. A snake has little or no feeling of parental obligation. As soon as the young are born, or hatched from the egg as the case may be, they must fend for themselves. Someone probably killed a female rattler, opened her, and finding in her living young that had not yet been born, at once jumped to the conclusion that she had swallowed them.

One of the gentlest and most docile of all our snakes is the little DeKay's snake, named after James DeKay, an early American naturalist. My two children kept one as a pet for quite a long time.

Rather than objecting to being handled, it seemed to like it and would crawl up their hands and arms the minute they extended them toward it. It is one of our smaller snakes, rarely exceeding a foot in length. It is fairly secretive in its habits, preferring to remain in seclusion among stones or under flat rocks during the daytime. It is not uncommon in such localities, even being found quite frequently

DE KAY'S SNAKE

in considerable numbers within the limits of some of our large cities. It almost never attempts to bite.

One of the most maligned of all our harmless snakes is the hog-nosed snake, or " puff adder " as it is more commonly called. Owing to its habit of drawing back into a striking attitude, flattening out its body and particularly its head, and hissing furiously, it presents a really deadly appearance which causes it to be feared by anyone not familiar with its ways, as being a deadly poisonous species. In some sections of the country it is even thought that the exhalation of its breath is poisonous. Besides the name puff adder it is known by other equally formidable ones including " flat-headed adder," " spreading adder," " blow snake," etc. It really is a terrible fake, for it is one of our most gentle and harmless species. It sometimes makes a half-hearted strike, but is careful that it never reaches its objective. It cannot be induced to take hold of one's hand, or to bite in any manner, no matter how roughly it may be handled. Moreover it has no fangs, and it secretes no poison.

If it finds that its fake ferocity will not scare away an intruder, it feigns death, hoping that it will then be left alone. So cleverly and persistently is this done that it may be picked up and thrown over

BLACK SNAKE WITH CAST SKIN

the limb of a tree where it will swing perfectly limp or slide off and fall to the ground, where it will lie on its back perfectly still. Or it may be tossed about in any manner, and show no sign of life. While lying on its back on the ground if we turn it over on its belly it will immediately come to life, turn over on its back, and again apparently become lifeless.

Another interesting fact about this snake is that it is found in two distinct color varieties. So greatly dissimilar are these that at one time, not so long ago, they were thought to be two distinct species. Later, however, they were determined to be but color variations. The commonest, and the one most often seen, has a ground color of dull yellow, light brown, or reddish, with an irregular pattern of large blotches of dark brown extending from the neck to the base of the tail and from there on forming half rings. On each side, in alternation to the spots on the back, is a row of smaller spots. The other variety is of a uniform black over its entire body with the exception of the under portions, which are white fading into gray posteriorly. Occasionally there are some indistinct markings in this latter variety in the form of slightly lighter blotches.

Two of our snakes so closely resemble each other, although belonging to different genera, that a novice would probably be unable to differentiate between them. I am not exaggerating when I say that both are distinctly beautiful. These are the rough green, or summer snake, and the smooth green, or grass snake. The coloring of the upper parts of both these snakes is a uniform, bright, shining, emerald green. The under parts of the rough green are bright yellow, while those of the smooth green are greenish white. The main difference between the two species is that the scales of the former are keeled, while those of the latter are smooth. Both are gentle and harmless in the extreme. They never object to being handled even when newly caught, and they make very acceptable pets. They are arboreal in their habits, spending much of their time in bushes and small saplings where they blend well with the foliage. One authority on snakes writes: " A more innocent and dainty reptile cannot be imagined than one of these creatures, and the spectacle of a tiny green serpent beaten to death on the roadside should provoke pity for the human individual who so ' bravely ' engaged in combat and succeeded in destroying, with the aid of a substantial club, about twelve or fifteen inches of diminutive body that would have real difficulty in battling with a fair-sized grasshopper."

The largest of our harmless snakes is the bull snake which attains a length of nearly nine feet and a body circumference of six inches. It is orange, or reddish-yellow with a row of dark reddish brown blotches on its back. It is fairly common from southwestern Canada southward into Mexico. It is closely followed in size by its near relative the pine snake which attains a length of almost eight feet. It is white with black blotches, and can never be mistaken for any other snake for it is our only white species. It is found from southern New Jersey southward, and is particularly abundant in the pine woods of the coast region. While it can be classed among our harmless species as it secretes no poison, it is a decidedly bad-tempered reptile and savagely resents being handled.

Among all the snakes of this country, both harmless and dangerous, the rattlesnakes are pre-eminent both from point of interest and deadliness. There are among the members of this tribe some of the most dangerous serpents in the world, whose " bite " in many instances is sure death. And yet the rattlesnake is a gentleman. He never attacks; will almost invariably retreat if offered the chance; and always gives warning of his presence in ample time to avoid all unpleasantness. Nor is this cowardice on his part, for there is probably no living animal possessed of a more cold-blooded, deadly fearlessness than a rattlesnake. Cornered he will fight, and he is an antagonist which anyone would do well to fear.

Some people will probably disagree with my characterization of the rattlesnake as a gentleman. To them let me say that I have made many photographs of different species, and although I have undoubtedly annoyed them considerably by forcing them to remain on one spot, I have never been bitten and not one of them has ever even offered to strike at me or at the stick with which I was herding it. These were not museum specimens, and in every instance they were photographed within a few days of their capture, and always in the open with no protective barrier between me and them. Also, and this may seem almost unbelievable, my hand when manipulating the camera was frequently within striking distance of my subject. Furthermore I have never known one of them to attempt to move toward me. If they moved at all, it was in the opposite direction. More often, however, they would remain absolutely still for an almost indefinite period in the pose first struck by them when liberated.

I cannot say as much for the copperhead, for I consider it to be the most treacherous snake that we have. It gives no warning, will not move from one's path, and strikes at the first opportunity.

In its ordinary movements the rattlesnake is rather sluggish, traveling slowly and deliberately. But when it strikes, its movement can only be compared with the proverbial streak of lightning, for it has reached its objective and is back in striking position before the eye can properly register its motion. No snake can strike more than about one-half of its total length, nor much more than a foot above the ground. All of the myths concerning the leaping powers of snakes are simply figments of the imagination. Therefore if one stands four feet from a six-foot rattler, he is perfectly safe so long as he moves no closer. The rattler knows this and will not even attempt to strike.

Rattlesnakes are represented by one or more species of one or both of the two genera *Sistrurus* and *Crotalus* in practically every locality throughout the entire United States. It is rather a strange fact that the smallest of them all, the pygmy, or ground rattler (*Sistrurus miliarius*), and the diamond-back (*Crotalus adamanteus*), which is the largest, are both found in the same localities in the far southern states, and are both most abundant in Florida. The diamond-back is probably the most dreaded of them all, and not without reason. It ordinarily grows to a length of about five or six feet, but specimens have been taken which were as much as eight feet long. A full-grown diamond-back has fangs which are frequently as much as an inch in length, and when the strike is delivered these are driven so deeply into the flesh of the victim that the poison is injected where the blood stream immediately takes it up and distributes it throughout the body.

Besides the diamond-back, there are some eighteen or twenty species and sub-species of the genus *Crotalus*, and three of the genus *Sistrurus* distributed throughout the country. Most of these are inhabitants of the western and southwestern states. Of them all, the most widely distributed is the timber, or banded, rattlesnake (*Crotalus horridus*). It ranges from Maine to Georgia and Texas and through the Mississippi valley as far as Iowa. It is nowhere very common, which is probably fortunate. It occurs in two phases of coloration. The one most frequently seen consists of a ground color of bright sulphur yellow, crossing which are bands of varying widths, roughly hour-glass shaped, of dark velvety brown. It is a strikingly beautiful creature in this phase, as anyone must be forced to admit if he can, for a moment, forget his natural abhorrence of it is an instrument of sudden death. The coloring in the second phase ranges from dark olive-brown to almost dead black with indistinct markings which are frequently completely lacking in the darker specimens.

Specimens of this species average about four feet in length, but individuals have been taken measuring as much as six feet. While not so deadly as their southern relative, they are nevertheless sufficiently so to warrant the greatest care when working with them, for their bite has been known to cause death. In captivity they have been known to become so tame as to allow themselves to be handled without showing resentment. But I would not advise my readers to try this, as the results might not be entirely pleasant.

Rattlesnakes, strange as it may seem, make most tractable sub- jects for photography. When released they seldom attempt to es- cape, but will take a pose, usually in a striking attitude, and hold it almost indefinitely so long as they are not interfered with. This makes them extremely easy to photograph in characteristic poses,

TIMBER RATTLER READY TO DEFEND HIMSELF

but one must constantly bear in mind that his subject is ever on the alert for him to make the one false move that would bring him within striking distance. Also, if he wishes his subject to remain quietly posed he must make all of his movements slowly and deliberately, with no sudden, quick moves. A sudden motion will almost invaria- bly start a rattlesnake into action. In working with a rattlesnake all advice may be summed up by saying: treat your subject with the respect that is his due, and he will accord you the same treatment. Then there need be no difference of opinion between you.

There is a class of reptiles that possibly some of my readers might prefer to snakes as photographic subjects. I am thinking of the lizards which represent the sub-order *Sauria* of the order *Squamata* of the class *Reptilia.* The other sub-order is the *Serpentes,* the snakes. To those not very well acquainted with the lizards, it may come as somewhat of a surprise to learn that there are some twenty-five hundred known species in the world. Of these about one hundred and seventy-five species and sub-species are native to North America.

Lizards range in size from diminutive creatures only about two inches in length, to large powerful animals such as the monitors, which attain their greatest size in the giant monitor of the Dutch East Indies which reaches a length of more than ten feet. A superstition responsible for the popular name of these monsters of the saurian world credited them with giving warning of the approach of crocodiles. They are semi-aquatic, being powerful swimmers, and rapaciously carnivorous, seizing and devouring whatever animal they are able to overcome.

The skin of a lizard, like that of a snake, is in most instances covered with scales. These have a thin, horny coating which is shed periodically. In some species, however, the scales are replaced by tubercles which cause the skin to assume a glandular or pebbled appearance. Lizards vary considerably in color. Those inhabiting dry, sandy regions are usually drab colored, browns and grays prevailing, but those whose lives are spent in forests or wooded and grassy places are frequently highly colored and beautifully marked. They are able to change their colors to a limited extent, as is shown by the chameleons. This is used as a means of protection from their enemies, as it allows them to conform more closely to their surroundings. Many species have also a protection of spines and horns which more or less cover their entire body, as in the case of the so-called "horned toads." Some species have appendages which impart to them a most ferocious appearance. The famous bearded dragon of Australia, and many others, will assume a pugnacious attitude which is conducive to the belief that they are dangerous. However, with the exception of some of the larger species, most of them are gentle and will not even attempt to bite, or if they should do so their bite is harmless. So far as is known, there is only one genus (*Heloderma*) which is represented in this country by the Gila monster, that is poisonous.

The general appearance of lizards varies considerably, from the squat, broad form of the horned lizards, to the snake-like form, minus legs, of the " glass snake," and the worm-like forms of a few species. Generally speaking, however, it may be said that they have a well-formed head with a distinct neck connecting it with the body, which ends in a more or less lengthy, tapering tail. In many species the tail is important as a means of defense, as they are capable of using it as a whip-like weapon. Many species have the ability, also, of parting with it at will, without undue discomfort to themselves. Thus, when seized by the tail by a pursuing enemy, they can leave the tail with the astonished foe while they hurry to safety. As they have the power of growing another tail within a comparatively short time, they are not greatly inconvenienced by its loss. However, the new tail is not a perfect substitute for the original, as the extending of the real vertebrae seems to be an impossibility, their place being taken by a cartilaginous tube.

As a rule lizards are characterized by extreme swiftness and agility, running along the ground with considerable speed and climbing trees and exploring their branches with the greatest ease. There are, however, a few species that are more or less sluggish in their movements. Many of these are dwellers in the hottest, dryest regions and thrive in the heat and sand, while others are arboreal in their habits, preferring trees to the ground. Still others live among rocks, a few species are aquatic, and there is one marine species which is found in the ocean around the Galapagos Islands.

The spiny swifts of the genus *Sceloporus*, belonging to the family *Iguanidae*, compose the largest genus of lizards in the United States. They are well named, for all the species have large, coarsely-keeled and more or less sharply pointed scales covering the entire body. The name swift is also well applied, as they are exceedingly quick in all their movements. They are dull in coloring, gray, brownish-gray, or olive-brown predominating. The throat and abdomen of the males are ornamented with large patches of bright blue, which varies in different species and under atmospheric conditions. This coloration is confined entirely to the male sex.

Some thirty to thirty-five species are recognized in this genus, but owing to the fact that there is so little variation in color or markings among the species, it is sometimes extremely difficult to differentiate between them. By far the greater majority of them are inhabitants of the southwest, occurring in the greatest numbers in Mexico and Central America. However, they are distributed in somewhat smaller numbers from northern California and Washington throughout the central and southern latitudes from the Atlantic to the Pacific and one species, the pine tree swift, or fence lizard, is more or less common from southeastern New York to Florida.

As I have said, our only poisonous species is the Gila monster (the first name pronounced *heela*). It inhabits the hot, desert regions of Utah, Nevada, Arizona, and New Mexico and is particularly numerous in the valleys of the Gila River, from which fact it takes its name.

GILA MONSTER

Besides being our only poisonous lizard it is, with the exception of two of the Iguanas found in the cape region of lower California, our largest species, averaging a foot and a half in length. Its body is stout, covered with bead-like tubercles instead of scales, and with short, stubby legs and a short, thick tail. This latter is deserving of special attention as it serves as a storage for a reserve supply of nourishment for its owner. In a season of plenty, when the lizard finds enough to fully appease its appetite, the tail becomes large and round with fat. When a lean season comes, and food is scarce and hard to find, the tail gradually decreases in size as the supply of fat is drawn upon by the animal in lieu of other food. Its coloring is rather striking, being a glossy black marbled with a pale hue which ranges from light pink or pale yellow to deep salmon or orange.

These reptiles do not always eject their poison when biting, which has caused some people to consider them harmless and, unfortunately, they have put these ideas into writing. The poison fangs, situated on the lower jaw and toward the rear, are provided with simple grooves along which the poison exudes from the glands in the lower jaw, instead of being forcibly ejected through hollow fangs as in the case of most of the poisonous snakes. Therefore it is possible for one of the lizards to grasp with the solid teeth only, in which case

DOUGLAS'S HORNED LIZARD

no poison would enter the wound. The dangerously poisonous nature of these animals has been thoroughly established by competent scientists, and they should be treated accordingly.

There is one genus of North American lizards the members of which, in shape and general appearance, differ so considerably from all others as to set them in a class by themselves. These are the horned lizards (*Phrynosoma*) commonly, but erroneously, called " horned toads " from the fact that their broad, squat bodies and short stubby tails more nearly resemble those of a toad than a lizard. There are, in this country, some eighteen species and sub-species of these interesting little creatures, all of them indigenous to the more arid, sandy portions of the southwest. They are capable of withstanding a degree of heat that would quickly prostrate a human being, and they give every evidence of enjoying it, and are particularly active at midday when the sun is at its height. As night approaches, they bury themselves in the sand by the alternate use of their heads and the spiny borders of their sides, by a twisting, shovel-like motion

"Glass Snake," A Snake-like Lizard

that quickly hides them from sight. Their bodies are more or less covered by rather sharp spines, and in most species these are considerably elongated about the head. In color they are universally a drab or greenish-tan with darker markings. As a rule they are rather apathetic, and apparently indifferent to handling, but occasionally a specimen will exhibit the remarkable habit of ejecting a fine jet of blood from the corner of its eye. This is accompanied by a puffing up of the body and head, and the ejection is accomplished with considerable force. Dr. Ditmars tells of one which he was handling which hit a wall with such a jet at a distance of four feet in a level line from the spot where it was being held.

One of the most curious and unusual of all our lizards is the so-called " glass snake." It grows to a length of from two to two and one half feet, has no trace of legs, and its body is slender, closely resembling that of a snake. It has not the pliability, however, of a snake and it has well-developed eyelids and ear openings which are lacking in snakes. While many of our lizards, as I have described, are capable of parting with their tails, this species does so with the greatest facility and must be handled with the utmost care to prevent it. It is not uncommon over a widely distributed territory ex-

COLLARED LIZARD

tending well into the north, but not along the Atlantic coast. In the east it is common from North Carolina to Florida and southwest through Texas and northern Mexico. Owing to its retiring habits spending much of its time in burrowing, it is not often seen by the average observer.

Possibly the handsomest of all our native lizards is the collared lizard found in the drier regions of the western states from Arkansas and Missouri to eastern California. Its total length is about twelve inches, but most of this is taken up by the tail. The body color ranges from yellow to bright green, covered rather liberally with white or yellowish spots which become reddish on the sides. The throat is deep orange, and the under parts greenish. Immediately back of the head are two jet-black bands separated by a yellowish space. In the females these are usually much less pronounced, and sometimes even entirely wanting. Females are apt to be much less intense in their general coloring than the males. These really beautiful lizards are extremely quick in all their actions, running swifty over the ground, at first on all four legs but as they get up speed rising on their hind legs and running erect with their tails elevated over their backs. In this position they are adepts at dodging and eluding pursuit, as anyone who has ever tried to chase one has discovered. They are somewhat pugnacious and when cornered will rise on the hind legs, open their mouths to their widest extent, and hiss, presenting a really quite ferocious appearance.

The skinks are a family of small lizards with smooth shining scales. The *Scincidae* is one of the largest families of lizards, of which the greatest number of species inhabit the old world. The family is represented in North America by two genera and fifteen species. One species extends as far north as Massachusetts, south to Florida, and west to central Texas. This species has two distinct phases of coloration which causes it to be called by two popular names. In fact these were at one time supposed to be two distinct species. When young the specimens are black, with one bright yellow stripe along the back, and two on each side. These stripes extend from the head to the tail, where they lose themselves in a brilliant shade of blue. In this phase, the animal is commonly called five-lined skink, or blue-tailed lizard. As it reaches the adult stage the black fades to a dull brown, and the stripes disappear. Some females retain very indistinct stripes, but the males are a uniform brown with a bright red head which becomes swollen at the temples. The name by which they are commonly known in this phase is red-headed lizard, or " scorpion." This species is extremely active, swift, and difficult to capture. It is exceedingly wary, flashing to a place of concealment at the first suspicion of any approaching danger and refusing to emerge again until reasonably sure that the danger has passed. They average about ten inches in length, and are strictly diurnal in their habits, seeking their hiding places in late afternoon.

There are few of us, I am sure, who do not know our native American chameleon, sold by thousands by curio dealers in the south. It is the only representative in this country of the genus *Anolis*, of which there are over one hundred species distributed throughout Mexico, Central and South America, and the West Indies. The popular idea that this lizard can take on the hue of whatever it may be resting upon, is entirely erroneous. In reality it has but two distinct changes of color: green and brown, or grayish-brown, and it may assume the green color while on a brown tree trunk or weather-beaten fence and

Five-lined Skink

the brown color while climbing among green leaves. The change of color is automatically brought about by temperature and light, and also by anger and fear.

There are also the geckos, a family with small scales and soft skin, mostly inhabitants of tropical and semi-tropical countries, but of which five species are found within the confines of southern and lower California, Florida, and Texas. There are five species of iguanas found in the west and southwest. Also in the west and southwest are distributed a considerable number of species of one genus of race-runners or striped lizards, some of them resembling the five-lined skink. There are also the spotted lizards, and some others.

In working with the lizards I should advise confining them to a glass-fronted cage when photographing them. While some of the species, notably the horned lizards and the Gila monster are more or less sluggish and may be photographed in the open, the majority are so quick in their movements that, while they may be posing quietly in one spot at one minute, the next they may be ten feet away and traveling with great speed. In a cage, however, especially after they have been allowed to become somewhat familiar with it, they will always take natural poses and hold them.

To those of us whose knowledge of the *Testudinata* (the turtles) is more or less limited it may come as somewhat of a surprise to learn that there are no fewer than sixty-five species and sub-species native to the United States and that they are fairly well distributed, both on the land and in the water, from the Atlantic to the Pacific, and from Canada to Florida.

The names "turtle," "terrapin" and "tortoise" have always been more or less confused by the majority of people. Dr. Hornaday, long the director of the New York Zoological Park, and one of our foremost zoologists, was the first to make a classifying suggestion. He advised that all of these reptiles that are entirely terrestrial in their habits be called tortoises, as the giant tortoise of the Galapagos Islands; that all those living a completely or partially aquatic existence in fresh water ponds, lakes, and watercourses be called terrapins; and that all marine forms be called turtles. This is a sensible and logical classification, and one that has been adopted by most zoological writers. Tortoises are more or less restricted to semi-tropical regions. The giant tortoises of the Galapagos Islands, that I have already mentioned, are restricted entirely to those islands. They are supposed to be survivals from the age of giant reptiles, and are excellent examples of the tortoise group. The three species that inhabit North America are found only in arid regions; the gopher tortoise, found from the Carolinas to Florida and into Texas in barren stretches of sandy country; the desert tortoise, found in the deserts of Arizona and southern California; and Berlandier's tortoise restricted to the sandy areas of southern Texas and northeastern Mexico. They all dig deep tunnels in the sand, often as long as ten or twelve feet, enlarged at the end into quite a roomy chamber. In these they spend the daytime in order to escape the intense heat, coming forth in the early morning and late afternoon to forage.

The marine species include the loggerhead, leatherback, green, hawkbill, and Kemp's turtles which inhabit the coastal waters from Maine to Florida. They all crawl up on sandy beaches along the coast, particularly in the south, to lay their eggs, and at such times may be easily photographed if found. The leatherback, or trunk, turtle is the largest. Its total length from tip of snout to end of tail averages about six feet, and it attains a weight of one thousand pounds or more. Specimens as heavy as fifteen hundred pounds have been taken. Next in size is probably the green turtle which sometimes reaches a length of four feet and a weight of five hundred pounds, although one of this size is not often nowadays encountered. This is the turtle so greatly prized for the delicious quality of its flesh. Its habits are typical of those of all the marine species. From April until June the female may be found crawling up on a sandy beach well above high-water line. Here she digs a hole some two or three feet deep, using her hind flippers to make the excavation, and in this she deposits between one and two hundred eggs. She then covers them with the sand which she has taken out of the hole, smoothing it down until it takes a sharp eye to detect the spot. Unfortunately she cannot obliterate the tracks made by herself in coming from and returning to the water, and these lead the egg hunters to the nest, for these eggs are esteemed as delicacies and command high prices in the markets. The turtle never returns to her nest, leaving her eggs to be hatched by the warmth of the sun. The young turtles are possessed of what is known as an egg tooth, a hook-like protuberance on the tip of the upper beak with which they cut their way through the tough shell of the eggs. They then dig themselves out of the sand and immediately make for the water which many of them never reach, because the sea birds, land crabs, and other predatory animals are exceedingly fond of these delicate morsels. Those that reach the water immediately become the prey of many different sea creatures, and it has been estimated that only a very small percentage of those hatched ever reach maturity.

The loggerhead, the commonest species of them all, is next in size, averaging about three feet in length of shell and in weight about three hundred pounds. It is the commonest turtle along the gulf coast of Florida, and it is no unusual sight during the spring season, especially on the sandy beaches of the lower end of the peninsula, to see numbers of them reposing on their backs in which position they have been turned by the turtle hunters to await shipment to the Key West markets, for in this position they are entirely helpless. The flesh is not nearly as fine as that of the green turtle, but it is much more often found in the markets and much of the so-called green turtle soup is made from the flesh of the loggerhead.

Kemp's turtle seems to be intermediate between the green and the loggerhead species, with characteristics of both. It is much smaller than either, averaging only about two feet in length. The hawksbill, the smallest of the marine species, is rarely over two feet in

YOUNG BOX TERRAPIN AND EGG SHELLS

length and often considerably under. It is from this turtle that the so-called tortoise shell is obtained. This species has been pursued for centuries for this purpose so that today it is seldom seen along our coast.

Of all the *Testudinata* the box "tortoise," as it is erroneously called, is undoubtedly the commonest. The name tortoise is a misnomer since it is classed with the fresh water species, or terrapins. In fact it is a connecting link between the aquatic terrapins and the terrestrial tortoises. The greater part of its time is spent on the ground, preferably in open wooded territory near streams, but it is frequently found in the water, crossing streams, etc. It is a strong swimmer, while the true tortoise will drown if placed in water. The box terrapin is capable of protecting itself from its enemies much more effi-

ciently than are any other of the reptiles. The lower half of the
" box," the plastron, is provided both front and rear with hinged sections that are capable of being closed so tightly against the upper
portion of the shell, the carapace, that it is next to impossible to in-
sert even a thin knife blade between the two parts. Moreover the
muscles that control these hinged portions of the shell are so powerful that it is difficult to pry the shell apart. Once the animal has

SNAPPING TERRAPIN

withdrawn its head and limbs within the shell and closed the hinged
parts, which it does at the first sign of danger and with surpassing
quickness, there are few living creatures, with the exception of man,
that can do it any harm.

The common snapping terrapin, with the exception of the sea turtles, is one of the largest species in the United States. It frequently
attains a length of two feet or over from the tip of its snout to the
end of its tail, and a weight of more than thirty pounds. It is almost
entirely aquatic in its habits, spending most of its time in muddy-bot-
tomed ponds, watercourses and marshes. The female leaves the water in the late spring or early summer to lay her eggs. In some damp
spot not far from her watery home, she scoops a hollow large enough
for her to crawl into. In this she moves about until the loose soil
which she has thrown out falls on and completely covers her while de-

positing the eggs which range in number from six or seven to a couple of dozen. When they are laid, she crawls forth, tilting her upper shell as she does so to allow the loose soil to fall off and cover the eggs, and again seeks the water with no further thought to her family, leaving the eggs to hatch by themselves by the aid of the sun. A species that exceeds her in size is the alligator snapper of the southern states which often reaches a length over all of four or five feet and a weight of more than a hundred pounds. The snappers are rather dangerous, as they are vicious and apparently fearless. They are almost unique among the *Testudinata* as they defend themselves, and attack, in much the same manner as the snakes, by striking. The rapidity with which they can dart the head forward at anything that comes within their reach almost equals that of the rattlesnake. They are not poisonous, but their mandibles are provided with an exceedingly keen cutting edge and the muscles that control the jaws are extremely powerful. To amputate a finger at a single snap is no difficult task for even a medium sized specimen of the common snapper, while a large-sized one can inflict a much greater injury. It is said that the alligator snapper can sever a broomstick as quickly and cleanly as though it were done with a sharp-cutting tool. These creatures must be handled with extreme care by anyone using them as subjects for photography. Fortunately they cannot turn quickly and as long as one's hand is kept behind them, there is no danger. In picking them up, or moving them in any way, always do so by the tail. In carrying them, however, never allow the head to come within reach of your leg, or you will be very apt to lose a chunk of flesh from it. In one respect they make good subjects for the camera as they are far from being shy and will not withdraw their heads. In fact, they are incapable of completely withdrawing the head within the shell as can most other species.

Next in size to the snappers come the soft-shell terrapins. There are four species of these in this country: the southern, spiny, brown, and Emery's. The southern is the largest, attaining a length of shell of about eighteen inches and a weight of about thirty pounds. The others are smaller, ranging from about seven inches in the brown to about fourteen in the spiny. They are entirely aquatic and, as their name implies, their coverings are soft and leathery in texture without the horny plates that are characteristic of all other species.

Their necks are fairly long, their heads narrow, and the upper jaw is provided with a slender proboscis. Despite their inoffensive appearance they are really quite vicious. Their jaws are powerful and with knife-like edges, although these are concealed by soft, flesh-like lips. They strike in the same manner as do the snappers, being the only other species that will do so, and are capable of inflicting a somewhat severe injury if one is careless in handling them. They are cold-blooded and fearless, and as such must be treated with consideration.

Next to the green turtle, the species of greatest economic importance is, undoubtedly, the diamond-back terrapin. From a gastronomical standpoint its value is so great that, because of its rapidly diminishing numbers owing to the extent to which it has been caught, the United States Bureau of Fisheries has established a station at Beaufort, N. C., in which to propagate it and thus attempt to save it from complete extinction. It is rather a small species, averaging about six inches in length of shell. It inhabits the salt coastal marshes from Massachusetts to the Gulf of Mexico, being most numerous in the warmer southern waters.

It is probable that of all the terrapins the little painted terrapin is the commonest and, aside from the box terrapin, the best known. When one purchases a young turtle in any pet shop to place in an aquarium, it is likely to be the young of this species. It is one of our handsomest species, beautifully marked about the edges of its shell with crimson lines and blotches which are particularly brilliant in young specimens. Its neck and head are black, streaked more or less with bright yellow. When fully grown it measures only a little more than four inches in length of the carapace. It is common in all ponds and watercourses.

The mud terrapin and the musk terrapin are quite similar in appearance with the exception that the latter has a somewhat pointed snout, while that of the former is blunt. They are both dark brown in color with shells usually so encased in dried mud that it is impossible to determine the true color. They both emit a disagreeable musky odor which is more pronounced in the musk terrapin. The musk terrapin is not common, but the mud terrapin is one of our commonest species. It inhabits ponds, small lakes and sluggish watercourses with muddy bottoms, so thickly that sometimes every tussock of grass, protruding log or stump, rock, or anything else upon which they might climb, is black with literally hundreds of the creatures and as many more swimming about in the water waiting for a chance to climb to some spot vacated by one of their fellows. At the slightest sound from an intruder, however, they all slide from their resting places with a combined splash that can be heard for a considerable distance.

The wood terrapin, or sculptured terrapin as it is sometimes called, is another species which, like the box terrapin, could almost be classed as a tortoise since it is not aquatic and nearly all of its existence is passed on land in damp woods and swamps. It can swim readily, however, and, as is the case with the other terrapins with the single exception of the box, mating takes place in the water, or very close to it.

The photographing of members of the *Testudinata* is not difficult provided one has the patience to await the pleasure of the subject. The only method that is really successful is to place the subject on the spot selected, focus upon it and wait until it is ready to protrude its head and legs from the shell. This may mean a wait of only a few minutes or it may extend into a considerable period. Sooner or later, however, the subject will slowly thrust out its head and when it has reached nearly its full extension it will be turned from side to side in order that its owner may give its immediate surroundings the once-over. After this the front legs are thrust forth, and then the hind legs appear. It is at this moment that the exposure must be made, for at that very instant the little shell-back will decide to move, and he does so faster than at any other time of his life, always turning away from the camera.

OCTOBER

RECALLING the many years during which I have been occupied with nature photography, I am convinced that no season of the year is so attractive for a field or woodland ramble or for camera work, as the month of October. The air is clear and invigorating with just enough warmth to make tramping a joy, even though we may be burdened with a photographic outfit.

Not only is this the finest time of the year for a tramp through the woods and fields, but one need have no fear that there is any dearth of photographic material. There is a plentiful supply of subjects in all the different fields, but there is one group of subjects that are to be found most plentifully at this time of the year to which I wish to call particular attention. I am speaking of our wild fruits.

I am not using the term " fruit " in its popular sense as meaning merely those few pulpy seed coverings that are used as articles of food. The definition of the word fruit is: " In flowering plants the matured seed vessel and its contents, together with such accessory or external parts of the inflorescence as seems to be integral with them." In simpler words, it is that part of the plant which bears the seeds and all that pertains to them.

All plants bear seeds of some sort, or they would cease to reproduce themselves and thus the species would die out and become extinct. In some plants, such as the fungi and ferns which do not bear flowers, these seeds are very minute and dust-like, and are called spores. Of these I shall have more to say later. In the majority of plants, the seeds are produced from flowers, and the fruiting portion of the plants are more or less conspicuous. Without becoming too technical and giving a botanical description of the various kinds of fruit, it might help if I described them as simply as possible in order that camera workers may be able to classify them with some degree of understanding.

Fruits are divided into four classes — simple fruits, aggregate fruits, accessory fruits, and multiple fruits. The simple fruits may again be divided into dry, stone, and baccate fruits. In the simple class the dry fruits that are dehiscent (that is opening in some manner to discharge their seeds) are the follicles, such as the milkweeds, dogbanes, etc.; the legumes, such as the beans and peas; and the capsules, of which the common plantain and henbane are good examples. The dry fruits that are indehiscent, not opening to discharge their seeds, are the samaras which have a one-seeded fruit provided with a wing, such as the maples, the elm, and the ash trees; the achenes, one-seeded dry, hard, seed-like fruit, of which the best examples are the dandelions, buttercups and all the members of the sunflower family. In all of these the style remains as some kind of an appendage. With some it takes the form of a feathery tail, as in the case of the dandelion; with others it is merely a short hook as in the buttercup; while in the *Compositae* (the sunflower family) the upper edge is ornamented with a set of scales, teeth, or tuft of hair called pappus. Grain is a term applied to dry, indehiscent fruit of the grass family including corn and all cereals. Those hard, one-celled and one-seeded, indehiscent fruits, such as the chestnut, hickory, oak, etc., are called nuts. The smaller, nut-like fruit of the mint and borage families are called nutlets.

The stone fruit are the drupes, the pome, the pepo, and the berry. The drupes are the one, or rarely, two-seeded fruit in the ripening of which the outer portion of the pericarp becomes fleshy, or pulpy, and the inner portion much hardened. The best examples are the cherry, plum, peach, etc. The term is also applied to similar fruits of the dogwood, hackberry, etc. The pomes are those fleshy fruits in which a number of seeds are held in parchment-like cells, such as the apples, pears, etc. The pepos are represented by such well-known examples as the melons, squashes, cucumbers, etc. The berries are simple fruits in which several seeds are covered by fleshy pulp contained within an outer skin and without an inner hardened coat, such as the grape, gooseberry, banana, tomato, etc.

The aggregate fruits are those in which otherwise simple fruits are crowded together into one mass on the receptacle. The members of the blackberry family are perfect examples of this class.

HAZELNUT FRUIT

Accessory fruits are those in which some conspicuous portion of the fruit is derived from some portion of the flower not organically connected either with the ovary or pistil. The fruit of the wintergreen, in which the fleshy part is merely a considerable enlargement of the calyx of the flower, forms a perfect example of this class. In the strawberry the fleshy part of the fruit which makes such delightfully palatable food, and comprises practically the entire fruit, is merely an enlargement of the receptacle of the flower, called the torus. The seeds, small and insignificant, are scattered over the surface of this pulpy mass.

Multiple, or collective, fruits are those in which several flowers come together to form one mass, as in the pineapple and mulberry. The simplest form is the fruit of the partridge berry.

This brief description is sufficient, I imagine, to give one a fairly good idea of the different kinds of fruit and enable him to differentiate between them with little or no difficulty. Incidentally, it will be noticed that the popular term " berry " is rarely used correctly, for none of those fruits that are generally called by this name belongs in the same class with the true berries.

The fruits of many of our deciduous trees have ripened and fallen before October: the willows and poplars early in the season immediately after the blossoming period; the maples a little later; and others in June, July and August, but there are a goodly number whose fruit does not mature until late September and October. Foremost among these are, of course, the nut bearers, the hickories, black walnut, butternut, beechnut, etc. Our hickories, which include twelve species, are true native Americans as all but one, which is found in Mexico, occur in the eastern part of the United States. Of them all the shellbark, or shagbark, is the best known and most popular for the edible quality of its fruit. Its name was given this hickory because of the loose, shaggy appearance of the bark on the trunks of the older trees. It hangs in strips from a few inches to three or four feet in length, attached to the trunk only at the middle. These strips are easily torn loose without injury to the tree. This and the pecan are the only members of the hickory group whose fruits are really edible. The pecan, which attains the greatest size of any of the hickories, when growing in rich, watered bottomlands, sometimes reaches a height of one hundred and seventy-five feet with a trunk diameter of five or six feet. It is our only native nut tree that has been cultivated for the value of its fruit, the meat of which is generally conceded to be the sweetest and best flavored of any of the family, although the shellbark runs it a close second. While its natural range was restricted to the lower Mississippi valley, it has been planted in large groves for commercial purposes so extensively that it is now fairly common throughout many of the southern states. Of the other hickories, the pignut is probably the most common, although both the bitternut and the mockernut are fairly plentiful. The names of the last two are suggestive, the fruit of the bitternut, as the name implies, being decidedly bitter in taste, while that of the mockernut so mocks in appearance the fruit of the shellbark that it is often mistaken for that edible species. The mistake is discovered as soon as we try to open one of the nuts only to find that the shell is hard and thick, and the meat small and of poor flavor.

SHELLBARK HICKORY, FRUIT

Both the black walnut and the white walnut, or butternut, belong to the same family with the hickories, the walnut family (*Juglandaceae*), and both have fruit ripening at the same time. The black walnut is growing scarce because its wood is so fine-grained, hard, durable, and capable of being finished with a high luster, that it is used extensively in the manufacture of airplane propellors, gunstocks, furniture, and cabinet work. Unless some considerable replanting of it is done, it bids fair to disappear completely from our forests before very long.

The chestnut and its small brother, the chinquapin, both mature their fruit in the fall. The chestnut was abundant throughout the greater part of the eastern states until about 1910 when a blight which was imported from China attacked this very important tree, killing them literally by the thousands until the species was practically exterminated. They have begun to come back again to a small degree, but whether or not they have been able to develop an immunity to the disease is not certain at this writing (1942). The chinquapin is a dweller of the southern states, ranging from southern New Jersey to Florida, Missouri, and Texas. It is a much smaller tree than the chestnut, with smaller fruit and usually with but one nut occurring in each bur. In flavor, the meat is equal to that of the chestnut.

The oaks, which must be included among the nut-bearers, all mature their fruit in the fall. There are in the United States about fifty species that may be divided into four groups: the white oaks, of which the white oak, the swamp white oak, bur oak, post oak and chestnut oak are prominent species; the black oaks, comprising the red oak, black oak, scarlet oak, pin oak, willow oak, black-jack oak and others; the live oaks found in the south and on the Pacific coast, whose foliage remains green throughout the year; and the scrub oaks, represented by the scrub oak, California scrub oak, and scrub chestnut oak, all shrub-like growths rarely attaining the dignity of a small tree. The members of the white oak group are sometimes called annual oaks because their fruit (acorns) are developed in one season. The black oaks are all biennials, that is, their fruit occupies two full seasons to reach maturity. This fact should be borne in mind when searching for these fruits to use as photographic subjects.

There are two trees, found commonly in the eastern United States, whose fruit may be photographed in this month, that are not natives of this country. These are the horse chestnut, planted extensively in yards and parks as an ornamental tree, and the ailanthus, or Tree of Heaven. The horse chestnut was introduced into this country from its native home in the Greek mountains about the middle of the eighteenth century, has been planted far and wide until it can be found in every state in the Union, and in most of them it is one of the more common ornamental trees. It has escaped from cultivation to such an extent and is found so commonly along highways near habitation that it deserves to be included in our sylva as a naturalized member. The two buckeyes, that are members of the same family, are natives of this country. It has been said that the name was given them because of the fancied resemblance of their brown nuts to the eyes of a deer. The sweet, or yellow, buckeye is a large and handsome tree attaining a height of ninety or a hundred feet. Its clusters of flowers stand upright like those of the horse chestnut, but are yellow instead of white, and the husks of its nuts are smooth, without the spines of those of the horse chestnut.

The ailanthus I have already spoken of in an earlier chapter. Its fruit, in the shape of brilliantly colored orange and yellow samaras, is borne in large, pendent clusters, matured in the early fall and persistent on the trees throughout the winter.

Two of our native trees have fruit, maturing in the fall, closely resembling each other in that they are both borne pendent on long slender stalks. These are the sweet gum, or red gum, and the plane tree, also called sycamore, buttonwood, and button-ball tree. Here the similarity ends, however, for the fruit balls of the gum tree are made up of capsules arranged compactly and each ending in a projecting irregular spine, while those of the plane tree have no projecting spines but are composed of tightly packed green seed covered with a hairy down. In both cases these fruit balls are very apt to hang on the tree throughout the greater part of the winter, especially in the case of the plane tree. The leaves of the sweet gum form a perfect means of identification as they are unique in their shape of a five-pointed star, with a sixth point missing where the stem joins. The twigs and small branches often develop projecting wings of a cork-like substance which are constant throughout the year.

The plane tree is also easily recognized and identified by both its fruit and leaves, but more particularly by the bark of its trunk and limbs. This is dark brown, but in early summer it flakes off in large pieces, exposing a whitish, yellowish, or greenish inner bark, imparting to the tree a peculiarly leprous appearance. It is one of our largest trees, occasionally reaching a height of one hundred and fifty to one hundred and seventy-five feet, and with a trunk diameter of ten feet or more.

Next to the oaks in importance are the conifers, the cone-bearers. They may even take precedence over the oaks, for they are of great value in different ways. They include the sequoias, or big trees of the west coast, that are not only the largest but the oldest of any living organism. Some of those now standing were undoubtedly in existence when Christ was born. Of the pines there are about eighty species, many of which are of the greatest economic value. Of them thirty-four are natives of the United States, ten being found in the northeastern region. Besides these there are a number of introduced species.

Of the larches, there are but three species in this country, two in the west and one in the east. There are three species of spruce in the Atlantic states, one in the middle section of the country, and three on the Pacific coast region, all native trees. There is besides one introduced species, the Norway spruce. Of the seven known species of hemlock, four are natives of this country, two in the east and two in the west. Ten of the twenty-eight species of firs are found in this country, eight in the Pacific coast and Rocky Mountain regions and two in the Atlantic states. All of the cone-bearers mature their fruit in the fall, and it is persistent on the trees throughout the entire winter.

The winged fruit (samaras) of the eight or nine species of ash persist in hanging in heavy bunches from the branches of the trees until well after the leaves have left. It has been said that the Indian designed his paddle from a seed of the white ash, as well as made it from the wood of the tree.

The locust and the catalpa are both in fruit in October. The common locust, a member of the pea family, whose lovely, sweet white blossoms are well known to us, retains its fruit pods even after the leaves have fallen, as do also its relatives the clammy locust, yellow-wood, and honey locust. The catalpa's distinctive fruit resembles a long, round bean pod or a slender cigar which has caused it to be given two popular names, " Indian bean " and " cigar tree." A near relative of the catalpa is the Paulownia, named in honor of a Russian princess. It is the only member of the figwort family in the north temperate zone, and was brought to this country from Japan and escaped from cultivation years ago. The flowering dogwoods that delighted us in late April and May in their dress of snowy white, are now maturing their scarlet drupes. The clustered, bright red, berry-like pomes of the mountain ash will remain on the trees to beautify them until the birds eat them. And in the swamps and low damp places, the gray-white, berry-like drupe of the poison sumac, borne in loose, pendent clusters, is persistent on the small trees, or overgrown shrubs, throughout the entire winter. Be careful in handling them as they are virulently poisonous to some people. The harmless members of the same family, the staghorn, smooth, and black sumac produce red fruit borne in upright, tight clusters, and these are also fully matured at this season.

The different members of the holly family (*Ilex*) are all maturing fruit in this month which will remain on the plants well into the winter, or until the birds devour it. The best known, of course, is the American holly, which we use extensively as Christmas decorations. Besides this species we have, more or less common in different parts of the Eastern states, the dahoon holly, yaupon, and meadow holly, natives of the southern states; the evergreen winterberry, or inkberry, and the smooth winterberry, both found from Maine to Florida; the

CREEPING WINTERGREEN FRUIT

large-leaved holly, found in the mountains of the eastern states; and the Virginia winterberry, common from Nova Scotia to Florida. The fruit of all of these is a bright red drupe, erroneously called " berry," with the exception of the inkberry whose drupe, as the name implies, is black.

Among the shrubs, vines, and herbaceous plants there are many that bear fruit in October. Many of these fruits serve as food for the birds that remain with us throughout the winter, and without them many of these birds would fare poorly. The partridge berry, or twin flower, which grows in tight mats of dark, shining, evergreen leaves in the woods from Nova Scotia to Florida and west as far as

Arkansas and Texas, is one of these. Its bright red " berries " which remain on the vines throughout the winter months, form one of the principal foods during the winter for the bobwhite and grouse who will dig down through deep snow in order to get them. Another woods plant that helps to feed these birds through the winter is the creeping wintergreen, which, by the way, is not a wintergreen at all but a member of the heath family to which belong the blueberries and huckleberries. We all know the spicy, bright red " berry " of this plant that ripens in late September and early October and, if left alone, will still be hanging on the plant in the spring. It is not a berry at all but merely the thickening of the calyx of the flower to protect the five-celled ovary containing the minute seeds, and is called an accessory fruit. This fact, however, need not detract from its beauty or usefulness as a photographic subject.

Of our wild grapes, the largest, and probably the best known, is the northern fox, or plum, grape. When fully ripe, especially after a frost, these grapes are deliciously sweet, although rather thick-skinned. From them have been derived the Concord, Isabella, and Catawba varieties of cultivation. The summer grape and the winter grape both bear much smaller, bluish-black fruit which is sour, but edible. The riverside, or sweet-scented grape, ripens in late July or August, but its fruit will frequently remain on the vines until late fall. The frost, or chicken, grape, on the other hand, ripens fully only after frost. A well-known member of the grape family is the Virginia creeper whose dark blue berries and bright red leaves, making a lovely contrast, adorn many an old fence, stone wall, or dead tree throughout the country in late September and October.

In the northern woods are large patches of that lowly member of the dogwood family, the dwarf cornel, or bunchberry, of which I have spoken in an earlier chapter. Its lovely white flowers have given place now to equally as attractive bunches of bright red, berry-like fruit from which the plant takes its common name of bunchberry. Throughout the woods and thickets those two members of the smilax family, the carrion flower with its tight bunches of blue berries, and the catbriar with berries of the same color in rather loose clusters, have now fully matured their fruit. The name carrion flower is extremely appropriate as its flowers give forth a most offensive odor similar to decaying carrion. This odor disappears with the fading

of the flowers, and the fruit is entirely without it. I am sure that anyone who has ever tramped the woods and fields knows and has reviled
the catbriar. Its long snaky branches, armed with sharp thorns,
reach out and grasp one's legs with a hold that it is almost impossible
to break. To try to force one's way through a tangle of these vines,

FLOWERS OF THE WITCH HAZEL

results only in badly torn clothing and flesh. The leaves, which turn
orange and red in the fall, make a lovely contrast to the blue of the
berries. The familiar " smilax " which may be bought at any florist
shop, is a native of the Cape of Good Hope and is not even remotely
related to the smilax family (*Smilaceae*).

In sandy fields and along the shores, the bayberry may be found
full fruited not only throughout the month, but during the entire
winter. Its grayish-white fruit grows in tight clusters about the
stems of the plant, principally where they join the main stem, and is
really most attractive.

The witch hazel is a shrub, or small straggling tree, that produces its flowers late in this month or early in November. It is somewhat of an anomaly since its blooms open after all other flowering plants have passed their fruiting stage. It is rather difficult to say if it is the last or the first of the flowers to bloom. Its straggly golden blossoms adorn its bare branches long after the last of its leaves have fallen. Continuing the anomaly, this rather strange plant matures its fruit from the flowers of the previous season at the same time that the flowers of this season are opening. It distributes its seeds far and wide in a rather unique manner, for they are actually shot from the capsules with a distinct report and a force that carries them for several feet. This is accomplished by a contraction of the horny lining of the capsule upon the hard, smooth-surfaced seed until it is discharged in much the same manner as one may propel a moist melon seed by pinching it between thumb and finger. One may obtain photographs of both flowers and fruit at one trip and upon the same branch, which may rarely be accomplished with any other plant. The English immigrants gave this plant its two names — the *hazel* because its leaves reminded them of their own hazel tree (which is a member of the elm family), and the *witch* because its twigs were used as divining rods with which to locate water, minerals, etc.

It is interesting to know what really extensive travelers some of our commonest wild flowering plants are, and how they manage to get from place to place. Many of our commonest plants are naturalized immigrants from other countries and some of them, notably the white daisy, have gradually covered the entire continent from coast to coast. The dandelion is one of the greatest travelers of all our nomadic tribe of wild flowers. It is a lowly plant, often considered a pest, which has migrated from its original home in the central part of Europe to practically every section of the civilized globe. How do these plants that of themselves are utterly incapable of progressing even the smallest distance, thus project their hordes across oceans and continents to all parts of the earth? The answer is, of course, by their seeds. Through ages of development, the great majority of our plants have adapted their seeds to traveling, in one way or another according to species, for considerable distances.

A very large number of plants, notably many members of the thistle family (*Compositae*), furnish their seeds with a tuft of feathery pappus that transforms them into miniature balloons, or parachutes, that the slightest breath of air will carry away. One of the best examples is that pest of our lawns already mentioned, the dandelion. After the flowering head has withered, it closes tightly until it resembles the opening bud. The scape, or stem, gradually lengthens until it stands erect, frequently as much as ten or more inches tall so that the seeding head may easily be reached by passing breezes. The closed flower then expands once more, but this time into an airy, delicate, white ball composed of scores of tiny parachutes, each one attached to a seed, ready to float away on any wandering zephyr. I venture to say that there are few of my readers who, as children, have not blown upon these heads to tell the time of day, thus setting free myriads of the seeds to start their journey. In the hay used as packing, they travel to foreign lands, and the plants are so hardy that they readily adapt themselves to practically every condition that they meet, no matter how forbidding or hopeless it might seem. It has been established that immersion for a full month in the ocean, or in any other water, does not destroy the ability of these seeds to germinate. This is a sufficient length of time to allow them to be carried for many miles along a coast or down a river course. Across country, heavy winds carry them for almost unbelievable distances before depositing them again on the ground. This little plant is so well equipped for the struggle for existence, that probably the last piece of vegetation, growing upon the last square inch of fertile soil, on an otherwise frozen world, will be a dandelion.

There are many plants that produce ballooning seeds. In the early spring the willows and poplars, noticeably the cottonwood, have filled the air with their fluff and covered the ground and streams with downy windrows of their cottony plumes. From then until late fall or early winter, each month brings its quota of plants to produce this type of seeds and start them on their journeys. The air of summer and fall is full of them. They are caught in every briar patch, and each spider's web, especially those of the orb spinners, will be sure to hold half a dozen or more of them. It is interesting to know them and be able at a glance to name the plant from which they come, and a camera will help us very greatly in studying them.

Many of the trees produce winged seeds that, while they are incapable of floating away as do the plumose seeds, are nevertheless so adapted that they will not fall directly downward but are often borne for some distance from the parent tree, especially when there is a stiff breeze blowing.

John Burroughs, in his delightful volume " Wake Robin," refers to the weeds as " the tramps of the vegetable world." He says " They are going east, west, north and south. They walk, they fly, they swim, they steal a ride; they travel by rail, by flood, by wind; they go underground, and they go above across lots and by highway. But like other tramps, they find it safest by highway. In the fields they are intercepted and cut off, but on the public road every boy, every passing herd of sheep or cows, gives them a lift."

This latter part describes very accurately that great class of plants that do not use the wind as a means of distributing their seeds, but depend entirely upon more mundane agencies. These are the plants that attach their fruit, by various methods, to whatever brushes against them and these are known by the various popular names of " beggar's-lice," beggar's-ticks," " stick-tights," " stick-seeds," " pitchforks," and other aliases. There are a number of different groups of plants that use this method of sending their offspring out into the world. Probably the largest group is composed of the various species of the genus *Meibomia*, the tick-trefoils. There are in the United States some forty odd species of this genus, all of them producing more or less similar seeds. These are the queer green, or later brown, triangular affairs that usually come attached to each other in chains composed of several individuals. Another group, using a different method of attaching their seeds to any person or thing passing by, is composed of the plants of the genus *Bidens*, the bur marigolds, beggar's-ticks, and tickseed sunflowers. There are twenty odd species of these in this country, and many of them produce handsome, sunflower-like flowers. In the fall, however, when the flowers have transformed themselves into what another author calls " armories bristling with two-pronged, and finely barbed, pitchforks," we can see no pleasure in coming into contact with them. The " pitchforks " attach themselves with altogether too great readiness to anything that touches them, and cling with too great perseverance.

Fungi, a species of plant life that is plentiful during the fall, appear in many and varied forms, some extremely unattractive, but

many more not only attractive but really beautiful both in coloring
and form. One author has called them the grotesques of nature, and
this is not an inapt name for them, as the shapes which they assume
are frequently extremely ludicrous. The mildew that appears on
clothing and other objects in damp weather, the mold which frequently ruins our food stuffs, the rusts and smuts of our grain fields
which are the despair of the farmer, and the dry rot which causes
lumber to crumble and from which a pale, ghostly light will frequently emanate at night, are all forms of fungus growth. These,
however, are the unattractive and injurious forms that we could well
do without. There are many others with which it is well worth while
to become acquainted, and there is one of the unattractive forms that
is highly useful, the fungus from which we get our yeast.

The fact that many forms of fungi inhabit damp and unhealthy
places has caused them to be somewhat despised and abhorred as
rather gruesome growths, and the fact that some of them are extremely poisonous has helped to enhance this idea in the minds of
many people. But there are many that are beautiful as well as many
that are extremely useful articles of food.

All fungus growths are either parasites dependent upon living
plants or animals for their existence, or saprophytes dependent upon
dead organic matter or products from plants or animals. All plants,
as well as animals, must feed in order to live and grow. The fungi
have lost the power, or possibly never had it, that all green plants
possess, of assimilating inorganic matter and turning it, by means
of their leaf green, into organic substance. Therefore fungi, in order to exist, must feed upon material which has already been made fit
for their use by green plants.

Fungus growths may be described, in a general way, as plants that
have no flowers and therefore produce no seeds, but reproduce themselves by means of minute, dust-like bodies called spores. Ferns and
other plants, of which I shall speak in the next chapter, reproduce
in the same manner, but these are possessed of leaf green which is
entirely absent in fungi. These spores are borne, in various species,
in different parts of the plants. In the ordinary capped " mushroom," or " toadstool," they are borne on the gills on the underside
of the cap. If we will take one of these caps, place it with the under,
or gill side, down on a piece of white paper, and allow it to remain

for a few days, it will drop its spores and make a very pretty picture of the radiating gills of the plant.

To the majority of people the only fungus growths known are divided into two classes. Those species that are considered edible are called mushrooms and all of the others are grouped together under the name toadstool, as being not only uncanny but actually poisonous. This distinction is absolutely without foundation and has no scientific basis. In fact there are no such things as toadstools, as a great many of the species that are popularly classed under that name are not only edible but delicious food, while only too often poisonous

THE POISONOUS FLY AMANITA

species are picked as mushrooms. Furthermore, while a number of fungus growths have slight poisonous qualities, and a few are really deadly, these are greatly in the minority.

Fungi, in one form or another, may be found almost everywhere. In damp places, particularly cellars, the molds and mildews flourish. Our wheat, corn and other grains produce the rusts and smuts, some of which (ergot) are used medicinally. In the woods, fields, and open places are the capped fungi, among which the finest edible, as well as the most poisonous, species occur. In the woods are found many of the so-called " bracket " fungi, which grow from standing tree trunks or fallen logs, projecting outward in the form of brackets and often superimposed one above the other to form quite a considerable mass.

They appear in many different forms and colors, and some of them make excellent food. One in particular is highly esteemed by mushroom lovers. This is the beefsteak fungus (*Fistulina hepatica*), so-called on account of its fancied resemblance to a piece of raw beef. It protrudes from some decaying stump or log like a huge, livid red tongue, which caused the French to give it the name of *langue de bœuf*.

In similar situations grow the hydnums, the " fungi with teeth," so-called because they bear their spores on downward projecting,

Boletus Edulis

awl-like teeth. Some of them, particularly the bear's-head (*Hydnum caput-ursi*), and the Medusa's head (*Hydnum caput-medusae*), grow to a considerable size. In this genus are a number of important edible species.

On the ground, and also on decaying stumps similar to the preceding, grow the dainty coral fungi (*Clavaria*). It needs only a glance at one of these fungus growths to understand the reason for their name. They come in delicate colors of pink, violet and gold, and their growth closely resembles that of the branched coral. Most of these are edible.

Along the edges of the woods, and in open spots in the woods themselves, we will find the *Russulas*, green, red, purple, pink, blue and orange, and all the different shades thereof. In similar places, as well as the deeper woods, are innumerable species of the genus *Boletus*. With but few exceptions they grow upon the ground and always in groups of from two or three to many individuals. Many of them are extremely beautiful and they occur, as do the *Russulas*, in practically every color and color tone. They are readily distinguishable from any other fungus growth from the fact that the underside of the cap is provided with close-fitting tubes, or pores, instead of the radiating gills, or lamellae, of the other parasol-shaped species. Among them are many edible species, and also many that are somewhat dangerously poisonous.

Species of the genus *Amanita* may also be found in the dry woods and fields. It is in this genus that some of the most poisonous species are found. In fact a few of them are so deadly that they have been given such significant names as death-cup, destroying angel, etc. While there are a few species of this genus that are edible and one, (*Amanita caesarea*), that is considered delicious, many of them are so poisonous that to be on the safe side all should be avoided. All the species of this genus are readily distinguishable as they have both a ring (*Annulus*) around the stem a short distance below the cap, and a cup-like wrapper (*Volva*) about the base of the stem which is usually bulbous. Other genera have one or the other of these characteristics, but no others show both in the same plant.

Growing everywhere throughout the fields and woods are the many species of that unique group, which children delight in stepping on in order to see the " smoke " puff out, the *Lycoperdales*, or puff-balls. These differ from all other forms of fungi in that they are more or less round, and the spores, the smoke, are borne inside the plant. When young, their interior is fleshy, with a cheese-like consistency, at which time they are all edible and many very palatable. The flesh gradually darkens with age, until it turns to a mass of dark brown, or black, dust-like spores. The plant then opens, usually at the top, to allow these spores to escape, which they do in clouds with every least pressure on the outer surface.

The genus *Coprinus*, the ink caps, is another genus in which all of the species are not only edible but are generally conceded to be among the most delightfully flavored. Their name is derived from the fact that very soon after maturity they dissolve to a sticky, ink-like mass of putridity. The species of this genus are nearly all almost literally twenty-four hour plants. They spring up in the night, last through the day, and by another night have started to deliquesce into a rotten mass. For eating purposes they must, of course, be picked before this deliquescence has started. Most of them grow in groups so tightly packed together that only those on the outer edge retain their true shape.

EARTH STARS

Another genus among whose species there are none that are not edible, is *Psalliota*, of which *P. arvensis* and *P. campestris* are the two species that commonly find their way to our tables and are grown extensively for that purpose.

In fields, pastures, on lawns and hillsides, the *Oreades* form " fairy-rings," so-called because in olden days, when the existence of fairies was firmly believed, it was said that these rings were the spots in which the fairies danced nightly. This pretty myth was dispelled when science revealed the true cause of these rings. One fungus plant will exhaust the soil immediately beneath it of the food necessary for its growth and so only the spores that fall outside of this exhausted space will survive and produce other mushrooms, and so a small ring of them is formed. This yearly grows larger as the spores continue to reach outward for ground that is not impoverished.

Some of the strangest forms of fungus growth are those commonly known by the name of stinkhorn. While this is not a pretty name, there is no other that could so adequately describe them. They notify us of their whereabouts while we are still some distance

A STINKHORN

from their hiding place, by the strong fetid odor that reaches us. It is suggestive of the effluvium arising from a mass of decaying flesh. By this, if by nothing else, these plants may always be known, for there are no other fungus growths that have such an offensive quality.

The *Geasters*, or earth stars, belong to the *Lycoperdales*, and are among the most curious of all the fungus growths. The early growth is a ball sunk in the earth and covered by two layers of skin,

the outer thick and leathery, the inner not nearly so tough. This
ball is gradually pushed to the surface of the ground where the outer
skin bursts, forming lobes which gradually dry and stiffen and become reflexed, so that the inner ball is lifted from the ground where
it sits upheld by a star-shaped dais. The largest, and probably the
most common, is the water-measuring earth star (*Geaster hygro-
metricus*) found practically all over the world. When the weather
is damp, the points of the lobes become viscid and fasten themselves

DELICIOUS MOREL

with considerable firmness to the ground; but when the weather is
dry, these points become hardened and curl up again loosely around
the inner ball. If there is a wind blowing, the plant will roll about
and its spores are thus scattered from the hole in its apex. These
growths are found in dry fields, dirt banks, sides of roads, and similar
places. They are not uncommon but their drab coloring, closely
matching that of the ground upon which they rest, make them so inconspicuous that they easily escape notice unless one looks closely.

A rather peculiar little growth is the bird's-nest fungi (*Cyathis
striatis*). When mature they are not over one-third of an inch in di-

ameter, and resemble miniature birds' nests containing eggs. When young, they are but small pouches, but as they mature they open at the top to form the nest. The eggs are small, globular cases in which the spores are contained. These are jelly-like and when fully ripe are expelled from the nest. This is accomplished by the formation of gases beneath the spore cases which expand until the cases are pushed out. These little fellows are found either on the ground in groups, or on well-rotted logs in damp places.

In swamps and all moist wooded places throughout the world the slime molds, or slime fungi (*Myxomycetes*), grow in abundance. They are most peculiar and interesting organisms. Certain phases of their life histories are strongly suggestive of animal life, while other phases, especially the fact that they produce spores in spore cases, are decidedly characteristic of plants. At all events, they lie close enough to the borderline that separates animal from vegetable life to make it impossible, as yet, for scientists to come to a decision as to whether they should be classified with the one or the other, although it has been stated that these organisms have been the objects of study for at least two hundred years. In many cases the growths are individually minute. Although the mass may cover a large portion of the rotten log which is the abiding place chiefly chosen by them, one needs a microscope, or powerful magnifying glass, in order to observe their shape and beauty.

Besides the forms of fungi about which I have written there are, of course, many others which the seeker after subjects for his camera will discover for himself. A genus with a number of large, wood-loving species, none of which are poisonous and many excellent eating, is *Pholiota* of which a representative species is the fat pholiota (*Pholiota adiposa*). Another tree-loving genus, *Polyporus*, contains some conspicuously handsome species. One that should be well known as it may be found growing even from telegraph poles, is the sulphury polyporus (*Polyporus sulphureus*). It is a large, fleshy form growing in clusters from dead wood, the stemless caps, which are often as much as seven or eight inches broad, overlapping each other. In color they range from a bright sulphur yellow to an equally brilliant orange. The genus *Pleurotus*, mostly fleshy, tree-loving forms, growing in masses closely overlapping, are all of them edible and one species, the so-called oyster mushroom (*Pleurotus ostreatus*) is considered by many to be one of our most delicious species.

While the fall months, from September through November, offer the most and best opportunities for the finding of specimens of the fungus growths, they are to be found throughout the summer months, but in lesser numbers. There is also one genus, at least, of which the species are early spring growers appearing in May and June. This is the genus *Morchella*, the morels, of which the delicious morel

POLYPORUS SULPHUREUS

(*Morchella deliciosa*) is considered the finest of the fungus growths.

That delight of European epicures, the truffle, is also a fungus. There are several species of the genus *Tuber*, none of them very common, and all found in central and southern Europe. They are entirely subterranean, growing about a foot below the surface of the earth, frequently in groups of a dozen or more. They are used extensively in the preparation of many dishes. Dogs and pigs are trained to seek them, readily discovering their underground location by smell. Attempts have been made to grow truffles in the United States but, so far as I know, these have been unsuccessful.

NOVEMBER

I FEAR that I have but little sympathy for those deluded people who, with the poet, believe that with November come " the melancholy days " and that therefore there is little or nothing in the woods and fields worthy of the effort to find and photograph. It is true that in the days of late autumn and early winter the sky is often overcast; the leaves that have not fallen are brown and wrinkled; the grass and herbage is dead and brown. Photographic subjects, it goes without saying, are not nearly so plentiful, or as easy to find, as they were during the spring and summer months.

There are, however, many days during this month that are far from being melancholy. Some are bright and cheerful, fairly warm but with just enough tang in the air to make a jaunt through the woods and fields something to look forward to with the keenest anticipation. Furthermore, to offset the diminution in the numbers of subjects that one may find, is the fact that many of those that are to be found are either peculiar to this season of the year or else at this time in their best condition. Moreover the searching for them is made easier and much more pleasant from the lack of the extreme heat of summer.

By the first of November practically all of the flowering plants have dispersed their seeds and died, with the exception of the perennials whose basal leaves still remain green. There is, however, a group of plants the members of which are more or less numerous throughout nearly the entire month, and these the nature photographer will do well to hunt for and photograph. I am speaking of the cryptogams, a general term applied to those plants that have no flowers and, therefore, produce no seeds. The principal members of this group are the ferns, mosses, lichens, lycopodiums, or club mosses, horsetails, liverworts, and fungi. The name cryptogam is derived from two Greek words, cryptos, hidden, and gamos, marriage — in other words a hidden reproduction of the species.

Of them all, the ferns are undoubtedly the most familiar to the majority of people. It is, however, only a very few of the more common and conspicuous species, found nearly everywhere, that are really well known, and these are usually known only under the general name of fern. It is unfortunate that some of the most beautiful forms are so rare that they are seldom seen by the casual observer. Ferns are more or less numerous over the entire world, there being about eight thousand known species. While most of these are found only in the tropical and sub-tropical regions, there are still a considerable number that inhabit the temperate zone, and in North America north of Mexico there are more than two hundred and fifty known species. Many of these are more or less rare, but a sufficient number of them are common enough to make them easy subjects for photography.

Ferns were among the earliest plants to appear on the earth, and it is very probable that the number of extinct species is far greater than the number of those still living. As far as it has been possible to ascertain from fossil remains, they appeared on the earth in the early part of the Paleozoic era and reached their greatest abundance during the Carboniferous period. Since then they have been largely replaced by plants of a higher organization. At the present time they form only about one-fiftieth of the total plant life of the globe.

They vary greatly both in shape and size. There are some species that are almost moss-like in their growth, with delicate, filmy leaves. In the tropics there are forms that resemble trees, rising fifty or more feet in the air with leaves fifteen to twenty feet long forming a crown at the top. In the United States our smallest species is one of the so-called filmy ferns (*Trichomanes petersii*) whose overlapping fronds are scarcely half an inch in length. It grows mostly on rock ledges where it is kept constantly wet by the spray from waterfalls. Its diminutive size and manner of growth is so nearly like that of some of our liverworts that it is easily mistaken for one of them. Our largest species are the cinnamon fern (*Osmunda cinnamomea*), the royal fern (*Osmunda regalis*), and the ostrich fern (*Onoclea Struthiopteris*), which reach a height of from five to eight feet.

It is sometimes difficult for the novice to distinguish between the different species. There is, however, one infallible rule by which one may soon learn to know them. I take it for granted that my readers know that ferns are members of a class known as flowerless plants which have a plentiful supply of foliage but are without flowers and, therefore, produce no true seeds. Instead, the plants produce spores, dust-like bodies which are the reproductive agents. These are borne in what is known as spore-sacs, or cases (sporangia), on the backs of the segments of the fertile fronds. These, in the formation which they assume, are called sori, or fruit dots. One must bear in mind that in a plant there are many more sterile fronds that bear no sporangia than there are fertile ones. The distribution of these sori, as well as the shape of the sporangia and the positions which they occupy on the pinnules, or segments of the fronds, varies in the different species, but is constant in each one and, therefore, absolutely distinctive. As an example of this, the sporangia of the common bracken, or brake, are placed on the extreme edge of the underside of the pinnae, sometimes curling for an infinitesimal distance on the upper side, and so close together that they form a continuous, unbroken edging around each leaf of the frond. Again, in the polypody, the sporangia have the shape of perfectly round dots arranged close together in a line on each side of the midrib of each pinna, but usually only on the upper half, or possibly a little more, of each frond. The Christmas fern is another species that bears its sori only on the upper half, or frequently less, of the fertile frond. In this case, however, the sporangia are so crowded together as to give the appearance of a solid mass almost completely covering the underside of the pinnae. Thus, as I have said, each species has its own individual manner of bearing sori and no two are exactly alike. In some cases both fertile and sterile fronds may occur upon the same plant, while again all the fronds on a single plant may be either fertile or sterile. The upper sides of the pinnae, in the majority of cases, show no material differences between those that are fertile and those that are sterile, and so the underside must be examined in order to determine which is which.

FERTILE FRONDS OF POLYPODY FERN, SHOWING SORI

There are certain species, examples of which are the royal, cinnamon, ostrich, sensitive, and Clayton's, whose fertile fronds are so distinctly different from the sterile ones that there is no possibility of mistaking them. In these species the pinnules are rolled up into berry-like bodies which hold the spore-cases.

This individuality in the shape, position, and arrangement of the sori in the different species forms an absolutely infallible means by which to determine the species. One of the best methods to learn to know the ferns is by making a series of photographs of them, not only of the plants growing, but of the underside of the fertile fronds to show the arrangement of the sori clearly.

Ferns can be found almost anywhere and everywhere, and although many are lovers of the damp places, still there are others that flourish only in the most arid places. Such a one is the star-cloak fern, found in the deserts of the southwest, whose beautiful fronds spread wide in damp weather but roll into tight balls during a dry spell, to await the first touch of dampness when they will again unroll and spread themselves, none the worse for their drying out. The common bracken, or brake as it is more often called, and the hay-scented fern, two of our larger and commoner species, especially in the eastern states, are partial to dry fields and hillsides exposed to the full force of the sun. In wet marshes and damp fields are found the *Osmundas*, the so-called " flowering ferns," because the fertile fronds (so different from the sterile, as I have said) may by a great stretch of the imagination be comparable to the inflorescence of a flowering plant. They are the royal, cinnamon, and Clayton's, or interrupted, ferns. The interrupted fern is so-called because the fertile and the sterile leaves are borne on the same stem, the fertile leaves interrupting the continuity of the sterile ones. Those two species of another genus, the ostrich and the sensitive ferns, may also be placed in this class. The chain ferns (*Woodwardia*), are found in swamps, often standing in water. The commonest is the Virginia chain fern which, standing from two to three feet tall in clumps, frequently extend over a considerable area of swampland. The dry woods produce the oak fern, beech fern, and other closely allied species, while the well-known Christmas fern (the " dagger-fern " of commerce), the evergreen wood fern (" fancy fern " in a florist's shop), maidenhair, shield ferns, and others as well as the hart's-tongue, one of our rarest species, are more partial to the deeper woods where the ground is richer and damper. On rocks and damp cliffs, often in the deepest woods, grow the dainty spleenworts, cliff brakes, and walking ferns; while the polypody, one of the commonest and most lovely of our wood ferns, may be found in similar situations or on steep, rocky banks, preferably along streams. It frequently grows in quite large colonies, covering considerable space, on a cliff or steep hillside.

The climbing, or creeping, fern grows in the shape of a vine, climbing over the surrounding herbage. While it was never found commonly, it was at one time much more plentiful than it is now. There are but few places where it is to be found at all, and one of these is the pine barrens of New Jersey. It is in its prime in the month of October, but can be found in equally good condition in November or, in fact, until the killing frosts arrive.

Of all our ferns the bracken, or brake, is undoubtedly the commonest and also of widest distribution. It extends, in one form or another, over practically the entire world. It is probably well known to most of my readers as its habitat is the dry fields, hillsides, and

CHRISTMAS FERN

open woods. Wherever it is found it grows extensively, covering a considerable extent of ground, often as much as several acres. In the eastern United States it grows to a height of from one to three feet, while in the Andes it is said to attain a height of fourteen or fifteen feet.

Two of the most curious of our native ferns are found in Florida. One of these is the grass fern, or shoestring fern, whose string-like, tufted fronds are leathery, about an eighth of an inch in width, and several feet in length, and look very much like large bunches of shoestrings. It grows upon the trunks of trees, principally the cabbage palmetto. Another curious fern is the hand fern, which also grows pendent from tree trunks. Its fleshy leaves, a foot or more in length, are divided into fingers that closely resemble the human hand.

There are, of course, many other species of ferns that are native to the United States. The rattlesnake fern, grape ferns, and adder's-tongue are all small ferns whose sporangia are globose and separate and always borne on the terminal branches of a special stalk. In one form or another the rattlesnake fern is quite common over most of North America. Its best growths may be found in the deeper dry woods. The maidenhair fern and the Venus's-hair fern of the south, both belonging to the genus *Adiantum* in which there are about two hundred species, are very similar. They both have delicate, finely divided blades, and dark, polished stalks. Their names were given to these plants from the fancied resemblance of their lustrous stalks to women's tresses. The sensitive fern is a rather coarse-looking plant, usually growing in low damp situations. It has, however, one distinction in the manner in which it produces its spores, or at least the appearance of its fertile fronds, which is almost unique among our native species. These are developed in late summer and do not appear to belong to the same plant as the sterile fronds. The erect stalks, fairly thick, are surmounted by the lobes tightly rolled into small, hard balls, inside of which the spores are held. At first these are green, but as they mature they turn brown. When fully ripe they burst open to release the spores, but the stalks, retaining the dead, opened cases, remain erect well through the year.

In photographing ferns one should, naturally, be careful to select such plants as show the individuality of the species clearly, and make the exposure from such a point of view as will show the distinguishing features as distinctly as possible. Often ferns are crowded among other herbage so closely that their outline and distinctive features are completely lost. If you can find no better specimen of this particular species in a better location, then some of the surrounding herbage must be cleared away so that the fern will stand out clearly. This must be done carefully so that the elimination of the other plants will not be noticeable in the photograph.

Mosses, hepatics, or liverworts, and lichens — all flowerless plants — are closely related, and it is sometimes difficult for the novice to differentiate between them. The following distinguishing description, which helps to give the salient features for identification of the

PEAT MOSS

different groups, is taken from Miss Marshall's book on the mosses and lichens and always appealed to me as being particularly apt: " If a small plant, rootless, of almost any color except bright green, grows in a dainty mat — a *thallus* — flat or ruffled on its support, one may suspect it of being a lichen. If in addition to this habit of growth, it bears its fruits in flattened, colored discs one may know it is a lichen, also if the plants branch like corals or hang in fringes from the trees and are without leaves one may suspect that they are lichens, and may be pretty sure of it if the fruits are little colored discs or cushions on the tips of the branches. . . . If plants are small and green with leafy stems and have the habit of living in such close proximity as to form velvety cushions one may suspect them of being mosses, but if they have this habit of growth, or grow in clusters resembling tiny ferns or miniature trees, and bear their spores in little cases opening by lids, one may feel confident that they are the true mosses as distinguished from the hepatics. If the plants are green growing flat and ribbon-like, or as prostrate stems with paired, venous leaves and with fruits umbrella-like or with caps which do not open by lids but split irregularly into symmetrical valves in order to permit their spores to escape, one may know them to be hepatics." She might also have added that the majority of liverworts, or hepatics, are partial to damp situations, some often lying flat upon water and others in very wet mud.

Mosses are of almost universal distribution from the wet bogs, where the peat, or bog, mosses (*Sphagnum*) form a mat often so thick that ice may be found beneath it even in mid-summer, to the tops of the highest mountains, and from the equator to the Arctic and Antarctic circles. They may also be found, and photographed if we desire, the year round. All of the true mosses produce their spores in spore cases which are either at the summit or side of the moss stem, and may or may not be supported by a pedicil (stalk). Probably the best known and most often noticed of all the mosses are the hair caps. They are common everywhere in the woods, bordering the paths and wood roads, and frequently covering considerable areas of ground, to the exclusion of all other forms of vegetable growth, especially in open places. Their spore cases are borne on quite long pedicils rising from the ends of the moss stems, making them quite conspicuous.

One of the loveliest of all our mosses is the dainty Knight's-plume moss (*Hypnum crista-castrensis*), so named by Linnaeus for its resemblance to a military plume. It is found in deep woods frequently completely covering rocks or decaying stumps or logs. The branches of the stems somewhat resemble a miniature fern frond and might readily be mistaken for one of these plants by the uninitiated. It is of fairly wide distribution and not uncommon. As its spores do not mature until autumn, it remains green until quite late in the year.

The closest relatives of the mosses are the liverworts (*Hepaticae*). In fact these two groups of plants form the two primary sub-divisions of the *Bryophytes*, one of the four primary groups of the plant kingdom. Liverworts grow under a variety of conditions; some float upon the water, many live in damp places and many on the barks of trees, but in general they are moisture-loving plants. With but very few exceptions the plants lie close to whatever they are growing upon. Probably one of the more common forms is *Riccia fluitans* which grows in considerable patches on pools, ponds, and slowly running watercourses, forming, with its small, two-lobed leaves, an almost solid green mat. It undoubtedly is familiar to most of us although not all of us may have been able to name it. It is easily photographed if we will be sure that the water upon which it is resting is absolutely motionless so that the sharpness of detail will not be blurred. Found in similar places, often mingling with it, but with

LIVERWORT

considerably larger, fan-shaped leaves, *Ricciocarpus natans* is quite a conspicuous and rather beautiful species.

Lichens are found all over the world from the far north to the depths of the equatorial forests, and from the lowest, most dismal swamps and bogs to the absolute peaks of the highest mountains. They appear in spots where no other plant will grow and in places where it would seem impossible for them to obtain any sustenance. They have no need of soil and the smoothest rock is all-sufficient as a resting place for them. At one time it was a general belief that they sprang up spontaneously. Research and investigation, however, finally proved that the lichen is not an individual plant, but the result of the joining together of two separate forms of plant life, an alga and a fungus. As one author puts it, the lichen is probably the earliest instance of a division of labor in which, for mutual benefit, one party to the pact manufactures and supplies the food while the other serves to protect it from outside dangers and interference during its labors. In this instance the food is supplied by the green alga, while the fungus, which is incapable of supplying food for itself, repays by shielding the alga from the sun's rays, and also absorbs water for its work. The alga would quickly perish if exposed to the sunlight and dry air, but when protected and kept moist it is capable of capturing certain elements from the air and transforming them into plant food.

Lichens grow in many beautiful and intricate patterns, especially in the genus *Parmelia*, the members of which grow exclusively on rocks, tree trunks, and branches. When we find a rock in the woods or pastures more or less covered with a grayish-green growth closely adhering to it, or a tree with its trunk, and sometimes its lower branches, mottled with patches of the same growth, especially on the north side, where it is shaded, we may be fairly certain that it is one of the various species of lichens of this genus, although the members of another genus, *Sticta*, closely resemble them. They are sometimes also found on old rail fences, on deserted unpainted buildings, on log piles in the woods, and in other similar places. The " old man's beard " (*Usnea*), which hangs in festoons from dead or living evergreen trees, is another of our lichens, although it is frequently miscalled " moss." The parula warbler builds its nest of this lichen, hollowing out a thick bunch of it and adding a little soft lining. The yellowish growth which we find extending itself along old fence rails, old walls, tree trunks, rocks, etc., usually near water, is another form (*Thelochistes*). Covering cliffs for a considerable area, or on large rocks in damp forests, grows one of the most curious forms, the " rocktripe " (*Gyrophora dillenii*). When wet the " leaves," which are then a dark velvety green, lie flat against the surface of rock or cliff, but as they dry out the edges curl up until the under surface, sooty black, is fully exposed to view. At the approach of damp weather it again uncurls and lies flat on the supporting surface, twisting and writhing about in the process. Its form is so constantly varying at every atmospheric change that it may show us a different

LICHEN ON TREE TRUNK

aspect each time we find it. It was used quite extensively as an article of food by the Indians and was supposed to be instrumental in saving Sir John Franklin from starvation when he was exploring the Arctic. Another species, the lungwort (*Sticta pulmonaria*) so-called because of the fancied resemblance of its pitted undersurface to the surface of a lung and also because it was supposed to be a sure cure for any lung trouble, has much the same habit. It clings to the bark of trees, fallen logs, or rocks, showing its green upper side when damp. Upon drying it curls in the same manner as does the rock-tripe, but its under surface is white instead of black.

The ruby-throated hummingbird is very familiar with these lichens and makes good use of them by attaching small pieces, principally of the rock- and bark-loving *Parmelias*, to the outside of its nest in order to camouflage it. When viewed from below it causes the nest to have the appearance of a lichen-covered knot on the tree limb. The pewee, one of our flycatchers, whose nest is saddled upon a horizontal limb in the same manner as is that of the ruby-throat, also uses bits of lichens for the same purpose.

It may be well to correct an erroneous idea that many people have. The so-called " Florida moss," which hangs in pendent masses from many of the trees throughout the south, particularly the live oaks, and which is supposed to be either a moss or a lichen, is neither one, but a true flower-producing plant with stamens and pistils. The flowers are insignificant and escape notice, but the seed capsules can readily be seen after the flowers have gone.

Many of the fungi, of which I wrote in the last chapter, are still in excellent condition for photographing during this month. Especially is this true of the so-called bracket fungi and other tree-loving species, such as some of the *Hydnums,* the *Pholiotas* and others. Those who are interested in the fungi as photographic subjects need never suspend their activities until well into December. Among the more common forms of fungi that are more or less plentiful during this month are the different species of the genus *Fomes.* These are those stiff, hard, shelf-like fungi that project from the trunks of dead or living trees. Their tops are hard and horny, usually brown, grayish-brown, or reddish-brown, while their undersides are usually pure white and smooth. The slightest scratch on this surface will leave a dark mark, and they are often found in curio shops with pictures etched on them. A very lovely little tree-loving fungus, which may also be found in this month, is *Schizophyllum commune.* It is pure white on top and looks exactly like a small frosted cake, while the dainty, branching gills of the underside are delicately tinted with lilac, pink, or blue. It is a small species, each individual rarely exceeding an inch in breadth, but it grows in groups of a number of individuals on the faces of cut logs, dead branches, etc.

Among the mammals, the beavers are finishing their houses and strengthening their dams to secure them for the winter months, but the muskrats, at this time, have frequently not much more than commenced to build their winter quarters. They will complete them, however, before there is any danger of really cold weather coming to shut them in. Thoreau wrote: " The muskrats have added a new story to their houses since the last flood. They are uncommonly high: I think a full four feet by five or more in diameter, a heaping cartload. I opened one. It was composed of coarse grass ponte-

deria stems, etc., not altogether in mouthfuls. This was three and a
half feet above water, others quite four. After taking off a foot I
came to the chamber. It was a regularly formed oval or elliptical
chamber, about eighteen inches the longest way, and seven or eight
inches deep, shaped like a pebble, with smooth walls of the weeds, and
bottomed or bedded with a very little dry grass — a mere coating of
it. It would hold four or five closely packed. The entrance, eight

Muskrat

or nine inches wide, led directly from the water at an angle of forty-
five degrees, and the walls are of such a breadth at the bottom that
the water in the gallery probably never freezes." However, the ar-
chitecture of the muskrat house differs considerably according to location and the idiosyncrasies of the builders.

The frogs, toads and snakes have mostly disappeared for the winter, but there are, occasionally, some still to be found if we care to
look for them. As far north as New Jersey some few snakes are still
abroad, and others come from the hiding places to sun themselves
during the warmer part of the day. They are more or less torpid,
however, and therefore when found are easily photographed.

If we search beneath the rocks in damp woods, especially near watercourses and springs, we will be sure to find several species of sala-

manders, in particular the red-backed, four-toed, and two-lined; for in such situations they spend the winters. The newts may still be taken in shallow pools or roadside ditches. The tadpoles of those species of frogs that occupy two years in the completion of their metamorphosis are nearly full-grown and may be taken by dredging the bottoms of the pools with a heavy net, and this will also often produce a mature frog.

November is a month when one may expect surprises as he walks through the woods and fields. One day in late November I was passing through a small tract of woodland when a rabbit, "cottontail," started to life almost at my feet and departed in long and rapid jumps that soon took him out of sight. Anyone not well acquainted with the habits of the cottontail might have watched him as long as he was within sight and then passed on without another glance at the spot from which he had started. Those acquainted with these little rodents, however, know that they have a habit, especially at this time of the year, of sitting motionless for hours at a time in what is known as their "form." This is merely a place on the ground which they have hollowed out in the grass, dead leaves, or low herbage, to exactly fit their bodies, and in which they crouch with the tuft of white down, glorified by the name of tail, tucked under them. Here they are practically invisible because the color of their coats so exactly matches that of their surroundings. Of this they are well aware and frequently depend entirely upon it for their safety, allowing an enemy to pass within a few feet of them without stirring. Had I not almost stepped upon him, the one that I started up would undoubtedly have remained in his form absolutely still, allowing me to pass by without suspecting that he was there. As it was, I gladly grasped the opportunity to make a photograph of the form.

At another time, in the late fall, I was walking through a meadow when I was somewhat startled by a diminutive creature that leaped from the grass at the very spot upon which my foot was descending, and went sailing away in jumps that were almost incredible for such a small creature, each one covering six or seven feet. I realized at once that I had scared up one of our smaller rodents, unique among its fellows, the kangaroo, or jumping, mouse (*Zapus hudsonicus*). I followed him as quickly as possible, hoping that I might be able to catch him, but he was altogether too quick for me and some fifty yards or so from where he started he disappeared down a hole in the ground and I knew that he had reached his haven of safety, his underground burrow, and that I would see him no more. I consoled myself, however, by making a photograph of the entrance to his burrow.

The jumping mouse is unique among American mammals in sev-

RABBIT "FORM" IN WOODS

eral ways. It is dull, brownish-yellow in color, is possessed of a very slim body some three inches in length, with a remarkably long and slender tail usually more than twice the length of its body. Its hind legs are also long and slender, although strongly developed for jumping like those of the kangaroo whose name it bears, but its front legs are short. It is also provided with cheek pouches, similar to those of the gopher, in which it carries food to its underground storehouse. Its long tail serves as a balancing pole when executing its really remarkable feats of jumping. If it should suffer the loss of this useful

ICHNEUMON FLY COCOONS IN COCOON OF CECROPIA MOTH

appendage, its leaps would deteriorate into a series of awkward som-
ersaults which would carry it nowhere. Jumping mice are distributed over most of northern North America from Labrador to Alaska
and south to North Carolina, New Mexico, and California. They
are, however, nowhere very common. They are entirely nocturnal in
their habits, and they excavate burrows from two to three feet deep
in which they live and sleep through the winter months. The burrow is enlarged at its end into a chamber which they line with dried
grass, plant pappus, and other soft materials. Their summer nests

COCOON OF CECROPIA OPENED TO SHOW PUPA

are placed in shallow burrows, behind loose bark, in a hollow log or tree, or any similar situation. In these the young, numbering from two to eight, are born some time between May and September. The kangaroo appearance of these little rodents, and the fact that they are so named, has given rise to a more or less popular belief that, like their namesake, they are marsupials and carry their young in a pouch. This, of course, is not so. The only member of the marsupial family which is native to this country is the opossum.

November is a good month in which to search for cocoons of the moths in order to keep them until spring when the adult moths will emerge, perfect specimens for photographing. Do not, however, keep these cocoons in a warm room else their inmates may emerge long before there is any suitable foliage upon which to pose them. It is always a good idea to cut open a cocoon of each species of moth that you have, in order to photograph the enclosed pupa. This must be done with great care not to puncture the pupa. Occasionally

Sphinx Moth Caterpillar Covered with Cocoons of Ichneumon Fly

when you cut open a cocoon, instead of finding the pupa you expect, you may find it packed full with what appear to be other much smaller cocoons. This is exactly what they are, the cocoons of an ichneumon fly.

The ichneumon fly is what might be called one of our beneficial insects. There are many species, and they are all parasitic on the larvae of other insects, each different one being a specialist on those of some particular species. The one whose cocoons we are most apt to find when we open a cocoon, is a brown, wasp-like insect about the size of the common brown wasp (*Ophion macrurum*), whose larvae specialize on the larvae of the *Cecropia* moth. It lays quite a number of eggs in the body of its prey. These hatch and the young larvae feed upon the fatty portions of their unwilling host, always careful not to attack any vital part until the victim has spun his cocoon, and they are ready to do likewise, when they finish him off and spin their own cocoons inside the one he has already made, completely filling it. Viewed from the outside it is impossible to tell whether the cocoon holds the pupa of its maker or the cocoons of the little fellows who have devoured him. Other, much smaller, species attain their full growth and emerge from the body of the caterpillar who has been their food supply before he is ready to pupate. They then attach their tiny cocoons to the body of their victim where they remain until the perfect flies emerge. Incidentally, the larva upon which they have been living, dies.

DECEMBER

R EAL winter weather rarely begins before the middle or latter part of this month. Even then, although the temperature may fall below freezing, snow seldom remains on the ground for any length of time until after the holidays, and a white Christmas is rare except in the extreme northern parts of the country.

All this is a decided help to the nature photographer who would continue work with his camera during the winter months, and let me say that no one who desires to make a really worth-while collection of photographs of the wild things can afford to allow mere cold weather to stop, or even seriously curtail, his endeavors to make additions to that collection. Naturally there is not the wealth of material that is to be found in many of the other months of the year, but December has photographic material well worth making a search for if one does not allow the cold weather to deter him.

Nature begins fairly early to prepare her offspring so that they may survive the cold weather. It is true that she always prepares for an average season. When an exceptionally cold winter comes there is almost always an unusual amount of mortality in both the vegetable and the animal world. We always regret that this should happen, but we are told that it is necessary and is merely one of nature's methods of eliminating the weaker and less wanted of her offspring, and thus raising the general average. In other words, it is a test for the survival of the fittest, which is one of the great laws of the universe.

The special preparations that are made each fall by the various members of nature's family are many and ingenious. In the vegetable world the thick and often waxy scales that cover the leaf buds of the trees are one of these precautionary measures to keep the buds from freezing, as is also the wooly down with which many of these bud coverings are lined. A series of close-up photographs of these winter buds of the various trees, showing the different forms which these coverings take, is extremely interesting and instructive, for on every different species of tree the form varies. Another very good reason for making such a series is that these buds form an almost perfect means of identification of the winter trees, one that is unfailing once we have learned to know the different buds.

There are other plants besides the trees that protect their buds in a similar manner. Notable among these are those early spring plants, the hepatica, or liver-leaf, and the trailing arbutus, or mayflower. The leaves of both of these plants are evergreen and their flower buds are formed in the fall and lie beneath the snow throughout the winter, efficiently protected by a furry covering, all prepared to burst into full bloom at the first touch of warmth in the spring. Photographs of these evergreen winter leaves of the herbaceous plants, surrounded by the dead herbage, are always well worth while. They are some of the subjects that one should search for in December.

There are other herbaceous evergreens that one should search for during this month and which may be found in the woods at any time, even after the snow falls. Of course if the snow should be deep they will be covered, but with merely a light fall of snow they stand out perfectly for photographing. One of the handsomest of these, and probably the best known of them all from the fact that it is used extensively for Christmas wreaths and festoons, is that really lovely little member of the genus *Lycopodium*, or club mosses, the trailing Christmas green (*Lycopodium complanatum*). This little plant is well called " trailing " as it is a running vine, hugging close to the ground and covering it with a thick carpet in places. Not so very long ago it was extremely common in our woods. I have quite frequently found it covering the ground in patches of up to an acre in extent. It has been hunted and pulled up so ruthlessly in late years to be made into wreaths and festoons to decorate our walls and windows on Christmas day that it is rapidly becoming more and more rare. It may become extinct before very many years unless it receives some protection, but at the present time it may still be found in patches of considerable size in the deeper woods on almost any day of winter when the snow is not so deep as to completely cover it. The snow in the open may be fairly deep, but in the woods where this plant grows it is so well protected by the trees that form a heavy canopy overhead that it will seldom be found with more than a light covering. The little snow that is there will only add to the beauty of the photograph and show at what time of the year it was made.

Another member of the same genus and one that is used almost as extensively for Christmas decorations is the ground pine (*Lycopodium obscurum*). This is more of an erect plant than the former, standing from six to twelve inches high so that a little snow on the ground interferes in no way with the photographing of it, but has the advantage of causing it to stand out more distinctly from its surroundings. It, also, grows in deep, damp woods and may be found in considerable quantities in places by anyone having the patience to search for it, although the use of it for decorative purposes is rapidly depleting it.

Another member of this genus, and probably the commonest, is the running-pine, or club moss (*Lycopodium clavatum*). It is extremely common throughout the northern woods, especially in the Adirondacks, but is also found as far south as North Carolina. Besides these three, which are typical of the genus, there are a number of other species, about one hundred in all, divided between the temperate regions and the tropics, the largest occurring in the Andes of South America and the Himalayas.

The name " club moss " was given to these plants because in the manner and appearance of their growth they somewhat resemble moss, their stems being clothed with short, pointed scaly leaves. They belong to the flowerless plants which reproduce by means of spores. In the case of the Lycopodiums, these are borne on a club-shaped fruiting stem. These fruiting heads, when fully ripe, discharge their spores in the shape of a copious sulphur-colored powder that will turn our shoes and trouser bottoms yellow if we brush through them. This powder is also inflammable, as we can quickly ascertain if we take one of the fruiting heads when it is fully ripe and shake it gently over a lighted match or candle. We will discover that we have a nature-made sparklet. This powder is used to some extent in theaters to simulate lightning and other effects, and is also used in the manufacture of fireworks.

There are many others of our common plants whose leaves remain green throughout the winter which could therefore very well have the term evergreen applied to them. Besides the hepatica and arbutus, of which I have already spoken, there is the trailing wintergreen from which we obtain our wintergreen flavoring, and whose bright red " berries," which are in reality not berries at all but merely a thickening of the calyx to protect the seeds, that will remain on the plants all winter unless taken off, are a delight to both birds and children. This plant, by the way, is not a member of the wintergreen family at all, despite its name, but belongs to the *Ericaceae*, or heath family to which family also belong the arbutus, the azaleas, the rhododendrons, the laurels, and other lovely plants. The true wintergreens (*Pyrolaceae*), of which there are about fifteen species, are all members of the northern hemisphere. They comprise the pyrolas, of which the commonest and best known is the shin-leaf, so-called because, as Neltje Blanchan says: " By reason of the old custom of clapping on a so-called " shin-plaster " to every bruise, regardless of its location on the human body, a lovely little plant, whose leaves were once counted a first aid to the injured, still suffers instead under an unlovely name." The other two genera in the family are the one-flowered wintergreen, in a genus of its own, and the spotted wintergreen and prince's pine, or pipsissewa, which, with one other species on the Pacific coast, are members of the genus *Chimaphila*. Then there is that lowly little plant the partridgeberry, or twinflower, that covers the ground in places with a veritable mat of small, round, dark green leaves. Its waxy white flowers, which grow in pairs, slightly tinged with pink and faintly fragrant, are a delight in the spring. Its right red berries, really drupes, remain on the vine all winter and are a godsend to the bob-whites and grouse (partridge) who will often dig down through a foot or more of snow to get at them.

Another class of plants whose leaves, or at least part of them, remain green all winter are the typical biennials, the plants that spend one year in making a rosette of leaves close pressed to the earth, and the next year to send up their stalks and produce their blossoms, and then die. There are also in this class some that are perennial, such as the plantain. These renew their rosettes each year from the same root. These rosettes are the basal leaves of the plants. They lie close to the ground and remain green all winter and may be successfully photographed at any time during that season, but I venture to say that very few of the great army of camera users have ever done so. Nevertheless they are quite beautiful and a series of photographs of them is interesting, instructive, and valuable, from a botanical as

ROSETTES OF MULLEN

well as from an artistic standpoint. All of them are more or less symmetrical in outline, many of them almost absolutely so, and they might be used to great advantage as models by the decorator, wood carver, or designer of fabrics and wallpapers. They are frequently so perfect as almost to suggest a conventional design of some artist, but the designer who has conventionalized them is the greatest artist of all, nature.

There is one point that must be considered in the making of a series of photographs of these rosettes, especially for him who does not care for extended tramps in the cold weather. One need not go far afield in his search for subjects. Any waste piece of ground, a vacant lot or old field, even a back lot, may be found to produce a dozen or more of them, although the farther we extend our search, the greater the number of different species we will be likely to find. They are everywhere and one can hardly go amiss in his search for them. Of course, when the snow is deep upon the ground, the finding and photographing of them produces greater difficulties, but even then it can be accomplished. Nearly every weed stalk which we see protruding above the snow has one of these rosettes lying flat upon the ground at its foot. If the snow is not too deep it may be brushed aside and blown away and the rosette will be found as perfect as when it was first formed. It will add considerably to the interest of the resulting picture if it is clearly shown that it was made when the plant was actually surrounded by snow.

December and often well into January is by far the best time to photograph these plants because then there are many days when the ground is bare or, if there is snow, it lies only in patches here and there, and the rosettes when found are in the very best condition. Search for the most perfect specimen of each species and do not be satisfied with the first one that you happen to see. There are usually many of them, and one can always take his choice. Many of them are imperfect in some respect. Some of the leaves may have been eaten by insects, or have dried and shriveled up, or have grown unequally and so formed a not very perfect type of rosette, which is often due to the fact that something has impeded the free growth of the plant. There are a great many things that are likely to happen to spoil the perfect symmetry of the rosette, but one should always have the patience to continue his search until the perfect specimen of each species is found, which will inevitably happen if one persists.

When such a specimen is finally found, it should be thoroughly cleaned of all particles of dirt, dead vegetation, or other extraneous matter that does not belong to it. Every piece of dead grass, leaf, or weed stem that would intrude into the picture must be removed with the greatest care not to disturb in any way the arrangement of the leaves of the rosette. The ground immediately surrounding the subject should be carefully cleared of all objects that intrude, and it is often not only justifiable but actually best to pull up all dead vegetation surrounding it, and thus leave the ground absolutely bare. The rosette will then stand out with much greater distinctness than if the outline was blurred by other small growths. In making the picture, the camera must be pointed directly downward at the subject to show the true arrangement of the leaves. This can easily be accomplished with the aid of a tilting top to your camera. A camera with a rear extension of bellows greatly simplifies the work as it is much easier to focus by the use of the rear extension.

The arrangement of the leaves in the rosette is in exactly the same progressive sequence as will later be found in the leaves on the stalk.

WINTER ROSETTES OF THISTLE

As one author has put it: " If we imagine the stem of the plant to consist of an elastic cord at full tension, then our rosette would represent the result of its contraction to the ground."

Photographs of these rosettes are a great aid in the study of our native wild plants. Not many people can identify wild flowers by their leaves alone. The basal leaves of many plants are entirely different from the stem leaves, and this is confusing until we have studied them. One of the commonest, and at the same time most beautiful, of these rosettes is that of the common thistle. One need never mistake this for any other, for its leaves are exactly the same thorny kind that have deterred us from picking the handsome purple bloom

in the summer. There is another beautiful one, however, composed
of heart-shaped leaves which the uninformed would never suspect be-
longed to one of our common asters. Another, equally as beautiful,
belonging to the rattlesnake weed, one might puzzle over for a long
time unless he was familiar with our hawkweeds. All of them, however, are fairly easy of identification by the use of a good botanical
work. After studying and photographing these rosettes for a while,
one's knowledge of the wild flowers that he sees every day throughout
the summer is very much greater than it was before.

BASAL LEAVES OF HAWKWEED

Among the mammals many have already started their winter's
sleep of hibernation, some even as early as the latter part of November, but there are quite a number that remain active throughout the
winter. One may wonder how these creatures endure the sometimes
intense cold of midwinter. Nature has adequately provided for this
by causing a semi-annual change of pelage in the mammals or plumage in the birds, which occurs in spring and fall. At the fall change
there is added a second and downy coat of fur or feathers, as the case
may be, underneath the main coat and this is discarded during the

spring molt. Thus the animals don their heavy underwear as cold weather approaches, and take it off again when warm weather returns. Some mammals and birds that live where snow is more or less constant throughout the winter, for protective reasons alter the color of their coats during the fall change to pure white, which causes them to become practically invisible against the snow, and so protects them from their enemies. Among these is that scourge of the smaller mammals, the weasel. This animal's red-brown summer garb with white only on the belly and the inside of the legs, is replaced by white over the entire body, except the tip of the tail which is black, and the weasel, or stoat as it is also called, becomes the ermine, so valuable as a fur bearer. Mr. W. E. Cram, writing in one of his delightful books on nature, says of this little animal: "Late in the autumn, or early in the winter, the ermine changes from reddish brown to white, sometimes slightly washed with greenish-yellow or cream color, and again as brilliantly white as anything in nature or art; the end of its tail, however, remains intensely black and at first thought this might be supposed to make the animal conspicuous on the white background of snow, but in reality it has just the opposite effect. Place an ermine on new fallen snow in such a way that no shadow is cast, and you will find that the black point holds your eye in spite of yourself, and that at a little distance it is quite impossible to follow the outline of the weasel itself. Cover the tail with snow and you can make out the position of the rest of the animal; but as long as the tip of the tail is in sight you see that and that only." This has been definitely proven by conclusive experiments. Some birds, such as the ptarmigan and the snow bunting, which are exclusively ground feeders and which change their plumage to white in the fall, thus making themselves almost invisible against the pure white snow, also retain some spots of dark color which helps in their protective color scheme.

Dame Nature also provides special appliances for some of her offspring whose winter stamping ground is the north where the snow usually lies deep for at least three or four months of the year, so that they can more easily get about to procure their food. Thus there grows upon the toes of the ruffed grouse, in the late fall, a fringe of stiff feathers which act as snowshoes, enabling it to walk in deep snow without sinking in too much, and so procure the berries and plant buds upon which it lives in the winter. It also enables its wearers to scoop a hollow in the snow and lie there well sheltered and fairly comfortable at night. The feet of the ptarmigan, that member of the grouse family that lives in the far north, are similarly clothed, else it would have difficulty in progressing at all in the deep snow that covers the earth of their habitat for nearly half the year. Some mammals are similarly provided for. The varying hare of the northern United States and Canada, so-called from the fact that

WEASEL

it is one of those animals whose coat turns from brown to white in the fall, has hair on its feet that grows so long and stiff as winter approaches, that it is frequently called " the snowshoe rabbit."

The red squirrels are the true imps of the woods. They are abroad and active all winter — ever on the alert, and almost constantly in motion. No one at all familiar with the different voices of nature's offspring fails to know their rattling bark; and one can hardly take a stroll through the woods either in summer or winter without hearing it. The tones of the squirrel's voice are varied. There is a great difference between his angry bark; his cry of fear; the chattering monologue with which he addresses an intruder upon his domain;

and the running fire of repartee which is the constant accompaniment of the antics of a pair at play. The long rattling roll call which he utters apparently from sheer enjoyment of his voice or as a challenge to some unseen enemy of his own tribe, often reverberates through the silent woods with sufficient force to carry half a mile. Especially is this true in the winter time when almost the only other sounds which one may hear in the woods are the cracking of the frosty limbs and the occasional thud of snow falling from some overladen branch. If we listen for a moment, when we hear one of these challenges sent forth, we may hear it answered from some distant point, the sound coming to us so faintly that we cannot be certain it is not an echo of the first call. Some other male has heard the challenge and detecting the self-satisfied note in it, has answered. We may be sure that the challenger has heard the answer and that the two are hastening toward each other, each with the full intention of annihilating his impertinent foe or, at least, teaching him a severe lesson. The different calls of the squirrels are as distinctive of the different emotions as the calls of any animal can be, and to those well acquainted with them the lack of words is but a small obstacle in the way of perfect understanding.

The red squirrels build their winter nests of the strippings of hemlock and cedar bark or similar soft material, often placing them in some cavity in a tree or dead stump, or taking possession of a deserted nest of a hawk or crow which they roof over with strips of bark, moss, etc. If they feel particularly energetic, they will build a complete nest of soft materials placed on a rough platform of sticks lodged in the crotch of some tree, preferably a hemlock or cedar. Bird houses are also sometimes taken possession of by them, and they have even been known to enter human habitations and build in some corner of the garret. They are somewhat erratic in their storing of food for the winter. They sometimes fill a hollow in a tree, stump, or beneath a stone with a quart or more of nuts, but quite as often they deposit only a few nuts in several different places.

The little flying squirrel, which is consistently a nocturnal animal, stores his winter's supply of food which consists of thin-shelled nuts, corn grains, etc., in a like manner. He is a partial hibernator, his winter home a hollow, often a deserted woodpecker's nesting hole, in some tree. Here a number will congregate, often as many as ten or a dozen and sometimes even more, and roll themselves into a warm ball to sleep through the coldest weather, only occasionally venturing forth when it moderates somewhat, to draw rations from the general storehouse. If one can find such a sleeping place of the little fellows, it is not difficult to take them out and photograph them. Wear gloves, however, in handling them for they have sharp little teeth and know how to use them.

It may be well to correct here an erroneous idea which some people have. A flying squirrel does not fly in anything like the true sense of the word. There is a loose skin which connects its fore and hind legs, and which, by extending its legs to their full length, it can stretch tight, thus forming a sort of parachute. By means of this it can sail through the air, but always on a downward plane, and its only upward motion is at the end of the flight when the impetus of its descent enables it to shoot upward for a distance of half a foot or so in order to alight upon some tree trunk or limb. In these flights it must always start from some point considerably higher than the one it wishes to reach, and during the descent it cannot change its direction to any extent, nor acquire new impetus.

The chipmunks, those little striped ground squirrels with which we are all familiar, are the only true hibernators of this group of animals. Late October, or early November, usually sees them preparing for their winter's sleep in their snug underground retreat, where no cold nor any enemy can reach them. Here they doze through the long, cold days and nights, not knowing or caring how the storms may rage above them, and only waking, when hunger demands it, sufficiently to draw from their store of nuts and seed with which they have stocked their larder in the fall. They will not come forth again until the spring winds have tempered the air and melted away the snow.

The gray squirrel secretes his winter food in a much different manner from that of any of his relatives. Instead of having one or perhaps three or four storehouses, he has several hundred receptacles. Did you ever watch a gray squirrel gathering his winter's supply of nuts? It is a process that is well worth observing. He takes a nut in his cheek pouch and hops along beneath the trees, testing the ground every few feet with his front paws. When he has found a spot entirely to his liking, he will scoop out a shallow hole, place the nut in it, and cover it with loose earth. Then stamping this down and patting it into shape, he soon has so precisely restored the looks of the ground that it is difficult for one who has watched the entire operation to locate the exact spot. This performance he will repeat again and again in that and other localities, until he has hidden away in this manner a large quantity of nuts. It is no exaggeration to say that one squirrel will thus bury several hundred nuts. In the winter he unearths them whenever he wishes, and it is very remarkable how unerringly he can go to his various caches even though, as is frequently the case, they may be covered with a foot or more of snow. What sense it is that so surely directs him to the exact spot in which he has buried one of these nuts, remains a mystery although numerous conjectures have been made. These conjectures, however, have been mere guesswork and none of them is based upon any foundation of solid fact. It does not seem possible that these little animals can remember with such unerring exactness each individual spot in which they have secreted a nut, and yet it may be so. It seems equally incredible that their sense of smell can be so acute as to guide them, especially when the snow is lying deep upon the ground. Whatever sense it is that they bring into play, it serves them well, although it is entirely probable that a number of these storehouses are missed and that a percentage of the nuts buried are never exhumed by their owner.

Another source of food for the gray squirrels is the pine and spruce cones. If they can find none of these under the trees, they will search them out in the trees themselves, nip them off and allow them to drop to the ground, and go down after them. They do not eat the cone itself, but the seeds of which one is located at the base of each scale. And how do they get at them? Did you ever try to extract one for yourself? If so you must realize how admirably a squirrel's teeth are adapted to this kind of work. Thoreau describes the process as follows: "The squirrel has the key to this conical and spiney chest of many compartments. If you would be convinced how efficiently armed the squirrel is naturally for dealing with pitch pine cones, just try to get one open with your teeth. He who extracts the seeds from a single closed cone with the aid of a knife will be constrained to confess that the squirrel earns his dinner. The plucking and stripping of a pine cone is a business which he and his family understand perfectly. He does not prick his fingers, nor pitch his whiskers, nor gnaw the solid cone any more than he needs to. He holds in his hand a solid embossed cone so hard that it almost rings to the touch of his teeth. He knows better than to cut off the top and work his way downward, or to gnaw into the sides for three quarters of an inch, in the face of many armed shields. He whirls it bottom upward in a twinkling, and then proceeds to cut through the thin and tender bases of the scales, and each stroke tells, laying bare at once a couple of seeds. Thus he strips it as easily as if the scales were chaff, and so rapidly, twisting it as he advances, that you cannot tell how he does it until you drive him off and inspect his unfinished work." The generic name of the squirrels (*Sciurus*) is derived from Greek words which mean shadow-tail, referring to the fact that these animals sit under the shadow of their tails; and this they most certainly do. The tail, however, is not a useless ornament, but serves its owner in various ways. As a balancing pole to help the squirrel in retaining his footing when running along the swaying branches, it is indispensable, and in the winter it is undoubtedly of use as a wrapper to help keep its owner warm. It is frequently the cause of his downfall, for his flirting tail which he finds difficulty in keeping entirely still, will often disclose his whereabouts to an enemy when otherwise he might have been passed by unnoticed.

Squirrels may be photographed in the wild state by anyone who has the patience, and it takes a lot, to systematically bait a spot, preferably the top of some stump, and watch it for several days. The squirrels learn that in that place they can always find a supply of the kind of food they prefer. When they have begun to come after it regularly, set up the camera focused on the food, leaving enough space on either side in the picture for the subject to occupy, so that his entire image will be on the plate. Attach the remote shutter control, retire to some good, near-by hide out where there is little danger that the squirrel will spy you, and wait with what patience you may be able to command for the subject to appear. This may be several hours or only a short time, and again it may not happen at all, especially if the wary little animal has discovered you preparing the camera. It will help materially if when you start baiting the spot you will set up a dummy camera just where you intend to place the real one. This may be merely a box of about the size of the camera fastened on a stick stuck in the ground and covered with a black cloth. It will help very greatly to accustom the squirrels to the presence of a somewhat suspicious-looking object near their feeding place. When replacing it with the real camera do so as quickly and unobtrusively as possible.

This may seem a very uncertain and decidedly wearisome way in which to obtain photographs of these little rodents, but it is the only manner in which they may be successfully photographed in their really wild state. Of course they may be trapped and photographed in such a glass enclosure as I have already described, but squirrels do not tame easily unless caught when young, and it would be some days before they could be photographed in this manner without their showing that they were badly frightened. If there is a public park in your neighborhood, it is almost certain to be the home of quite a number of semi-tame gray and sometimes red squirrels. These are usually easily enticed before the camera by the offer of nuts.

By the middle of the month at latest, except in the south where he is active all winter, the opossum has usually sought some hollow log or tree stump in which he can make a bed of dry leaves and sleep away most of the winter, rarely venturing forth when there is any snow upon the ground. He is a member of an almost tropical race and therefore is to be found in greatest abundance in the southern states. If one can discover the sleeping quarters of one of these little beasts, he will find him to be a most excellent and easy subject for photography. He is an adept, however, at feigning death, or " playing 'possum," and will lie perfectly motionless on the ground for minutes at a time, even allowing himself to be picked up, without showing any evidence of life. Once he has decided, however, that his ruse is useless, he will come to life and pose with entire equanimity for as many pictures as may be desired. All that he asks is to be allowed to return to his snuggery as soon as the photographing is over.

The opossum is the only member of the *Marsupialia* that we have in this country. The headquarters of these animals is Australia where there are a large number of species which completely dominate all other mammals and form the most characteristic feature of the fauna. The largest of these, and undoubtedly the best known, is the kangaroo. Outside of Australia the only known marsupials are the opossums, and of these there are about twenty species, all native of

GROUNDHOG OR WOODCHUCK, NEAR ENTRANCE TO BURROW

Central and South America with the exception of the one found in the United States, which is the largest of the species, some of the others being no bigger than rats. The chief characteristic of the marsupials is that the young are born much sooner than are those of any other mammal and consequently are very small. When born the young, including those of the kangaroo, are only about half an inch in length, and they are immediately placed by the mother in a pouch situated on her belly, where they continue their development, attached to her nipples, until able to care for themselves. Even after they are fully able to run about and procure their own food they will return to the pouch for shelter.

That extreme sleepyhead, the woodchuck, or ground hog, has retired to his burrow long before this. In fact he is the first of all the animals to seek his burrow for his winter's sleep. Having retired from active life he will not again reappear until mid-March, or even considerably later if the cold continues. Once out, however, he does not go back to sleep no matter what the weather, despite the adage concerning him and his shadow. He is one of the laziest of all animals, spending much of his time in sleep. During his waking hours he is usually eating so that in the fall he is what might be termed a really ludicrous object of obesity. This fat, however, carries him through the winter, for he lays up no supply of food for that season. Once he has retired to his burrow it is utterly impossible to entice him forth until he is ready to come, and so it is useless to try. A photograph of the entrance to his burrow, however, is a good addition to the collection of photographs of any nature lover, although it may seem to some of my readers to be a waste of time and material to photograph a mere hole in the ground.

The field mice are all semi-hibernators, sleeping only part of the time during the winter, rousing when hungry and leaving their nests to forage for food in the night, as is proven by the number of their tracks that one will find in the early morning on freshly fallen snow. In early December, however, before the snow begins to fall, they have not even gone into partial hibernation, but are still very active. In fact their nests frequently contain young at this time of the year. These nests, particularly those of the white-footed, or deer, mouse, are often built in a deserted bird's nest which the little creatures simply dome over with dried grass, etc., and line with some soft material. The winter nest of the little white-foot is also often a round ball of soft material placed in a hole in some decayed stump, in a deserted woodpecker's hole, under a wood pile or fallen log, or any similar place. The meadow mouse, while it occasionally uses the nest of some low-nesting bird, such as the blackbird, more often makes a round, compact ball of a nest of dried grass placed in a slight hollow on the ground of a meadow, well hidden in a tangle of grass. Should we, at any time in December before the snow comes, go to some low meadow and look beneath the matted grass we will be sure to find the runways of these little rodents, little paths that lead in all directions under the tangled grass. If we have the patience to follow one of these paths, paying no attention to any of those that cross it at very frequent intervals, we will find that it leads to one of the nests of the little path makers, for these runways are the roads between their nests and feeding grounds. If we are lucky it may even contain a litter of young. Before opening it to see, we should always photograph it

YOUNG MEADOW MICE IN NEST

as it is found, then open it carefully and photograph the young if they are there. Before leaving, restore the nest as nearly as possible to its original condition and rest assured that the mother will return and finish repairs on it or else remove the young to some other nest. These runways, occasionally lead to a burrow in the ground which is rarely more than a few inches to a foot deep, at the bottom of which the nest is made and the young reared.

There is not much doing for the nature photographer in the way of insect life during December except for the chrysalids and cocoons of the butterflies and moths that can be collected and photographed. Have you ever, however, searched the woods in the winter for well-rotted stumps or logs that may be easily broken apart in a search for the larva and pupa of wood-boring beetles, as well as for the beetles themselves? The results are sometimes very interesting and often provide subjects for photography. One quite cold day in the latter part of December I broke open an old stump that was pretty well decayed, and out fell a beautiful, large specimen of one of our largest elaters, or " snapping beetles " (*Aleus occulatus*). He was an ex-

" Snapping Beetle " on Rotten Log

ceedingly large specimen, measuring nearly two inches in length, and was completely dormant, as any beetle found at this time of the year is bound to be. At first I was undecided as to whether he was dead or not, but after holding him in my hands for a short time he came to life sufficiently to crawl slowly to the top of the stump and pose there for me while I made a couple of photographs of him. I decided that he really deserved some consideration from me after serving me so well, and so I replaced him in the spot from which he had fallen, covered him over again with the piece of the stump I had pried off, and left him to his slumbers, and I am quite sure that he remained there in safety for the rest of the winter.

There are still plenty of water insects active in the bottoms of the ponds, pools, and ditches, even though a film of ice may cover them. If anyone cares to break through this ice and drag the bottoms with a heavy net, he may still bring up quite a number of these interesting creatures. But it is rather unnecessary for one to numb his hands at this work in ice cold water when it can all be done so much more easily and comfortably in warmer weather.

JANUARY

OF the twelve months of the year, January is the one of least activity in the outdoor world. It is the time when nature is resting almost completely, preparing and strengthening herself by storing up energy that will enable her to again resume her arduous duties when the time comes for her to do so. She is very far from being dead, however. She is only in a deep sleep from which she will presently awaken with renewed strength. Although this is a quiet time of the year, there is much to be found in the way of beauty and usefulness for the nature photographer. While much of the wild life is at a standstill, there are many pictures to be had if we will go out with our cameras and search for them.

The trees, with the exception of the so-called evergreens, the conifers, have long since discarded their leaves and stand forth in all the beauty of their nudity, displaying the full strength and symmetry of their trunks and branches which cannot be seen when they are fully clothed in the summer. This beauty is, in the opinion of many, even greater than when the trees are fully bedecked in their summer costumes of leaves. It is a beauty that is well worth preserving in photographic records, even though it means going out in the cold to do so. Once we have learned to study these bare trees to find the best and most perfect specimens, and to determine the point of view that will bring out all their beauty to the best advantage, we will find that the results are ample payment for the time spent in the cold and snow of January.

Of course we should select with care the specimens which we intend to use. They should stand out by themselves with no other trees so close that their branches will overlap those of your subject and so interfere with the perfect symmetry of the outline. We should never use as a subject a tree that has any broken limbs or branches or whose growth is not symmetrical. The point of view should be far enough away to include the entire tree to the tips of the topmost branches, and the sun should, preferably, be quartering from one side to give roundness to the branches. It is never advisable to photograph a tree directly against the sun as that results only in a somewhat uninteresting silhouette. A cloudy day is not good for this work, because it results in flat lighting. It is a mistake to photograph from a position so close to the tree as to make it necessary to tilt the camera upward to include the entire tree in the picture. The result of such tilting is a much foreshortened image that gives an entirely erroneous impression of the true shape of the tree. Make the exposure from a distance great enough so that it will be necessary to tilt the camera only very slightly, if at all. If your lens is of the symmetrical type, the rear combination will give an image the full size of the negative at a distance sufficient to eliminate all distortion. Otherwise it is best to make an enlargement from the smaller image that you will obtain from the same distance with a short-focus lens.

Long before the month of January, the water which carries the sap containing the food and building material for the tree has retired to the ground, thus draining the tree completely of all moisture which would otherwise freeze and by expansion split the trunk and limbs and kill the tree. But while the tree is completely drained of its life-giving fluid, it is far from dead. This is evidenced by the plump leaf buds, kept from freezing by their many hard, fleece-lined scales which adorn the twigs, awaiting the advent of spring to burst open and again re-clothe the branches in green. These buds are well worth studying and photographing, as the buds of each species of tree are individual and by them the tree may always be identified.

While to a large extent the vegetable world is asleep, the conifers are still green and their cones are in perfect condition for photographing, and they form excellent subjects both from a botanical and from an artistic standpoint. Also many of the " berry " bearing plants still retain their fruit, which forms one of the chief sources of food for the many species of birds that remain with us throughout the winter months.

The majority of people have little idea of the really large number of wild things that inhabit the woods and fields within a reasonable walk of their homes, because one may tramp for miles and be lucky

WHITE SPRUCE CONES

if he catches sight of a single one of these small creatures. He may be certain, however, that probably hundreds of them have seen him, and that he has passed within a few feet of dozens, at least. So well have they learned how to hide themselves through ages of persecution at the hands of countless enemies, that in the majority of cases it is impossible for the keenest eye to discern them. Someone has said that it is impossible for any animal so to move upon the surface of the earth as not to leave some record of its wandering. One is apt to question this statement, somewhat, if applied to animals during the summer months. In the winter when the ground is covered with snow, it is different, for then no animal can venture abroad without leaving his signature in the telltale snow, and a trail that anyone can follow without difficulty.

There is real fun in following these trails. There are stories to be read if one's eyes are sharp enough to read them, stories that are most interesting as well as instructive, for there are records of tragedies as well as comedies clearly imprinted upon the white surface of the snow. These tracks are very well worth photographing. The best time for trailing is in the early morning after a light fall of not too dry snow. If the snowfall has been in the early part of the night, or the evening before, especially if the clouds have cleared away and there has been a moon shining afterward, we will find that we cannot go amiss in looking for tracks. They are everywhere, for it is on such a night as this that animals particularly delight to be abroad.

At first one will probably find it difficult to differentiate between the various tracks which he finds. It is always hard to distinguish between those of the dog, cat, and fox; the squirrel and rabbit; the mink and weasel; and many others whose tracks are more or less similar. Gradually, however, the knowledge will come and before long one will be able to tell at a glance just what animal passed, in what direction it was going, and whether at leisure or in a hurry. When one can read the story that nearly every track tells, he will follow them with ever-increasing interest.

The most distinctive of all tracks is that of the cottontail. Not everyone knows that the rabbit, in running, throws his hind feet in front of his front ones. Thus the two parallel footprints in front are those of his hind feet, while the two following, one behind the other, are those of his front feet. The gray squirrel, when traveling fast, sometimes makes a similar imprint. The usual track of this little rodent, however, forms a nearly perfect square with the hind feet making parallel imprints in front, and the forefeet parallel ones behind, but slightly closer together. But the two tracks need never be confused, for the squirrel tracks are much smaller than are those of the rabbit.

Probably the daintiest of all the tracks, also one of the most distinctive, is that of the little white-footed mouse. This is a series of parallel imprints usually leading in a fairly straight line for as far as the eye can follow, with a more or less continuous line running between the footprints, made by the dragging of the little fellow's tail.

The track of the meadow mouse is somewhat similar, but coarser and lacking the tail mark, for the tail of this rodent is too short to make a mark.

These animal tracks, as I have said, make interesting and useful photographs and one should always take his camera with him when he goes a-trailing. The making of these photographs does not present any very great difficulties but a few words of advice may help the beginner in this particular line of work. Whenever possible, point the camera in the direction in which the animal traveled, and choose a track leading either directly, or quartering, toward the sun so that the shadows in each imprint will be well defined, causing them to show clearly. Study the track you have selected and determine from what point it may be photographed to best advantage, before setting up your camera. Be extremely careful not to leave any of your own footprints near enough to the track to be included in the picture. Have the camera as close to the snow as it is possible to do while including not only those imprints close to the camera but those at a distance as well. If a bit of skyline can be shown at the top of the photograph, it will help the result considerably. Always focus sharply on the middle distance, then stop the lens down to its smallest aperture. This should give sharp definition of all the footprints included in the picture. To obtain the very best results use a panchromatic plate with a filter.

Possibly the clearest of all the trail records I have read in my tramps through the woods and fields was one which I found some years ago, which ended in a tragedy. I was walking one day in midwinter through a piece of fairly open woods. There had been a light fall of snow the night before, making ideal conditions for trailing. In climbing over an old stone wall which ran along one side of the woods, I saw the tracks of a gray squirrel along its top. That the maker of the trail had been in no particular hurry was evidenced by the fact that the tracks were fairly close together, showing that he had been progressing at an easy lope. Suddenly, a short distance beyond the spot where I first saw them, I found the distance between the imprints lengthen to nearly a full yard, showing that the squirrel had, between jumps, increased his speed almost to top notch. Looking about to discover what had caused this sudden burst of speed, I saw the trail of another, slightly larger animal approaching the wall

RABBIT'S TRACKS CONVERGING

from the other side at an acute angle. It took but a glance for me to realize that the little gray squirrel had been sighted by his arch enemy, the weasel. A short distance beyond, his tracks joined those of the squirrel on the wall, and for a distance of some fifty yards the two intermingled until, at the foot of a large oak tree, they both terminated abruptly. Carefully looking over the unblemished surface of the snow beneath the tree, I soon found what I feared I might, a dark spot far out beneath the ends of the branches. Upon going up to it, I found what was inevitable, a blood-stained hole in the snow from which led a single track, that of the weasel.

Unfortunately many of these trail stories are apt to end in tragedies such as this, for nature is not always kind to her offspring.
Many others, however, end in a more pleasant manner and such an
one was the story told by the exceedingly well-defined trail of that
dainty little dweller of the old fields, the white-footed mouse which I
found and photographed, one winter's day some years ago. It led
in almost a straight line from which the little fellow had hardly deviated for as far back and as far ahead as I could see it. From this,
and from the steady pace at which he had been traveling, as shown
by the fact that the separate sets of imprints were evenly spaced and
the mark of the dragging tail showed plainly between the footprints,
I felt certain that he had a definite object in view and, a little curious to learn what that object had been, I followed the trail. It led
me, without the slightest detour, across two fields, over a little rise
and to the edge of a piece of marshland where there was a small
thicket of white birch saplings. Here the little fellow had plowed
the snow into a veritable maze of tracks in his search for the seeds
dropped from the birches. He had evidently visited the spot before
and was well acquainted with the route that was most direct. I
searched for, and soon found, his returning trail, taken after he had
doubtless filled both his stomach and cheek pouches with the seeds,
and this again I followed until it ascended a bank and ended at a
hole in the snow. I then proceeded on my way happy in the thought
that, for one night at least, that particular little white-foot had
returned safely to his home with a supply of provender for the
family that undoubtedly awaited him there.

Still another track which I followed came near to being a tragedy,
but fortunately was not. While walking one day across a piece of
frozen bogland with about two inches of snow covering the ice, I came
upon the trail of a muskrat that clearly showed that but for the alertness of its little maker it would have ended in a tragedy. The spacing
of his tracks showed that he had left in a leisurely manner a hole in
the ice that was the exit from his winter home. He was probably bent
upon a foraging tour or, possibly, just out for a little jaunt. He
had returned in long bounds, evidently in a great hurry occasioned
by fear. Wishing to learn, if possible, what had so frightened the
little fellow, I followed his outgoing tracks for about two hundred
feet to the point where he had suddenly turned and started for home

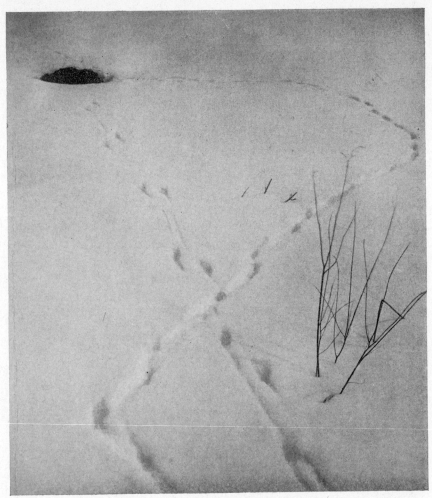

TRACKS OF THE MUSKRAT THAT LEFT ITS HOME LEISURELY AND RETURNED
IN A HURRY

in long leaps. Some half dozen paces beyond this point I found the cause for the sudden change in Mr. Muskrat's plans, the tracks of a passing fox. Fortunately for the muskrat, he either saw or smelled the fox before the fox caught sight or scent of him and managed to make a safe getaway without attracting his enemy's attention. But I could easily visualize him running for his burrow as fast as his little legs could carry him, each individual hair standing on end with fright, while the fox kept steadily on his predatory way unaware of the supper which he had missed by so narrow a margin.

Occasionally one is at a complete loss to reconstruct any kind of story from some particular track which he has found. This happened to me one day when I found where a crow had alighted in the snow, walked a few feet, and hopped into the lowermost branches of a small hemlock. That he did hop into the branches was evidenced by the fact that there were no wing marks where his track ended as there would inevitably have been had he taken wing directly from the ground. The wing marks showed very distinctly where he alighted and beat the tips of his wing feathers downward to arrest his flight. I searched carefully for evidence of the reason for this short walk but could find none. There was no sign of his having picked up anything, and had he come to join a comrade in the tree he would have alighted directly upon the tree itself. I therefore was forced to the conclusion that he had no definite reason for this little walk, and that it was just an evidence of the vagary of a crow's mind for which he is somewhat noted.

One morning after a night of brilliant moonlight following a light fall of snow, I started early on a tramp in search of trails. As I was entering a field on the edge of a piece of woods, I saw tracks of rabbits leading into it from all directions. Following one of these trails led me to an open, level spot near the edge of the woods where a rabbit convention had evidently been held the night before. The ground was literally covered with a network of tracks, the snow in places being actually beaten down hard by their little feet. There must have been at least a score of the little fellows present. How the word had been passed around that such a meeting was to be held upon that particular night is a mystery, but that the clan had gathered from far and near was plainly evident from the number of tracks that converged at this spot from every direction. Just what the object of the meeting was no one can say, but it was probably merely to frolic and play with each other, and I found myself wishing that I might have been present, invisible to their sharp eyes, to have watched their antics. I was glad to learn, from a careful survey of the ground, that no enemy had appeared to spoil their fun.

In making photographs of these tracks almost any camera can be used if it can be attached to a tripod. I have found the ideal outfit a 5 by 7 view camera with both front and back extension of bellows fitted with a lens that can be stopped down to secure great focal depth. Speed is of no consequence in this work as the track cannot move during the exposure, nor can any breeze sway it. Depth of focus is the principal consideration so that the picture will be perfectly sharp to the horizon.

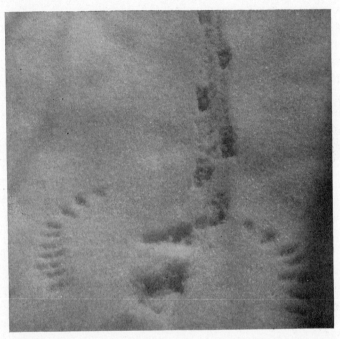

CROW'S TRACKS IN SNOW, SHOWING MARKS OF WING-TIPS
AS HE LANDED

One is very apt to think of the winter months as being completely devoid of all kinds of insect life. It is perfectly true that the majority of adult insects die from cold or starvation at the approach of winter, but there are quite a number to whom this rule does not apply. It would certainly seem as though such apparently delicate and fragile creatures as the butterflies and moths would succumb to the first touch of frost, and with the great majority of species this is true. The mature insect dies and the species is continued by the chrysalids of the butterflies hung from the stem or branches of some plant, hidden in the crevices of bark and similar places, or fallen to the ground and protected by the dead leaves; by the pupae of the moths snugly ensconced in their weatherproof cocoons; or by the eggs laid in the late fall which are uninjured by the cold storms of winter and hatch in the late spring when the leaves upon which the caterpillars feed have burst forth. Some species of butterflies migrate, and of this group a well-known example is the monarch butterfly whose caterpillar feeds upon the milkweed. They gather in immense swarms in the early fall and migrate to the south where they spend the winter, to return north when the weather is once more warm and the milkweed plants grown to a size sufficient to support the caterpillars which will hatch in a few days after the eggs are laid.

There are also others, the so-called " thaw butterflies " that hibernate for the winter under logs, fallen boards, rock ledges, in hollow trees, caves, and other similar places. There they remain in a more or less comatose condition until some particularly warm day, such as frequently occurs in midwinter, brings them forth for a few hours. I have seen them on numerous occasions in January flitting about when the ground was covered with snow. Among these thaw butterflies those most prominent are the species of the genus *Pyrameis*, which includes the red admiral, the hunter's butterfly, and the painted lady; the mourning cloak and the tortoise shell of the genus *Vanessa;* and the species of the genus *Polygonia,* the question mark, the comma, the satyr, the faun and others of the anglewings. These hibernators emerge from their retirement only upon particularly warm days and then only during the warmest part of the day, returning to their hiding places as soon as the air commences to become the least bit chilly, to await the next warm day. They are also the earliest to fly in the spring. The larvae of a number of the *Lepidoptera* also hibernate and there are some species of butterflies, existing in the arctic regions, whose development from the egg to the perfect insect covers a period of from two to four years, the larvae hibernating beneath the deep snow during the long arctic winters.

There are a number of species of butterflies whose habitats are the cold regions. The genus *Erebia,* medium-sized or small dark-colored butterflies, are called the Alpines from the fact that they are found only in the far north or upon the tops of the tallest mountains. The members of another genus, *Œneis*, are called the Arctics for they are found mainly above the Arctic Circle and also on high mountain tops. Probably the best known of them all is the White Mountain butterfly (*Œneis semidea*) whose habitat is restricted to the summit of Mount Washington, occasionally appearing also on the high mountains of Colorado and in Labrador. The caterpillars of these two genera, and also of some of the species of the genus *Brenthis*, often hibernate in a temperature of from forty to seventy degrees below zero. Of course they are frozen hard but, difficult as it is to believe, they come to life again as soon as the snow disappears and the weather becomes warm, or if brought into a warm room in the middle of winter, no worse for their experience. The apparent delicacy of these insects does not prevent them from enduring severe cold with no danger to themselves.

The hibernating caterpillars of our lepidopterous insects often occupy two or three years in that stage before pupating. The mature insect often lays her eggs in the late fall and, according to Mr. W. J. Holland, one of our most eminent entomologists, " Many caterpillars which hibernate do so immediately after emerging from the egg and before having made the first molt. The great majority, however, hibernate after having passed one or more molts. With the approach of spring they renew their feeding upon the first reappearance of the foliage of their proper food plant, or are transformed into chrysalids and presently emerge as perfect insects." Therefore, if you should happen to have, as winter approaches, some caterpillars in your breeding cages from which you are hoping to obtain some perfect moths or butterflies to photograph, and which refuse to pupate, do not be discouraged. Cover the bottom of your cage with an inch or so of dead vegetable refuse, dead leaves, moss, etc. A few pieces of loose bark will also help. In a short time you will probably find that your caterpillars have disappeared from view, having burrowed beneath the refuse to sleep away the winter. In the spring they will emerge and possibly pupate immediately, in which case you will have but a short time to wait for your perfect insect. Maybe it will be later in the summer when this happens or, perhaps, your guest will decide to sleep away another winter and you will be forced to await results until another spring. Nevertheless, if you have a sufficient amount of patience, you will eventually be rewarded by the appearance of the moth or butterfly, as the case may be.

The bees and wasps that, with the ants, form one of the most highly organized groups of our insect tribes, have little or no trouble during the cold weather. They live either in snug, well-constructed community houses or in burrows in the ground where they store their provisions and where, warmly sheltered from the freezing storms of winter, they sleep away the coldest part of the year in semi-torpidity. We all know the large, pear-shaped nests of the paper wasps, the so-called " yellow jackets." In these the grubs as well as the adult wasps sleep through the winter. If you should find one, cut it from the tree with a good-sized piece of the branch on which it is hung. Take it home and photograph it. Then, with a very sharp knife carefully cut it downward longitudinally through the center and make another photograph showing the sleeping insects and the arrangement of the interior of the nest. It makes an interesting picture, but I should advise anyone not to attempt it indoors in a warm room as it takes but little heat for a short time to bring these pugnacious little fellows back to active life, and the result might prove to be rather unpleasant.

Of course the farther south one goes, the more numerous and active are all forms of insect life, although even in the far south insects are much more numerous in the summer than in the winter. Where snow comes with the winter and the thermometer drops well below the freezing point, the majority of insects die in the autumn, some early and some late, so that there are in most groups extremely few, if any, adult individuals existing after the first hard frost.

Doubtless, if we wish to search for them, we will find a number of crickets, grasshoppers and locusts hiding in a semi-torpid condition in sheltered spots, particularly in hay lofts and stable corners where it remains warm enough throughout the winter to keep them from freezing. Also the burrowing or mole crickets are very much alive at the end of their burrows and may be dug out, but the trouble is to find the burrows. Any of these insects, when found at this time of the year, make excellent subjects for photography as they are still sufficiently alive to cling in a natural position to any support, but are lacking in sufficient energy to make a quick getaway.

There is one curious little insect, belonging to the order *Neurop-tera* (the lace-wing insects), that is very much alive at this time of the year. This is the so-called "snow insect," a wingless, cater-pillarlike little creature about the size and shape of a grain of rice. Some species are orange-red, others shining black. It lives among the mosses and is rarely seen except when snow is on the ground when it frequently appears in countless numbers on top of the snow. The orange-red species sometimes covers the snow so thickly over a considerable area as to impart to it a decidedly reddish cast, giving rise among the ignorant to the superstition that there is "blood upon the snow," predicting some terrible calamity.

Many birds are with us throughout the winter. I am speaking, of course, of those states in which the ground is covered by snow for at least a part of the winter. The farther north one goes, where the snow is deep and constant throughout the winter, the fewer birds will he find. The farther south he travels, the more numerous they become. In between these two extremes a much greater number of birds habitually pass the cold months with us than is generally sup-posed by the casual observer. I have frequently asked friends to name the birds that they knew could be found about their homes in the cold weather. With many of them the answer was, "Why, only the English sparrow." Some added the starling. A few went so far as to include the crow. And one or two were so bold as to tenta-tively place the blue jay on the list. Which tends to show how much the average person knows of the wild life that exists about him. To the nature photographer these winter birds of ours offer excellent opportunities for the use of the camera, and their pictures are easily obtained. A feeding station in the back yard, kept well supplied with the foods that the various species care for particularly, is all that is necessary. It is easy to induce the birds to come to such a place. Food is hard for them to find when everything is buried be-neath a heavy blanket of snow, and they lose much of their natural shyness when the food that they desire is freely offered them. At first they may show a little diffidence in approaching the station, but this diffidence will quickly wear off and each day will find them coming back in increasing numbers.

Of course the English sparrow, which was introduced into this country some sixty odd years ago in the forlorn hope that it would help to control the ravages of certain insect pests, is undoubtedly the most numerous year-round resident that we have. As a destroyer of insects it was a dismal failure, but as a thorough and unmitigated pest it has proved itself to be a complete success. Since its introduction it has rapidly increased in numbers and has extended its range until, over the eastern half of the United States and southern Canada, it is more numerous than any other species of bird or, in point of fact, than a number of other species combined. In the western half of the country it is not found in such large numbers, but it is more or less common all the way to the Pacific coast. Give it sufficient time and that part of the United States west of the Rocky Mountains will be equally as overcrowded with it as is the East at the present time. It is pugnacious, dirty, noisy, and with few if any redeeming features and yet we must accord it some admiration, albeit reluctantly, for its extreme hardihood and persistence, and its ability to overcome almost any difficulty.

Almost, if not quite as common as the English sparrow, at least from Massachusetts to Maryland and Pennsylvania, and equally as undesirable for many reasons, is that other pest mistakenly imported from England, the starling. After many unsuccessful attempts to naturalize it, it was finally firmly implanted in this country in New York City in 1890. At first its increase was necessarily slow, but each year since then has found it occupying more and more territory and it is only a matter of time until it will cover as much of the country as already does the English sparrow. I have called it a pest and those who have charge of public buildings will, undoubtedly, agree with me. It is an extremely dirty bird and its habit of gathering in considerable flocks and using the façades of these buildings as roosting places, fairly whitewashing them with excrement makes it a most undesirable citizen. It has, however, a few redeeming features, which can hardly be said of the English sparrow. It is rather handsome, especially the male bird, and when it condescends to sing, its song is rather a sweet, warbling whistle, much superior to the raucous note of the English sparrow. In the winter season starlings gather in flocks, congregating where food is more or less plentiful, especially in barn and poultry yards. They are therefore not difficult to entice to one's back yard by putting out a regular supply of food. The birds soon learn where food is to be found and will come every day, in increasing numbers, looking for it. The only drawback is that once having induced them to come, it is utterly impossible to force them to leave and their constant presence acts as a deterrent to the approach of other species.

Many birds come to us from their northern breeding grounds to pass the winter, and undoubtedly the most generally known is that neatly and modestly clothed little member of the sparrow family, the slate-colored junco. He must be well known to all of us, at least to those of us who have ever spent any time during the winter in the country or even visited a city park, for he is common everywhere during this part of the year, consorting with his English cousins. He is a sleek, trim fellow with a slate-colored coat and white waist-coat. A few breadcrumbs scattered on the snow in the same place daily will soon cause numbers of these birds to regularly visit that spot, making the photographing of them not very difficult.

Besides the junco, others that come to us from the north to pass the winter include the tree sparrow, fox sparrow, white-throated sparrow, red-poll, the two kinglets, golden and ruby crowned, the snow bunting, purple finch, crossbills, goldfinch, pine siskin and others. Some of these are more or less common, as the tree sparrow that frequently arrives in small flocks to mingle with the juncos and English sparrows. Others are rare or erratic visitors, such as the snow bunting and crossbill both of which may appear in fairly large flocks in some localities one winter and not be seen there again for several years. The latter is a completely irresponsible bird, staying in the far north one winter and migrating to the south the next. I have known a grove of conifers to be fairly alive with them upon a day in midwinter, busily engaged in prying the seeds from the cones with their bills which nature has specially adapted for that purpose, but upon the following day not one of them could be found nor did I see them again all winter. Some of these casual visitors may occasionally be enticed to the feeding stand and photographed by the use of the proper food and considerable patience. It cannot be said, however, that any of them make easy subjects.

Probably the most typical of our round-the-year residents, and one that not so very long ago was a very common one but whose numbers are now considerably depleted by the onslaughts of the hunters, is the bob-white, commonly, but erroneously, called quail.

No other bird remains so persistently in one locality throughout the year. A pair will raise a brood which remains intact until full-grown, forming a covey, and the following spring will find them still all together in the same locality provided nothing has happened to them in the meantime. Unfortunately, in about ninety-nine cases out of a hundred, something does happen to them. This very habit of remaining together in one locality is often their downfall, proving fatal to most of them. A hunter will mark down such a covey in the summer and, sure of finding them in the same vicinity, provided someone else has not found them first, will return in the fall when the season opens and gather them in. Moreover, as the bob-whites are mainly ground-feeding birds, when the snow is heavy upon the ground, particularly when it is covered by an icy crust, they find food difficult to obtain and many die of starvation. Another source of danger to these birds is the fact that they spend their nights upon the ground, grouped together in a circle, where they are easily discovered by their natural enemies, owls, foxes, weasels, etc. Here also they will remain even through a heavy snowfall, often allowing the snow to completely cover them. This, in itself, does them no harm, for in the morning they simply shake off the snowy covering and fly away. Should the snowfall end in a thaw followed by a sharp drop in temperature, thus forming a crust over them, as all too frequently happens, they are unable to break their way out and are very likely to starve or freeze to death before the crust melts sufficiently to allow them to escape. Thus, between the hunters, the hard winters, and his natural enemies, our little bob-white's existence is none too secure. Were it not for the fact that they are prolific breeders, the female often laying as many as twenty-five eggs in a litter and frequently raising two litters in a season, the bob-white would long ago have been numbered among our extinct species. As it is, their numbers are steadily diminishing. If one knows of the whereabouts of a covey of these birds it will be easy to bring them to a certain spot at practically the same time every day by keeping that spot baited with grain, thus making them not very difficult to photograph.

The blue jay is another of our rather common winter birds. Some, undoubtedly, come to us from farther north where they have spent the summer, but many are year-round residents. The blue jay is, beyond doubt, one of the handsomest and also, unfortunately, one of the noisiest of our birds. He seems to be excessively fond of his own voice for he will frequently sit in a tree top or fly about from one perch to another uttering the loudest, most unmusical screams imaginable, and all for no apparent reason. He might be called the scold of the avian world. That, and the fact that he is a robber of other birds' nests, makes him, despite his beauty, a somewhat

BOB-WHITE OR QUAIL

objectionable member of bird society. He is easily enticed to a feeding post in the winter season by baiting the post with unshelled peanuts. A friend of mine one winter tamed some of them to such an extent by placing peanuts on an open window sill of his breakfast room that they finally even entered the room and perched on the breakfast table, waiting to be fed. They eventually became so insistent in their demands for food that he was finally forced in self-defence to shut them out.

A large number of crows remain with us throughout the winter, although the majority form in great migrating flocks in late October and throughout November and leave for the south, whence they re-

turn in early spring. A sufficient number, however, remain behind
to place them in the list of winter birds. The crow is a most interesting bird in more ways than one. He is extremely sagacious and,
although he has rather deservedly a somewhat bad reputation, he is
not always as black as he is painted. The late Mr. E. H. Forbush
once said of him: " There is some reason for the low regard in which
he is held among men. First he is black, the color of evil. Then he
knows too much; his judgment of the range of a gun is too nearly
correct. If crows could be shot oftener, they would be more popular." Henry Ward Beecher once remarked that if men wore feathers
and wings a very few of them would be clever enough to be crows.
Also, as Dr. N. A. Cobb says: " The crow rises too early. We have
to get up very early in the morning to get ahead of the crow. Most
of us rarely see the sun rise, and while the sluggards still slumber
the early crow is up to some abominable mischief in the back yard.
It irritates us to have this disreputable fowl take such a mean advantage of us, especially as we know that it would not have happened had we been up and about as we know we should have been.
Then, according to human standards, the crow is a thief and robber.
He steals eggs, chickens, corn; he robs the songbirds of their eggs
and young, and so he is vilified and anathematized, pursued and
destroyed, at every opportunity; but all to no purpose, for we may
well believe that there are more crows in the country than there were
when the Pilgrims landed at Plymouth Rock. Today the crow is
the great American bird. Everybody knows him. How many
people have seen the American eagle except on the silver dollar?
But who has not seen the crow? If a person knows only four birds,
one of them will be the crow. The bird is well known because he
is large, ubiquitous, black and noisy. He is well worth knowing.
Each crow is a character. There is more difference in crows than
appears as they fly over."

Owing to his almost uncanny habit of keeping himself well out
of danger, knowing, as he seems to, that mankind as a whole is decidedly his enemy, the crow is an extremely difficult bird to approach
within anything like photographic distance. Also it is impossible
to entice him to any one spot. All in all, he is probably one of the
most difficult of our birds to photograph, and there are very few
good photographs of him extant.

Both the hairy and the downy woodpeckers are winter residents in the eastern states, the latter a year-round resident and much the more common of the two. They closely resemble each other and should anyone not well acquainted with both birds mistake one for the other, it could hardly be called a grave error of identification. The main difference lies in the size, the hairy variety averaging some two or two and one-half inches longer than the other and with a

SAW-WHET OWL

correspondingly longer bill. The coloring and markings of the two are exactly similar, black and white with a red patch on the head, with the exception of a slight difference in the markings on the three outer tail feathers which, in the downy woodpecker, are usually barred with black. Both of these birds are of considerable economic value because of the really tremendous number of insects which they destroy throughout the year. Mainly these consist of wood borers and, in the winter, of the egg masses which they search out in the bark crevices of the trees. Though they are, primarily, insect eaters, they are both fond of meat and fat, particularly in the winter. Therefore they may both be easily enticed to pose for their photographs by a piece of suet fastened to a branch of a tree in such a position that the camera may be easily focused upon it. There are others of the woodpeckers that are apt to visit us in the winter. They are, however, far from common. In fact all but the sapsucker might be called rare. Also they are extremely difficult to approach and so, as photographic subjects, they may be called negligible.

One of the most steadfast and by all means the cheeriest of our winter birds is that well-beloved member of the titmouse family, the black-capped chickadee. He might well be called the acrobat of the avian world for he is just as much at ease hanging back downward from a branch or swinging by one foot from a twig, as he is when standing upright. In fact he is more often upside down than otherwise. His cheerful song may be heard upon the coldest days of winter, the cold seeming to have no ill effect upon him as he flits from tree to tree in his search for insects or insect eggs hidden in the crevices of the bark. Chicadees are easy to photograph for they are very confiding little fellows, and will allow a near approach without showing any fear. They can even be tamed in a very short time so successfully that they will come to one's hand for food and have even been known to take it from between a person's lips.

The two nuthatches, white- and red-breasted, and the little brown creeper may be seen at almost any time on any day of the winter as they work their way up and down the tree trunks in their search for food. Although both the chickadees and the nuthatches are insect eaters, they are quite willing to visit the feeding station in order to pick at the piece of suet which should always be fastened there.

Many of our birds of prey, the hawks and owls, pass the entire winter with us. Among the hawks may be mentioned the red-shouldered hawk as well as the red-tail; the goshawk, sharp-shinned hawk and sparrow hawk, with the broad-winged hawk, duck hawk, and osprey occasionally. Of the owls the little saw-whet owl and the screech owl are permanent residents. I have frequently pulled them from their winter quarters in some hollow tree or stump. They both make good subjects for photography when taken from these quarters, but I should advise anyone trying it to protect his hands with heavy gloves when handling them, for their talons and beaks are sharp and they do not hesitate to use them.

The long-eared, short-eared and great horned owls are also year-round residents wherever they are found, as is also the barred owl. None of them are common, and should one have the opportunity to photograph any one of them he may consider himself fortunate. Also, as rare winter visitors from the far north, we occasionally have the great gray owl, snowy, and hawk owls. These last, however, should hardly be included among our winter birds as they very rarely leave their far northern haunts except when the weather is extraordinarily severe. Consequently their appearance with us is extremely infrequent.

FEBRUARY

EBRUARY is the last month of winter and like January, at least in our northern states, is a month when cold weather and snow-covered ground are to be expected. To all intents and purposes it is still midwinter so far as the temperature is concerned, with snow covering the ground for the greater part of the month and all the ponds, pools and watercourses securely locked with ice. February frequently averages more and greater cold than any other month. The thermometer is likely to keep well below the freezing point for days at a time, sometimes approaching or even passing the zero mark. Nature is still deep in her sleep of recuperation and it will be well toward the end of the month before she stirs and commences to rouse herself. These first stirrings are but tentative ones, however, and one must expect but few signs of spring before March. Subjects for the nature photographer are not any too plentiful this month but, if his enthusiasm enables him to ignore tingling fingers and toes, he can certainly go out into the woods and fields and find some. There are numerous good subjects to be found if we search for them understandingly, and are blessed with a bit of luck.

To anyone who really loves his work with camera and the wild things, the cold and snow of February are no deterrent to a tramp through the woods and fields in pursuit of suitable subjects. There is keen pleasure in such a tramp when the snow lies deep, the thermometer hovers about the freezing point, the sun shines brightly, and each breath of the clear, sparkling air sends the blood leaping

through the veins. If those who during the winter months remain
in the enervating atmosphere of indoors, close to a radiator or fire-
place, would but try this once, properly clothed, I am quite certain
that they would agree with me that the pleasure is greater than
from taking a similar walk on some hot day of midsummer when the
brightness of the sun is somewhat of a detriment rather than an
advantage. I would be glad to know that all my readers might
acquire the habit of taking their cameras out quite frequently during the winter months.

Winter is the season when one is undisturbed in possession of the
woods, fields, and byways, but not the highways which we should
studiously avoid whenever possible. In no other place where one
may ordinarily go, is the solitude and peace quite so complete as in
the woods, and in no other place is the change from the aspect of
summer to that of winter so great. The entire appearance and nature of things are completely changed. So radical is this change
that we cannot lay claim to any real knowledge of the woods unless
we have seen them not only in the summer but also in the winter
when they are completely denuded of the summer coverings of foliage
and stand out in all their unclothed glory, and the trickery of colors
is replaced by the monotone of gray and white. In summer it is
the covering of verdure and the almost infinite variety of color that
is responsible for the charm of every woodland landscape. In winter it is the beauty of pure form, the delicate tracery of bough,
branch, and twig, the rugged outline of bare trunks, and the exquisite purity of the violet-shadowed snow that make picture after
picture of surpassing loveliness for him who has eyes to see them.
To thoroughly know the woods one should be intimately conversant
with them during every month of the year, and even after many
months of such intimacy he will still be able to find something new
and beautiful in them, especially during the winter season.

To thoroughly enjoy all this, to learn to know the winter woods
and fields in their varying moods, to find the tremendous beauty in
them and become acquainted with their inhabitants and the various
things which are there, one should take his camera outfit and go to
them with a mind open and ready to receive impressions, to see and
to grasp the beauties that surround him and find the small signs
that will often lead him to the subject that he hopes to find. If not,

his walk will have done him no good and he will have failed completely to find any of those things which he might otherwise have found and photographed.

It is a clear, brilliant morning somewhere in the first part of February, with the mercury in the upper twenties. The ground is white with a light covering of snow that has fallen during the night. It is an ideal day for a photographic jaunt, for the air is still and bracing with no disturbing wind to make conditions uncomfortable and photography harder. Let us don heavy sweaters, high waterproof boots, warm caps with tabs to cover our ears if necessary, and fleece-lined gloves, or better still, mittens, and assemble our photographic outfit to fare forth not only to see the beauties of the out-of-doors, but also to discover suitable subjects to photograph.

We should not burden ourselves with a heavy outfit, for the less we have to carry, the more we will enjoy our walk and the further we will be likely to go. I always advocate the use, on such trips, of a camera no larger than a 4 by 5 or $3\frac{1}{4}$ by $4\frac{1}{4}$. A sharp negative, no matter how small if it is full of good clear detail, is always capable of being enlarged to almost any extent desired.

When we first start out we will, in all probability, be forced to follow some main traveled road. Let us choose one that will take us to the woods and fields as expeditiously as possible, for it is in them that we will find our subjects, and the sooner we reach them the better. Therefore when we reach a point from which the outlook for suitable subjects to photograph is inviting, we should leave the road and make a path for ourselves through the untrodden snow with our eyes ever on the alert for whatever camera subjects we may find. That we will find them, we need have no fear if we have learned the art of using our eyes effectively, and not just casually as so many people do.

I have spoken of the snow as being untrodden, but I meant only by the foot of man. The small inhabitants of the outdoor world have been there before us. In fact they have been abroad throughout most of the night, at least ever since it stopped snowing, and have delicately marked its otherwise spotless purity with their footprints. I have already spoken in detail concerning trailing and trails and how to photograph them, but I would like to show how the following of one may often lead to another subject for our camera. Frequently, if we take the trouble to follow one of these trails it will lead us to the nest of the maker, and not infrequently this nest will contain young. This happened to me one day in late February after a moonlit night following a light fall of snow in the evening. I was out early looking for tracks, for the conditions were ideal. I had gone but a short distance when I came upon an extremely well-defined track of the little white-footed mouse which stretched ahead

Brown Thrasher's Nest Which the Whitefoot Made Into a Nest for Her Babies

for as far as I could discern in an almost undeviating straight line. I knew by this that the little fellow knew where he was going and was anxious to arrive there as soon as possible. I decided that I had better find out just where he was going when he made the trail, and therefore followed it across several fields to a small thicket where, in a tangle of catbrier vines, I saw the nest of a brown thrasher which had been pre-empted by the little fellow and filled in and domed over with white cotton waste. It was a most conspicuous object for some distance, and as I came up to it I found, as I was certain that I would, that the trail ended at the foot of the sapling in which the nest was placed. I gave the nest a little shake and out popped the mother mouse, ran down the sapling to the ground, and disappeared in the underbrush. Gently inserting my finger into the nest, I discovered it to be occupied with young so nearly full grown that I knew that to take them from the nest and attempt to photograph them would be useless. I therefore consoled myself with a picture of the nest itself and left it undisturbed. I went but a short distance and hid behind a tree trunk, as I wished to see how soon the mother would return. Much to my surprise it was but a few minutes before she appeared, and much more to my surprise she ran up the sapling, entered the nest, and immediately reappeared carrying one of her babies in her mouth in much the same way that a cat carries her young. It was so large that she had difficulty in holding it, but after some struggling she managed to carry it down the sapling and into the underbrush where I lost sight of her. Presently she returned, took another young one away, and repeated the operation until she had removed four from the nest. When she did not return from the last trip, I went to the nest and found it empty. She had taken all her offspring to some other hiding place, after this one had been violated by me. I could undoubtedly have found the new hiding place by again following her trail, but I considered that I had discomforted her sufficiently, and so left her alone. Whether or not she took the young back to the original nest I do not know. Probably not, however, as they were almost old enough to fend for themselves.

Strange as it may seem to some of my readers, the winter months offer much that should be of the greatest interest to the nature photographer who is especially interested in botanical subjects. Naturally the cones on the evergreen trees are in the same excellent condition for photographing now as they were in January, and if we did not obtain them last month we should do so now without fail, for they are necessary adjuncts to our tree photographs.

The fruits of most deciduous trees and shrubs and herbaceous plants ripen and fall in the summer or early fall, but there are a few shining examples that retain their fruit practically throughout the winter for the winter birds, to whom these fruits are a blessing because they provide their principal source of food during that part of the year when the ground is covered by snow. These are the ones which we should search out and photograph on our winter walks. Visit almost any swamp, marsh, low piece of thicket-covered ground, or surroundings of a pool, at this time of the year and you will be almost certain to find some of the tall shrubs or small trees hung with thick clusters of brownish, berry-like drupes. If your skin is sensitive to vegetable poisoning be a little careful how you handle them, as they are the fruit of the poison sumac. To those who have never had any experience with this plant, let me say that its name is no misnomer. It secretes a more virulent poison than that of the poison ivy, causing a skin rash that frequently reaches serious proportions with those who are particularly susceptible. It is said that it is only the leaves that produce this poison and that it is therefore safe in the winter. As to this I cannot vouch. There are people, of whom I am lucky enough to be one, who are immune to its poison and can handle it with impunity. Unless one is sure that he is immune it would be well to wear gloves when working with these fruits. The drupes hang on the branches all winter, which makes it an excellent time to photograph them, which one may easily do by simply bending down one of the branches to within reach of the camera, which does not necessitate much handling of the plant. There are many others of these wild fruits that may be photographed at this season, but of these I have said more in an earlier chapter.

If we have not already made our photographs of the tree buds we should do so without further delay. They are in perfect condition now but some of them will soon be swelling, preparatory to bursting, and we should get them before this happens. There are two trees whose blossoms are full blown in February. One of these is the alder and the other the red cedar. There are several species of alder native to the United States and one that is naturalized from Europe. The commonest and most likely to be seen are the smooth and the hoary alders, both of which start their flowers in tassels (aments), in early winter and by February they are usually fully matured, from two to three inches long. The alders are members of the birch family, and the native ones are all shrubs or small trees rarely attaining a height of twenty-five feet. The naturalized species, the black alder, is a native of Europe, western Asia, and northern Africa. In its native habitat it reaches a height of seventy-five feet or more, with a trunk diameter of two to two and one-half feet. The naturalized species in this country are very much smaller. One of our native species, the mountain alder, is found only in high lands and is plentiful in the higher Alleghenies. The smooth and the hoary alders are inhabitants of low, wet localities from Newfoundland and the Northwest Territory to Florida and Texas. There are at least five species found on the Pacific coast, of which the Oregon alder is the handsomest. There is also a rather curious and interesting species, the seaside alder, which occasionally attains a height of thirty feet. It is distinct from all other alders in several respects.

STAMINATE BLOSSOM OF SCOTCH PINE

Its leaves are a glossy, dark green, a decided contrast to the dull green leaves of the other native species, and its catkins are of a golden color maturing in the fall rather than in the spring. It is restricted to two small localities, one near the coast in Delaware and Maryland, the other on the banks of the Red River in Oklahoma. In the mountain regions of Alaska and elsewhere the alders are the first arborescent growth to appear after everything has been swept away by the action of avalanches.

Also, toward the end of the month, we are almost certain to find the hazelnut bushes hanging fairly full with the flower tassels, somewhat similar to those of the alder. The hazelnut is a small bush, rarely attaining a height of more than five or six feet, bearing nuts that are ripe in August and which have a sweet, palatable kernel. It is also a member of the birch family.

The red cedar is usually a small tree or shrub, at maturity from twenty to fifty feet tall. Under the most favorable conditions, however, it sometimes reaches a height of one hundred feet. Its young growths, from a few feet to eight or ten in height, are familiar objects quite thickly scattered over old fields, especially on hillsides. It is found from Nova Scotia through the New England states, where it is particularly common, to Florida and Texas. Its flowers, which may be found from February until April, are extremely insignificant but should be photographed in order to complete a full series of this particular tree. If they can be somewhat enlarged in the photograph it greatly helps to show them in better detail.

In the marshes also, often well through the winter, stand the cattails both broad and narrow leaved, with their fruiting heads burst into fluffy balls. These should not be disregarded by us on our winter walks, for they lend themselves remarkably well to photography. With them also stand large patches of that tall reed-like growth, phragmites, reaching a height of from ten to fifteen feet, topped with heavily plumed heads. It is the largest as well as the most beautiful of our native grasses and its seeding heads remain intact well through the winter.

Though it may seem incredible, there is work to be done among the insect life in February, even though the ground may be covered deeply with snow. I have frequently seen some of the so-called thaw butterflies about in February in secluded, sun-warmed spots when everywhere else the snow was plentiful. In fact I have made a photograph of the question-mark angle-wing on a day in the latter part of February in an old orchard where it, and several fellows, were feeding on the sap that was exuding from cuts and broken places in the bark of the trees. An old orchard is an excellent place in which to search for these butterflies at almost any time of the year.

Mr. Holland says of the white admirals, butterflies of the genus *Basilarchia* that " the caterpillars feed upon the various species of oak, birch, willow, and linden. The eggs are laid at the extreme tips of the leaves, and the infant caterpillar, feeding upon the leaf in immediate proximity to the point where it has been hatched, attaches bits of bitten leaf by strands of silk to the midrib, thus stiffening its perch and preventing its curling as the rib dries. Out of bits of leaves thus detached, it constructs a packet of material which it moves forward along the midrib until it has completed its second molt. By this time winter begins to come on, and it cuts away for itself the material of the leaf on either side of the rib, from the tip to the base, glues the rib to the stem by means of silk, draws together the edges of the remaining portions of the leaf, and constructs a tube-like hibernaculum, or winter quarters, exactly fitting the body, in which it passes the winter." Incidentally the members of the genus *Basilarchia* are most interesting. There are a number of species found in the United States. Probably the commonest of them all, the viceroy (*Basilarchia disippus*), which is found everywhere from southern Canada and British America to the Gulf States, is an accomplished mimic. In its form, coloring, and markings it imitates our common milkweed butterfly, the monarch (*Anosia plexippus*), so closely as to make it almost impossible to tell the two apart. Practically its only difference is that, as a rule, it is somewhat smaller. This imitating is done as a protective measure because the monarch secretes a bitter juice that makes it unwelcome as an article of food to the birds, who have learned to leave it strictly alone. Thus the viceroy is also avoided by them.

Crickets may still be found in a dormant state underneath stones and haystacks and, if we care to drag the bottoms of the ponds, we will find that the larvae (nymphs) of the dragonflies, that will emerge in May as perfect insects, are now fully developed and ready to be removed from their natural habitat and placed in the tank for photographing.

Many of our mammals, as in January, are active and even become more so as the season advances. Mr. W. E. Cram, a very able chronicler of nature's doings, wrote: " I am persuaded that most of us would be surprised to learn how many wild animals of the bigness of a cat and upward pass their lives in the midst of cultivated districts without ever having been seen by men. In studying quadrupeds the chief thing to bear in mind is that, with the exception of the squirrels and woodchucks, and possibly one or two others, all of them have comparatively poor eyesight, at all events for daylight and apparently not much better for twilight or darkness. But with a sense of smell and hearing such as theirs, they are constantly aware of anything that takes place in their immediate vicinity with the exception of the one point toward which the wind blows. While the wind is at your back you will only get the most unsatisfactory glimpses of any of the fox or weasel tribe; but with it in the opposite direction you may study them at your leisure; and to a certain degree this is true of all wild animals." All nature photographers will do well to bear this in mind, for it will be of great assistance to them when stalking any of these animals with a camera.

At this time of the year the fur, or pelage, of all the mammals is in its very best condition, making it the very best time for us to photograph them. Also, when the snow is on the ground, is an excellent time to find them, for then one may easily track them to their nests or lairs. As I have said, the smaller mammals may be photographed in the wild by anyone who wishes to persevere in the attempt to do so. But by far the easier and perhaps the better way, is to set " catch-'em-alive " traps in their runways or near their nesting places, baited with some food of which we know they are fond. Having caught them, transfer them to the glass-fronted photographing cage which all nature photographers should own, which was described in the opening chapter of this book. Do not trap them on a night that bids fair to be very cold, for on such nights the little creatures seldom venture forth and should they do so and be caught, they would be likely to be frozen before morning. After the captive is placed in the cage, he should be allowed to remain there for several days with a plentiful supply of food, until he becomes somewhat accustomed to the confinement and is therefore less wild, before one attempts to photograph him. Some very excellent photographs of the smaller mammals can be obtained in this manner and the subjects can afterwards be liberated and suffer no ill effects.

The deer, at this time of the year, are sometimes hard pressed for food, especially if there is deep snow upon the ground. At such times they will frequently visit human habitations, particularly farms where there are cattle among which they can mingle and share their fodder. In the winter the antlers on the male deer are at their best. By the end of this month, however, they will begin to loosen upon their heads, and a little later will be knocked off against some tree trunk in order to allow the new pair to begin their growth. Therefore this is the very best time of the year to photograph these animals if we have the opportunity.

The porcupine, an inhabitant of the northern woods, wanders about practically all winter with the exception of the coldest spells when he will crawl into some hollow log and sleep until the weather turns warmer again. He apparently has no fear of man or beast

PORCUPINE EATING ROOT

and there are few wild animals that will attack him except when hard pressed by hunger, and then they are apt to pay dearly for their meal. When an enemy approaches, a porcupine never runs away but simply turns down his head to protect his face and throat, which are the only really vulnerable spots in his entire body, arches his back and with all his spines erected, awaits any onslaught which may come. The tail is armed with a multitude of spines and the instant that anything touches any part of his body, it is swung with a sudden strong sweep and any animal unfortunate enough to receive the blow is in extremely hard luck. The spines are driven deep into the body. Each one is fitted with a number of small barbs which keep forcing the spine deeper and deeper with every move that the animal makes, until it finally reaches a vital part. If the animal that attacked really killed him, the porcupine has avenged his death long after it occurred. The ability thus to drive the spines home and leave them deeply imbedded in the flesh has given rise to the idea that the porcupine is able to "shoot" these spines which is, of course, entirely erroneous. Because of his refusal to run from anything, the porcupine is a very easy subject for photography because there is never any difficulty in approaching him. Should you run across one in your rambles, as you approach you will see him quickly assume the attitude of defense and remain motionless. Do not attempt to touch him, as this would prove unfortunate for you. Set up your camera and focus while he remains in this attitude of passive defense, and then quietly await the moment when he decides that all danger has passed, when he will come to life again. At that instant, before he moves away, you can obtain your exposure and get a good picture. When working about one of these animals always beware of his tail, for if the spines with their barbed points are once driven into the flesh they are impossible to remove without making a jagged wound.

In the latter part of February the skunks come from their winter quarters to roam the woods and fields in search of whatever they may find in the way of food, for they have lived all winter on the fat which they accumulated the preceding fall. Probably no other animal is so well known and so much disliked as the skunk, because of his ability to eject at will a liquid which possesses a most potent and penetratingly malodorous scent. It is not true, as many people believe, that this liquid is thrown by the tail. The liquid is secreted in a small sac situated at the base of the tail, from which it is projected in fine jets through two small tubes opening on each side of the vent. Despite his method of defending himself from his enemies real and imagined, the skunk is really a rather likable fellow. He is extremely intelligent and good natured and easily tamed, especially when taken young. He makes a good pet as he is exceptionally cleanly and gives out no unpleasant odor except when forced by fear to make an ejection, and a slight operation will remove the scent sac so that there is no longer any danger of such an occurrence. The common skunk and its closely related species is one of our commonest mammals. It ranges from the Atlantic to the Pacific across both Canada and the

Entrance to Skunk's Burrow

United States and as far south as Guatemala. Skunks are to be found in almost any kind of situation and are particularly fond of settling near human habitations, frequently nesting and raising their young beneath outbuildings, porches, etc.

The mink, a near relative of both the skunk and the weasel, and as much or more of a scourge to the wild life of the woods as the latter, is active all winter. In late February he seeks a mate and the young are usually born in early April, in some recess among rocks or inside a hollow stump or log, never far from water. It is not at all likely that any of my readers will have the opportunity to photograph a mink in his wild state for he is an exceedingly shy and elusive animal. If one cares to go to the trouble of building an enclosure in his back yard of close-meshed wire fencing, at least four feet high and six or eight feet square, he can trap these and other animals too big for the cage, and enclose them in it after having built up a proper setting. It is possible to obtain some photographs in this manner, although they are not always successful. The best place to photograph these animals is in a zoological park or, in the case of the mink, in one of the numerous farms where they are raised for their fur. The mink is equally at home on the land or in the water. His very pliable spine allows him to turn and twist his long slim body into all kinds of contortions. His legs are short and in walking his progress is slow and rather clumsy, but when necessary he can travel swiftly in such long bounds that few animals can exceed him in speed. Mr. Cram, whom I have quoted several times, has to say of him: " I know of one spring under the steep river bank where the minks watch patiently until some unfortunate eel is brought into sight by the constant upward movement of the water, when it is quickly seized and dragged out upon the snow. But the struggle does not end here, for when the mink prepares to bear its victim away in triumph the latter is apt to wind its body around that of the captor, and generally succeeds in throwing him end over end more than once before being finally subdued and hauled away." And he goes on to say: " A mink will nearly always follow any open brook it comes to, even if obliged to change its course in order to do so, alternately swimming and wading or walking along the bank. On reaching the limit of the frozen water, he will often keep on beneath the ice, especially if the water has fallen away from it so as to leave an air space, and perhaps a narrow strip of turf uncovered along the edge of the water. For it is in just such places that the meadow mice spend the winter, their burrows opening out of the bank in the same manner as muskrat holes. And even the smallest brooks harbor young pickerel and eels as well as frogs and lizards." Unlike its cousin the weasel, the mink remains brown all winter but dons its underwear of an extra coat of fur to protect him from the cold.

Bats are one of the few mammals that actually hibernate throughout the entire winter, retiring to their retreats as soon as the cold weather starts and not reappearing again until it is definitely over. This might be accounted for by the fact that bats are entirely insectivorous animals, catching their food while on the wing. As they can find no such food during the winter, it is useless for them to be abroad and so they pass their time in sleep. They hang themselves, head downward, behind loose bark, in hollow trees, caves, empty buildings, etc. Often a large number will congregate in such a roosting place as a hollow tree, cave, or building. Once in Florida I was told that a large building used for packing oranges, was the daytime roosting place of a regular army of thousands of bats. I was a bit sceptical, but, wanting some bats as specimens, I thought I might possibly get a few by visiting the place. The roof of the building was some forty feet above ground, and looking up I could see no evidence of any such horde as I had been told I would find there. Still sceptical but willing to be shown, I threw a fairly good sized stone up among the rafters which it hit with a resounding bang. Immediately the air was full of bats and when I say full, I mean full. It seemed to me that my informer had underestimated the number. They swarmed about me, repeatedly striking me until I was forced to cover my face to protect it, and beat a hasty retreat. Returning with a stout stick, I soon had as many as I wished for specimens.

Bats are our only flying mammal, and Mr. Witmar Stone describes their wings as " abnormally-webbed forefeet " and goes on to say that " the bones of the forearm and fingers are lengthened and drawn out to such an extent that a man in like condition would have fingers at least four feet long. These slender finger bones are connected with each other and with the hind feet and tail by a thin, dark-colored, parchment-like, almost naked skin. The wing, as a whole, corresponds exactly with the accepted idea of a devil's or goblin's wing; and the short, puggy head, with its big shapeless ears and wide mouth and little blinking eyes, is of just as impish and devilish an aspect. Yet bats are the most gentle and friendly of living things."

Bats are entirely nocturnal in their habits, sleeping through the day and coming forth only at dusk to fly through the night in their quest for food. They devour large quantities of mosquitoes and other night-flying insects, which should make them our friends. They will often enter a room through an open window, but if left alone will also soon leave by the same means. They are accused by many people who know nothing about them, of carrying bedbugs under their wings, and also of attempting to get into people's hair. Of course neither of these myths has any foundation in fact. The bat has his own private species of body louse that will not leave him

RED BAT ON TREE

unless forced to, but he carries no bedbugs and he will never approach a person's hair if he can possibly avoid doing so.

The bats of this country are all small, the little brown bat which is common throughout all of North America east of the Rocky Mountains, being about the smallest. In the Oriental tropics, occur bats the largest of which have a wing spread of about five feet.

Probably the most noted of all the bats are the vampires because of the many myths that surround them. However, a few of them do subsist on blood sucked from animals and sometimes humans in their sleep. They are found in Neotropical countries, especially South America, and are mostly of small size and the injury done to human beings is undoubtedly greatly exaggerated although, where they are numerous, it is not always wise to sleep exposed in the open.

Bats are distributed in all parts of the world and there are about four hundred and fifty species recognized. The old adage, " blind as a bat," is entirely misleading for they all have most efficient eyes although in some species they may be small. A very bright light blinds them temporarily, but in the dark they can see well enough to

LITTLE BROWN BAT, ASLEEP

catch the small flying insects which form their food. They congregate in some such place as an old barn, and if we can find such a place we can obtain excellent photographs of them at this time of the year, because they are somewhat dormant and therefore easily handled. They should, of course, be photographed in their natural resting position, hanging head downward. They may be handled with impunity if treated gently, and will readily hang in their natural posture if we put their small hind feet against something which they can easily grasp.

All of our native mice are abroad more or less all through the winter. They have no real storehouse for food as do the squirrels, and so must go forth and forage for their food. As February advances, they become more and more active, so that now is a good time to try for photographs of them. John Burroughs says: "They lay up stores in the fall in the shape of various nuts, grains, and seeds, yet the provident instinct, as in the red squirrel and in the jay, seems only partially developed in them; instead of carrying their supplies home they hide them in the nearest convenient place. I have known

PIKA, LITTLE CHIEF HARE

them to carry a pint or more of hickory nuts and deposit them in a pair of boots standing in the chamber of an outhouse. Hence when the cold weather comes, instead of staying at home like the chipmunk, they gad about hither and thither looking up their supplies."

Mice as well as squirrels, may be enticed by baiting to a certain spot and then photographed, but it is a tedious operation and one which I do not seriously advise my readers to try. It has been done, however, both by myself and others, with considerable success. Some of the best examples of this method that I have ever seen were made by a friend of mine while photographing wild life in the Bitter Root Mountains of Idaho and Montana. This is the home of that curious and elusive little animal, the pika, cony, or little chief hare. While he is allied to the rabbits, he is more nearly like a guinea pig in shape, with a short, blunt head; broad, rounded ears; short legs; practically no tail; and a coat of long, furry hair. He lives among the masses of slide rock where he finds shelter in the numerous holes and crevices. In the lower altitudes he is more or less active all winter, but in the higher altitudes of six to nine thousand feet his home is frequently buried beneath many feet of snow, and he is seldom able to make his appearance much before June or July. He is most active and extremely quick in all his movements. If you are watching by a pile of rocks you may see him pop suddenly out of some crevice (if he does not see you first), look hurriedly around to be sure that no enemy is lurking about, and then after giving utterance to his peculiar little cry, scamper swiftly over the rocks to some spot where he can gather grass, or other herbage, which he arranges in little haycocks in some spot where it will be protected from the wind and will dry in the warmth of the sun. He is a diligent worker and, should a storm threaten, will often remain on the job all night gathering his hay to the common storehouse under the rocks where it will remain dry and where he can have easy access to it during the winter months, even though it may be buried under many feet of snow.

My friend watched one of these little fellows until he ascertained just where he was most apt to stop for a rest once in a while. This spot he baited, focused his camera upon it, concealed it well with branches and leaves, and secured a number of most excellent photographs of the little rock dweller, several of which he was kind enough to give to me. One must not imagine, however, that these exposures were all obtained within a few hours. In point of fact I believe that the making of them occupied some part of every day for two weeks or more.

February is far from being devoid of subjects that should be of great interest to the nature photographer, but he must not be afraid to brave the cold and must show some ingenuity in searching for them.

INDEX